Prepositions and Complement Clauses

SUNY series in Linguistics
Mark Aronoff, editor

Prepositions and Complement Clauses

A Syntactic and Semantic Study of Verbs Governing Prepositions and Complement Clauses in Present-Day English

Juhani Rudanko

STATE UNIVERSITY OF NEW YORK PRESS

Published by
State University of New York Press, Albany

© 1996 State University of New York

All rights reserved

Printed in the United States of America

No part of this book may be used or reproduced in any manner whatsoever without written permission. No part of this book may be stored in a retrieval system or transmitted in any form or by any means including electronic, electrostatic, magnetic tape, mechanical, photocopying, recording, or otherwise without the prior permission in writing of the publisher.

For information, address State University of New York Press, State University Plaza, Albany, NY 12246

Production by Cynthia Tenace Lassonde
Marketing by Bernadette LaManna

Library of Congress Cataloging-in-Publication Data

Rudanko, Martti Juhani, 1948–
    Prepositions and complement clauses : a syntactic and semantic study of verbs governing prepositions and complement clauses in present-day English / by Juhani Rudanko.
    p. cm. — (SUNY series in linguistics)
    Includes bibliographical references and index.
    ISBN 0-7914-2873-7 (hc: alk. paper). — ISBN 0-7914-2874-5 (pb: alk. paper)
    1. English language—Prepositions. 2. English language—Complement. 3. English language—Semantics. 4. English language—Clauses. 5. English language—Syntax. 6. English language—Verb.
I. Title. II. Series.
PE1335.R83 1996
425—dc20   95-22230
                                                            CIP

10 9 8 7 6 5 4 3 2 1

Contents

Acknowledgments   vii

1. Introduction   1
2. *Delighting in Frustrating One's Opponents:* On Verbs Governing *in -ing*   9
3. *Resorting to* and *Turning to:* On Verbs Governing *to -ing*   43
4. *Reducing Someone to Groveling:* On Verbs Governing NP *to -ing*   69
5. *Balking at* and *Working at:* On Verbs Governing *at -ing*   93
6. *Concentrating on Laying the Foundations:* On Verbs Governing *on -ing*   117
7. *Coping with Putting the Baby to Bed* and *Charging Someone with Stealing Something:* On Verbs Governing *with -ing*   135
8. *Dreaming of Changing the World* and *Accusing Somebody of Stealing Something:* On Verbs Governing *of -ing*   163
9. Concluding Observations   181

Notes   187
Bibliography   193
Index   199
Index of Verbs   205

Acknowledgments

It is my pleasure to thank SUNY Press for including the present volume in its series.

Parts of four chapters of the present book have appeared in article form. Parts of chapter 2 appeared in *English Studies* 72, no. 1 (1991): 55–72, under the title "On Verbs Governing *in -ing* in Present-Day English"; parts of chapter 3 appeared in *English Studies* 73, no. 1 (1992): 68–79, under the title "*Resorting to* and *Turning to:* On Verbs Governing *to -ing* in Present-Day English"; parts of chapter 4 appeared in *English Studies* 74, no. 5 (1993): 485–495, under the title "*Reducing Someone to Grovelling:* Aspects of an Object-Control Pattern in Present-Day English"; parts of chapter 5 appeared in *English Studies* 76, no. 3 (1995): 264–281, under the title "*Balking at* and *Working at:* On Verbs Governing *at -ing* in Present-Day English." I am deeply indebted to *English Studies* and to Swets and Zeitlinger bv, the publisher of *English Studies*, for their kind permission to republish materials that originally appeared in that journal. I also express my sincere thanks to WaltersgroepGroningen for their kind permission to quote selected material from H. Poutsma, *A Grammar of Late Modern English for the Use of Continental, Especially Dutch Students*, Part 1, *The Sentence*, Section 2, The Composite Sentence (Groningen: P. Noordhoff, 1905, copyright WaltersgroepGronigen); and from H. Poutsma, *A Grammar of Late Modern English*, Part 1 *The Sentence*, Second Half, *The Composite Sentence*, 2d. ed. (Groningen: P. Noordhoff, 1929; copyright WaltersgroepGroningen). I am also most grateful to Oxford University Press for granting me permission to include selected material from

H. Poutsma's unpublished Dictionary, which is copyright Oxford University Press.

I am also indebted to numerous individuals who were kind enough to help with the completion of this book in various ways, both academic and nonacademic. I thank Ian Gurney and Robert MacGilleon, of the University of Tampere, for giving most generously of their time to read through earlier versions of the book, to discuss specific issues, to offer suggestions with respect to English usage, and to act as informants. I am also deeply indebted to Jane Hill, of the University of Arizona, who was likewise kind enough to read through several chapters of an earlier version of the book, making numerous helpful comments. Readers for the publisher provided valuable comments as well. Further, I am indebted to David Lebeaux, of the University of Maryland, and to David Basilico, of the University of Alabama, for commenting on some aspects of control. No doubt the content of this book would have been improved if more of the comments and suggestions of these scholars had been incorporated into the text. I am also grateful to Robert Cooper, Virginia Mattila, Robert Hollingsworth, Yvonne Hyrynen, and David Robertson, all of the University of Tampere, and to Francine and Joe Galko, of the University of Texas, for their help as informants. Others who have helped with a number of informant judgments include Susan McAnsh, of the University of Oulu, and Gene Halleck, of the University of Oklahoma, and I am grateful to them. Frits Stuurman, of the University of Utrecht, was instrumental in securing access to H. Poutsma's unpublished dictionary for me, and I owe a debt of gratitude to him for his help. I am also grateful to Helena Halmari, of the University of California at San Diego, and Merja Kytö, of the University of Tampere, who helped me to obtain some other material that was difficult of access. I also want to express my appreciation to Hanna-Kaisa Manhela and Markku Kaunisto, my assistants at the University of Tampere, for their valuable help. Of course, the responsibility for the contents of this book rests entirely with me, being the sole author and the originator of all arguments not specifically attributed to others.

Tampere, February 21, 1995
Juhani Rudanko

1

Introduction

This book investigates the syntactic and semantic properties of an important set of complement clauses that are in construction with the prepositions *in, to, at, on, with,* and *of* in present-day English. [The term "present-day English" will be used in this book as in Rudanko (1989) to denote "contemporary English, twentieth-century English, of speakers who are alive today" (Rudanko 1989, 13).] More specifically, the types of complement clauses considered may be illustrated with the following sentences:

(1) a. John delights in frustrating his opponents.
    b. John resorted to denigrating his opponents.
    c. The rebuff reduced John to groveling before his idol.
    d. John balked at extending the deadline.
    e. John concentrated on winning the round.
    f. John coped well with putting the baby to bed.
    g. They charged John with stealing a car.
    h. John dreamed of changing the world.
    i. They accused John of stealing a car.

Sentences 1a–i share a number of salient properties. In each of them there are two verbs. The first, occurring immediately after the first noun phrase in 1a–i, is the matrix predicate. The other verb in each case occurs immediately after the relevant preposition in the sequence of expressed constituents. Each verb has its own subject. Here we might recall the projection principle and the theta criterion, which are two principles influential in guiding current syntactic work. Informal phrasings of the principles are sufficient for the present purpose. The projection principle says that "every syntactic representation (i.e., LF-representation and S- and D-structure) should be a projection of the thematic structure and the properties of subcategorization of lexical entries" [Chomsky (1981, 36)]. The theta criterion relates to arguments of verbs and says that each argument of a verb can have only one theta role and that "each θ-role is assigned to one and only one argument" [Chomsky (1981, 36)]. Given these two principles, it follows that in each of 1a–i there is an understood argument. The first NP in each sentence is the subject argument of the verb that immediately follows it, but given the theta criterion, this NP cannot simultaneously be the subject argument of the other verb of the sentence. At the same time, given the projection principle, the lower verb must have a subject argument. The subject argument of this other verb is not overtly expressed. In line with fairly recent work, the understood subject of the lower verb in each of 1a–i may be represented by the symbol PRO. This is a symbol for a pronominal element which has the features of number, person, and gender but has no phonetic realization. Earlier pretransformational and traditional work on English grammar did not use the symbol PRO but generally shared the basic intuition that there is an understood subject in each of 1a–i.

Given the presence of an understood subject in 1a–i, it follows that there are two sentences or clauses in each of them. In relatively recent work, sentences have been analyzed on the basis of progressively more hierarchical structures, including the S' node, originally proposed by Bresnan (1970), and the IP and CP projections proposed by Chomsky (1986a). Still further projections were proposed by Abney (1987) and Pollock (1989). For present purposes, such elaborate structures can be set aside, and the traditional "flat" structure may suffice. It is then possible to represent the sentences of 1a–i as in structures 1'a–i:

(1') a. [[John]$_{NP1}$ [delights]$_{Verb1}$ [in]$_{Prep}$ [[PRO]$_{NP2}$ [[frustrating]$_{Verb2}$ his opponents]$_{VP}$]$_{S2}$]$_{S1}$

  b. [[John]$_{NP1}$ [resorted]$_{Verb1}$ [to]$_{Prep}$ [[PRO]$_{NP2}$ [[denigrating]$_{Verb2}$ his opponents]$_{VP}$]$_{S2}$]$_{S1}$

  c. [[The rebuff]$_{NP1}$ [reduced]$_{Verb1}$ [John]$_{NP0}$ [to]$_{Prep}$ [[PRO]$_{NP2}$ [[groveling]$_{Verb2}$ before his idol]$_{VP}$]$_{S2}$]$_{S1}$

d. [[John]$_{NP1}$ [balked]$_{Verb1}$ [at]$_{Prep}$ [[PRO]$_{NP2}$ [[extending]$_{Verb2}$ the deadline]$_{VP}$]$_{S2}$]$_{S1}$

e. [[John]$_{NP1}$ [concentrated]$_{Verb1}$ [on]$_{Prep}$ [[PRO]$_{NP2}$ [[winning]$_{Verb2}$ the round]$_{VP}$]$_{S2}$]$_{S1}$

f. [[John]$_{NP1}$ [coped]$_{Verb1}$ well [with]$_{Prep}$ [[PRO]$_{NP2}$ [[putting]$_{Verb2}$ the baby to bed]$_{VP}$]$_{S2}$]$_{S1}$

g. [[They]$_{NP1}$ [charged]$_{Verb1}$ [John]$_{NP0}$ [with]$_{Prep}$ [[PRO]$_{NP2}$ [[stealing]$_{Verb2}$ a car]$_{VP}$]$_{S2}$]$_{S1}$

h. [[John]$_{NP1}$ [dreamed]$_{Verb1}$ [of]$_{Prep}$ [[PRO]$_{NP2}$ [[changing]$_{Verb2}$ the world]$_{VP}$]$_{S2}$]$_{S1}$

i. [[They]$_{NP1}$ [accused]$_{Verb1}$ [John]$_{NP0}$ [of]$_{Prep}$ [[PRO]$_{NP2}$ [stealing a car]$_{VP}$]$_{S2}$]$_{S1}$

As a point of terminology facilitating discussion, the symbol NP$_1$ is used in this book to designate the subject of a matrix clause, the symbol NP$_2$ the subject of a lower clause, and the symbol NP$_0$ the object of a matrix clause. Where there is no danger of confusion, these same symbols are sometimes also used, by way of a convenient shorthand, to designate the entities that are referred to by the NPs in question. As another point of terminology, the terms "*in -ing* pattern," "*to -ing* pattern," etc., will be used of the constructions in 1a–i and 1'a–i, even though, strictly speaking, in none of these is the preposition a constituent of the subordinate clause.

Examples 1'a–b, 1'd–f, and 1'h may be termed subject control structures, for in them PRO is generally, as in the sentences given, controlled by the subject of the matrix clause. On the other hand, 1'c, 1'g, and 1'i are object control structures, for in them PRO is frequently controlled by the object of the matrix clause.

The presence of PRO is an important feature shared by the patterns of 1a–i. Another important feature shared by the constructions concerns the syntactic status of the lower clause, designated S$_2$ in 1a–i. In each case without exception, the lower clause is a complement clause. This means that there is a close syntactic connection between the matrix verb, designated Verb$_1$ in 1a–i, and the lower clause. In particular, the focus of the present investigation on complement clauses entails a number of exclusions. For instance, it means that adverbial clauses will not be considered except in passing. An example, to be discussed more fully in chapter 2, may serve to illustrate the point. Consider sentence 2:

(2) John stammered in pronouncing the word.

Sentence 2 is similar to 1a in a number of ways. For instance, in 2, as in 1a, there is a PRO, and in both the PRO is coreferential with the subject of the matrix clause. However, in 2 the connection between the higher verb *stammered* and the lower clause introduced by *in* is less close than in 1a. One reflex of this is that preposing is more readily possible in 2 than in 1a. Thus compare 3a–b, with an adverb of manner added in each case to alleviate the artificial flavor of the sentences.

(3) a. ?? In frustrating his opponent John delights greatly.
    b. In pronouncing the word John stammered perceptibly.

The distinction between complement and adverbial clauses is important, but it is not always easy to make. More discussion of the question and, more broadly, of the delimitation of the patterns of 1a–i, will be provided in the individual chapters of this book. It will be seen that problems of delimitation do not always surface in the same way, but that adverbial clauses are a recurring theme.

The order in which the patterns of complementation are covered in this book is not based on some logical necessity. Nor is it alphabetical, based on the preposition. It is simply that in which the chapters were originally written. No doubt it would be possible to change the order, but this would affect little of substance, and consequently the order of conception has been preserved in this book.

Not all complement clause patterns involving control and introduced by prepositions in present-day English are covered in this book. For instance, sentential patterns introduced by *into, from,* and *for* are not included. The first two of these receive some attention in Rudanko (1989). As for *for* patterns, and other patterns not covered, their exclusion is not motivated by any desire to imply that they are unimportant in present-day English. Rather, it is dictated by practical considerations, including the limitations of space and time and the desirability of bringing the investigation of at least some central patterns to some kind of conclusion. It may also be hoped that the methods of analysis applied and illustrated here may be used in the investigation of patterns not covered.

Regarding data and sources of data in the present study, extensive use is made of two major corpora of present-day English, the Brown and the LOB corpora. In the collection of data in each chapter these two corpora are considered first. In an important sense, then, the present study is corpus-based. At the same time, the reliance on the Brown and LOB corpora does not mean that data collected by earlier grammarians should necessarily be discarded. In this connection, as will be seen, pride of place belongs to Poutsma (1905, 1929).[1] As far as sources of data other than corpora and grammars are concerned, Bridgeman et al. (1965) do not have a focus on documented usage, but it is beyond question that their lists of verbs selecting sentential complements in numerous types of constructions constitute another useful resource for the present investigation. From a broader perspective, data based on intuitions of native speakers should be taken into account. Indeed, recorded usage cannot be taken as an absolute guideline. Instead, it must be weighed against intuitions of native speakers. In the great majority of cases there is little conflict between these two sources of data, and for any given verb in any given construction there is a tendency for plentiful recorded usage to go together with native speakers finding the verb acceptable in the construction in question. In some other cases, relatively few in number, recorded usage offers examples that are clearly unacceptable to speakers today. An early example occurs in chapter 2. It is observed that in the LOB corpus, the verb *concentrate* is found construed with *in -ing*, as in *I concentrated in forgetting my trouble* (abbreviated from the example in chapter 2). However, there is a very pronounced tendency for speakers today instead to favor *concentrate on -ing*, as in *I concentrated on forgetting my troubles*, and on the basis of this introspective evidence, which is of course backed up by recorded usage of *concentrate on -ing*, the verb is not cited as taking *in -ing*, in spite of the one recorded example, but is restricted to taking *on -ing*. In a number of other cases, judgments are less clear-cut, and informants may have intuitions that are hazy or even conflicting. Mention will be made of decisions on including or excluding marginal constructions. It is observed repeatedly that marginal acceptability tends to go together with dearth of recorded usage in the corpora. The more general point is that introspective and corpus evidence must be weighed against each other, with the aim of doing justice—as best as one can— to what is current and acceptable in present-day English. This book will serve to demonstrate that both corpus data and data derived from introspection are valuable and necessary in the study of the complementation structures under review.

As far as the structure of the individual chapters is concerned, a broadly similar procedure is followed in each. First, an attempt is made to delimit the pattern or patterns to be considered as explicitly as possible. Second, there is the task of compiling lists of verbs. In this book, this task is as far as possible kept separate from that of characterizing and taxonomizing the verbs. This is to ensure that the process of classification does not interfere with that of deciding whether or not a given verb should be included in the first place. Taxonomies are preceded or followed in the individual chapters by discussion of the reasons for setting them up in the way done here. In all chapters, the taxonomies lead to further discussion of syntactic and semantic properties of the verbs included. Often it is possible to argue, partly on the basis of usage and partly on the basis of semantic analysis, that verbs selecting a pattern may be grouped into a relatively small number of core classes. Other recurring themes in the further analysis of the patterns in the light of the taxonomies include the question of whether the complement sentence in the pattern in question is always nominal and whether control properties interact with the semantic taxonomy proposed, and if so, in what way. The chapters also typically include discussion of the question of alternation, that is, whether verbs selecting the pattern under review select other patterns of sentential complementation, with the meaning of the verb in question remaining approximately constant. It is observed of the nine constructions investigated that verbs governing them permit differing amounts of alternation. Apart from the sheer quantity of alternation, it is also important to consider its quality, especially from a semantic point of view. It is suggested in the individual chapters that alternative construals—even when similar in meaning in some respects—often exhibit semantic differences on closer inspection, and that such differences may have a bearing on the degree of homogeneity that can be attributed to the pattern in question. Overall, the taxonomies, supplemented with discussion of core classes, of control properties, and of alternation, are helpful in pointing to at least some of the typical semantic functions associated with each pattern of complementation considered.[2]

With regard to the theoretical orientation of this book, the investigation draws on both traditional and more recent work on the syntax and semantics of English where such work bears on the analysis of one or more of the nine patterns of complementation in a fruitful way. At the same time, it is carried out in a fashion that is as independent as possible of any particular model of description, and especially of the technicalities of any model, so as not be an artifact of any one framework. It is grounded in facts of English relating to the nine patterns and their position in the complementation system of English that call for coverage in any paradigm, and overall, it is offered as a contribution to the grammatical analysis of English.

A comment might be appended on the relation of the present book to Rudanko (1989). It is certainly possible to find similarities between the two volumes. In both an attempt is made to gather and to consider a reasonable body of data for analysis, and in both the data are primarily from present-day English. Further, both share a concern with the syntactic and semantic analysis of the data and especially with the interrelation and the interface of the syntactic and semantic points of view. However, there are also important differences. For instance, the extensive use made here of corpus data—which I did not have at my disposal when I wrote the 1989 book—enriches the data base of the present investigation. More fundamentally, the subject matter of the two books is different. The nine constructions that are the focus of attention in the present volume are not the ones considered in the 1989 book. The difference in subject matter is accentuated by another consideration. Several of the constructions that were considered in the 1989 book—especially the nonprepositional *to* infinitive and *-ing* form construals, as in *John wanted to come along* and *John avoided committing himself,* respectively, and *that* complement clauses, as in *John asserted that he was innocent*—have been the object of intense investigation over the past thirty years or so. As far as the nine constructions that are the subject of the present investigation are concerned, Poutsma (1905, 1929) and one or two other studies have addressed some aspects of some of these. However, important features of the nine patterns, including the syntactic status of complements of prepositions in the structures, the question of control, and the possibility of core classes, have been more or less completely overlooked in the literature so far. Indeed, the neglect of the nine constructions over the past thirty years or so has been so pervasive that there is a sense in which the present book, by redressing this neglect and by focusing on sentential complementation dependent on prepositions from the vantage point of modern linguistic theory, introduces and defines a new research field. This may serve to provide justification for the project. In any case, as far as the relation of the present book to the 1989 volume is concerned, the two do not duplicate each other. Rather, they complement each other, and each of them is designed to stand on its own as an independent study.

2

Delighting in Frustrating One's Opponents: On Verbs Governing *in -ing*

I

Consider sentence 1 and structure 1', which is a partially bracketed representation of 1:

(1) John delights in frustrating his opponents.
(1') [[John]$_{NP1}$ [delights]$_{Verb1}$ [in]$_{Prep}$ [[PRO]$_{NP2}$ [[frustrating]$_{Verb2}$ his opponents]$_{VP}$]$_{S2}$]$_{S1}$

The present chapter examines the pattern of 1 as partially bracketed in 1'. (The term "*in -ing* pattern" will be used, even though, strictly speaking, *in* in 1' is not part of the lower clause.) Verbs will be listed and illustrated that can occur as Verb$_1$ in 1, that is, as the matrix verb in the pattern. A semantic characterization of such verbs will then be attempted. The examination of matrix verbs, it is suggested, will provide a suitable basis for discussing some other properties of the pattern, for example those of control.

With regard to sources of data, recorded usage will be drawn on. Apart from the Brown and LOB corpora, Poutsma (1905, 651 f.) and (1929, 897 ff.) will be referred to as well, for he is one of the relatively few grammarians of English to have devoted longish sections to the pattern. [For other discussions of aspects of *in* *-ing*, see, for instance, Mustanoja (1960, 572), Jespersen (1965, 115 ff.), Söderlind (1958, 194 ff.).] Another type of source is constituted by intuitions of native speakers, especially insofar as they relate to acceptability.

It should be emphasized at the outset that the present discussion is restricted to those constructions of type 1' where S_2 is a complement sentence. This means, roughly, that S_2 is closely connected with the verb of the matrix sentence, that is, that $Verb_1$ is subcategorized as taking an *in* and an *-ing* clause. This requirement has the effect of excluding adverbial clauses. The distinction between complement clauses and adverbial clauses is an important one. The odd ambiguous or indeterminate construction may be found, or devised, but in the great majority of cases it is not too difficult to separate these two kinds of subordinate clauses. This will be seen to be especially true of verbs such as *delight*. The question arises in the first place because *in* is quite capable of introducing adverbial clauses of time. As Poutsma (1905, 703) perspicaciously points out, in such clauses the "relation of time expressed by *in* is often mixed with other relations," such as instrumentality. It is worth quoting one or two examples: *This lunatic, in letting Scrooge's nephew out, had let two other people in* [Poutsma (1905, 702); from *A Christmas Carol*, 1]. *In so speaking, Rashleigh indeed played a winning card* [Poutsma (1905, 703); from *For His Sake*, 1, chap. 13, 224]. [For titles of Poutsma's sources here and elsewhere, cf. also Poutsma (1926, 835 ff.).] As Poutsma observes, in the first example, *in* introduces an adverbial clause of time, whereas in the second, time is mixed with instrumentality. It is worth noting that in the first example, *in* may be replaced by *when* without an appreciable effect on the meaning of the sentence. In the second example, *by* is a possible substitute for *in*, again without an appreciable effect on meaning. The possibility of such substitutions reinforces Poutsma's analysis.

It is possible to devise sentences with adverbial clauses that are close in appearance to the pattern being considered here. For instance, consider 2a–b:

(2) a. John stammered in pronouncing the name.
 b. John stumbled in climbing the stairs.

Sentences 2a–b have sequences of constituents that are seemingly similar to that of 1. Undoubtedly, 2a–b have PRO as well, in the same way as

1 does. However, the *in -ing* clauses of 2a–b have an adverbial force. In them the *in* and the *in -ing* clause are less closely tied to Verb$_1$. The *in -ing* clauses here express such adverbial notions as time, attendant circumstances, or perhaps manner. The adverbial character of the *in -ing* clauses in 2a–b is also brought out if questions are devised to which 2a–b could be responses. In such questions the question word is most properly *when, how,* or *why*. These are not possible in analogous questions with *delight* as Verb$_1$. For *delight,* resort must be had to *what*. On the other hand, *what* seems impossible or very awkward if an adverbial *in -ing* clause is to be elicited in response.

(3) a. Q. How did John stumble? A. He stumbled in climbing the stairs.
   b. Q. *How did John delight? A. He delighted in frustrating his opponents.
   c. Q. What did John delight in? A. He delighted in frustrating his opponents.
   d. Q. *What did John stumble in? A. He stumbled in climbing the stairs.

The contrasts in well-formedness among the sentences of 3a–d may perhaps also be taken to suggest that the *-ing* clause of 1' is nominal and that the *-ing* clauses of 2a–b are not, provided that we accept the view that nominal complement clauses exist. The suggestion is rendered plausible when it is observed that a similar difference in well-formedness between *delight,* representing verbs taking complement clauses, and *stammer* and *stumble,* representing verbs co-occurring with adverbial clauses, shows up in the replaceability of the *-ing* clause by other pronouns such as *it* and *that,* as well. [On replaceability of sentences by *it* as a criterion of NP status, see Kajita (1967, 15 ff., especially 17); on replaceability by *that* and *it*, see Quirk et al. (1985, 1049).] Thus a sentence such as *John delighted in frustrating his opponents and Jane delighted in it/that as well* is good, but sentences such as **John stumbled in climbing the stairs and Jane stumbled in it/that as well,* and **John stammered in pronouncing the name and Jane stammered in it/that as well,* are not. Further, the admissibility of right dislocation constructions may be invoked here as another criterion of nominal clauses. This confirms the nominal status of the lower clause in 1', for *John delights in it, frustrating his opponents* is conceivable. On the other hand, right dislocation is not possible in 2a–b, for neither **John stammered in it, pronouncing the name* nor **John *stumbled in it, climbing the stairs* is well formed. [For some discussion of this criterion, see Rudanko (1976, 97 f.) and Seppänen (1986, 31 f.).] The concept of a nominal clause is a traditional one, and it continues to be central even in recent grammars of English, for example that by Quirk et al. (1985). To be sure, some fairly recent work, especially within X bar syntax,[1] has the effect of casting some doubt on, or at least of clouding, its status and relevance, but in spite of this, the concept seems a useful one, and on the whole, it has stood the test of time. It will be adopted here and, accordingly, S_2 in the pattern of 1' will be considered a nominal clause.

The syntactic difference between *delight*, taking complement clauses, on the one hand, and *stammer* and *stumble*, co-occurring with adverbial clauses, on the other, is perhaps also reflected in their contrasting patterns of well-formedness in such pseudocleft sentences as those in 4a–c.

(4) a. What John delighted in was frustrating his opponents.
 b. *What John stammered in was pronouncing the name.
 c. *What John stumbled in was climbing the stairs.

It bears emphasizing here that these pseudocleft sentences should be read as specificational. That is, the approximate meaning of, for instance, 4a is something like 'John delighted in this: frustrating his opponents', rather than 'John delighted in X. Doing an X was frustrating his opponents', which would be an approximate paraphrase of the predicational reading (cf. Higgins 1973a, 16 ff.).

A full treatment of pseudocleft sentences cannot be attempted in the present context. However, it is clear that the adverbial clauses of 2a–b are not good in the focus position of pseudocleft sentences of the type of 4b–c. Sentences 4b–c are thus in contrast with 4a, which is good. [The well-formedness of 4a also reinforces the proposal that S_2 is an NP in such *-ing* complement-clause constructions as 1'; cf. the observations, admittedly tentative, by Higgins (1973b, 191), and cf. also the earlier and more definitive analysis of Rosenbaum (1967, 13 ff., 93 f.).] On the other hand, sentences such as *When/how John stumbled was in climbing the stairs* are better than 4b–c, again revealing the adverbial nature of their *in -ing* clauses, and contrasting with **When/how John delighted was in frustrating his opponents.*

Further, an adverbial *in -ing* clause may be preposed more easily than a complement clause. [For the criterion of preposability in more general terms, cf. Kajita (1967, 19).] Admittedly, the preposing of even adverbial *in -ing* clauses is not very common with such short predicates as *stammer* and *stumble*. However, 5a–b are still conceivable, especially if an adverb is added, but 5a is not, even with an adverb.

(5) a. *In frustrating his opponents John delighted (mischievously).
    b. In pronouncing the name John stammered (perceptibly).
    c. In climbing the stairs John stumbled (awkwardly).

On the other hand, as has been pointed out in relatively recent work, adverbial clauses are in general more resistant to the extraction of constituents out of them than are complement clauses. Thus there is a fairly clear contrast between 6a [from McCloskey (1988, 31)] and 6b [from McCloskey (1988, 41)]. (The one question mark in 6b is McCloskey's; the sentence might perhaps even merit two question marks.)

(6) a. I wonder what he said he wanted.
    b. ?Who did you lie while praising?

In 6a the *wh* constituent *what* has been extracted from, or, to put it more neutrally, is connected to a position in a complement clause, while in 6b the corresponding *wh* word *who* is connected to a position in an adverbial clause. [For further and more comprehensive discussion of the analysis of extraction of constituents out of complements and adjuncts, see, for instance, Cattell (1976, 38), Huang (1982, 487 ff.), McCloskey (1988, 40 ff.), McCloskey (1993, 499 ff.) and Chomsky and Lasnik (1993, 540 ff.).]

When extraction is applied to the kind of *in -ing* clauses that are under review in this chapter, contrasts such as those in 7a–b are obtained:

(7) a. Who did John delight in frustrating?
    b. *What did John stumble in climbing?

The contrast between extraction out of a complement and out of an adverbial clause seems a fairly robust one, at least in the case of *delight* and *stumble,* as illustrated in 7a–b.

Finally, it is symptomatic that *stammer* and *stumble* allow *when -ing* clauses, with meanings that are similar to those of 2a–b in their adverbial force, as in *John stammered when pronouncing the name* and *John stumbled when climbing the stairs. Delight,* of course, does not allow such *when* clauses: *John delighted when frustrating his opponents.*

Persist may take *in* and an *-ing* clause as well, as in 8:

(8) John persisted in frustrating his opponents.

Persist and *delight* are different, in that the former may omit the *in* and the *-ing* clause (with the meaning of the verb remaining at least approximately constant), but the latter cannot: *He persisted* is possible, but not **He delighted*. In this respect, *persist* resembles *stammer* and *stumble*. However, the resemblance is superficial, for the *-ing* clause of 8 is a complement clause, on the most likely interpretation of the sentence. An adverbial clause expressing attendant circumstances, instrumentality, or manner following *persist* is perhaps most appropriately introduced by *by*, as in 9:

(9) John persisted by interrupting me.

Sentence 9 allows the insertion of a pause, or of a comma in writing, after *persisted*, which is a sign of a looser connection between Verb$_1$ and the clause that follows. Example 9 is understood to contain a suppressed constituent, something along the lines of *John persisted (in what he was doing) by interrupting me*. By contrast, 8 may be interpreted as not containing any suppressed constituent of this kind, with the *-ing* clause expressing what John persisted in. Indeed, there is little doubt that this is the reading of 8 that comes to mind first. An adverbial interpretation of the subordinate clause in 8 seems less likely, though it is perhaps not altogether impossible, along the lines of 'John persisted (in what he was doing) in/when frustrating his opponents'. Setting the (rather fanciful) possibility of an adverbial interpretation aside, it is noteworthy that 8 calls for question-and-answer pairs such as Q. *What did John persist in?* A. *He persisted in frustrating his opponents*. Further, the pseudocleft sentence *What John persisted in was frustrating his opponents* is good. Finally, the contrast between the well-formed *Who did John persist in frustrating?* and the ill-formed **Who did John persist by interrupting* is rather striking. In the light of all these considerations, the *-ing* clause in 8 may be read as a complement clause.

In the following it seems advisable in the main to be guided by the considerations mentioned when selecting verbs as governing complement clauses. [For discussion of the complement versus adjunct distinction, see also Somers (1984, 508 ff.) and Somers (1987, 12 ff.).] Three or four of them seem particularly pertinent. The first of these is the ability of the verb in question to occur in question-and-answer pairs of the type of 3c. The second is the admissibility of pseudocleft sentences of the type of 4a, where the *wh* clause has the form *what... in*. The third is the admissibility of extraction out of the subordinate clause in question. The fourth relates to syntactic connectedness and the replaceability of the *in* that precedes the *-ing* clause. As far as complement clauses are concerned, substituting *by* or *when* for the *in* preceding the clause is either impossible or difficult without an appreciable change of meaning. It is impossible for matrix verbs such as *delight*, and it is difficult without a major change of meaning for matrix verbs such as *persist* (recall the understood constituent of 9). The difficulty of replacing the *in* seems a direct reflex of the close connection that exists between matrix verbs and the *in*s preceding complement clauses. On the other hand, in the case of an adverbial construction, the connection between the matrix verb and the *in* is much less close, and the *in* is more closely bound to the *-ing* clause that follows. (No doubt this is what makes it possible to prepose the *in -ing* clause, as in 5b–c.) In this case, the selection of *in* is not governed by the matrix verb, and it is then often possible to substitute either *by* or *when* for the *in* without an appreciable change of meaning.

The criteria are fairly straightforward, at least as applied so far. When they are considered more carefully, one or two comments should be added on the first two of them. Regarding the first criterion, it seems that for most verbs of the pattern it can be converted into the more powerful claim that the only means of eliciting an *in* and an *-ing* clause in a response is a question of the form of *what... in*. This holds for verbs such as *delight*, for as observed, question-and-answer sequences such as 3b are not possible. It also seems to hold for *persist*, which again is not felicitous in such question-and-answer sequences as *Q. Where/how did John persist? A. He persisted in frustrating his opponents.* However, there are verbs that are more compatible with *where* questions eliciting a complement clause in response. (On *how*, see below.) *Succeed* suggests itself here. We may consider a sentence such as *John succeeded in solving the first puzzle*. This sentence allows an adverbial interpretation. In the adverbial interpretation there is an understood constituent in the sentence before *in*, along the lines of 9: 'John succeeded (in what he was doing) in solving the first puzzle'. The adverbial interpretation should be set aside here. The sentence also allows a complement clause interpretation, and indeed this is the more likely reading of the sentence. In that interpretation the *-ing* clause expresses what John succeeded in, and there is nothing suppressed. However, even with the complement clause interpretation, question-and-answer sequences such as Q. *Where did John succeed?* A. *He succeeded in solving the first puzzle* are good, at least for many speakers. There are at least two reasons for the view that *succeed* governs a complement clause even here. First, if we apply the third criterion and replace the *in* by *when* or *by*, the resulting sentence is analogous to 9 in that it has an understood constituent and there is an appreciable change of meaning. The sentence is then not an appropriate answer to the question Q. *Where did John succeed?* It is clear that this question solicits information about the content of what John succeeded in doing rather than the manner, time, means, or instrumentality of how John succeeded (in what he was doing). The second reason is precisely that the *-ing* clause of the sentence *He succeeded in solving the first puzzle*, in response to *Where did John succeed?* expresses the content of what John succeeded in doing.

As far as *how* is concerned, a question such as *How did John succeed?* is ambiguous. (I am indebted to Ian Gurney for drawing my attention to the ambiguity.) Either it may be a question about the content of what John succeeded in, in which case an *-ing* clause as part of the response, as in *John succeeded in solving the first puzzle*, is a complement clause, or it may be a question about the means or manner in which John succeeded, or the degree of his success, in which case an *in -ing* clause as part of the response is an adverbial clause. In the latter case, a *by -ing* clause is perhaps more likely than an *in -ing* clause. In either event, in the adverbial case there is an understood constituent along the lines of 9 in the answer, and even in the question. (An approximate paraphrase of the question would be 'how did John succeed in what he did?') In the case of such matrix verbs as *succeed*, then, *where* or even *how* may be used in place of *what . . . in* to elicit an *in* and an *-ing* complement clause in response. However, because of the ambiguity of *how*, it seems best on the whole to set it aside in the following.

Of course, the first criterion given previously still covers complement clauses governed by *succeed*. Question-and-answer sequences such as Q. *What did John succeed in?* A. *He succeeded in solving the first puzzle* are possible. Indeed, there are speakers who definitely prefer the *what . . . in* question, to elicit the response desired. The comments in the two previous paragraphs, then, neither invalidate nor call into question the first criterion. The point is only that it is not quite possible to claim for all verbs taking *in* and *-ing* complement clauses that a question of the form of *what . . . in* is the only means of eliciting a complement clause in response.

The second criterion is the admissibility of pseudocleft sentences such as 4a. The criterion is straightforward as applied in 4a–c, but there is a factor that may detract from its usefulness elsewhere, even if the derivational properties of pseudocleft sentences are glossed over in the present context. This is that although pseudocleft sentences such as 4a and *What John persisted in was frustrating his opponents* are good, so, for most speakers, are such double *in in* pseudocleft sentences as 10:

(10)   What John delighted/persisted in was in frustrating his opponents.

There are speakers who object to such double *in in* pseudocleft sentences as 10, sometimes with vehemence, but others accept them, and one fairly common comment about them is that such double *in in* pseudocleft sentences have the advantage of being unambiguous in that there is no possibility of a predicational reading.

The complication for the pseudocleft criterion is that double *in in* pseudocleft sentences are often quite good even with adverbial *in -ing* clauses in the focus position, at least for many speakers. Thus *?What John stammered in was in pronouncing the name* and *?What John stumbled in was in climbing the stairs* are appreciably better than 4b and 4c, respectively, and even acceptable to many speakers. They seem to be variants of *Where John stammered was in pronouncing the name* and *Where John stumbled was in climbing the stairs* (Ian Gurney, personal communication), because of the semantic similarity. They are adverbial in character. It may be noted, however, that it is scarcely profitable to think that such double *in in* pseudocleft sentences as 10 are variants of pseudocleft sentences introduced by *where* or *how*, since sentences such as **Where/how John delighted/persisted was in frustrating his opponents* are bad. Rather, it seems that double *in in* pseudocleft sentences may arise possibly from an adverbial source, as in *?What John stammered in was in pronouncing the name,* as well as from a complement clause source, as in 10. A further point is that verbs such as *succeed* allow even pseudocleft sentences such as *Where John succeeded was in devising outrageous practical jokes,* at least for some speakers. However, neither the double *in in* pseudocleft pattern that is in general available for verbs taking *in* and *-ing* complement clauses, at least for many speakers, nor the *where . . . in* pseudocleft pattern that is available for *succeed* invalidates the pseudocleft criterion. After all, *delight* and *persist* occur in the pattern of 4a, as was observed above. *Succeed* occurs in the pattern of 4a as well, for *What John succeeded in was devising outrageous practical jokes* is good (and indeed the preferred pseudocleft construction with *succeed* for many speakers). The comment on the pseudocleft criterion only amounts to the caveat that the criterion cannot quite be extended into the stronger claim that verbs governing *in* and *-ing* complement clauses allow pseudocleft sentences of the type of 4a only, where the *wh* clause has the form of *what . . . in* and the focus consists of an *-ing* clause only.

Apart from adverbial clauses, two other exclusions are worth noting. First, the requirement that S_2 be a complement clause has the effect of excluding nongerundive *-ing* participle clauses. When these follow a combination of an intransitive verb and *in*, the resulting sentence bears a superficial similarity to 1, as in *John walked in, suppressing a yawn*. No doubt the *-ing* clause here contains a PRO as well. However, there is a clear break between *in* and *-ing*, emphasizing the lack of a syntactic connection, and the *-ing* clause is not a complement clause.

Also, the present investigation is restricted to constructions where the matrix predicate is verbal. Constructions where the higher predicate is an adjective, or even of the form *be* Verb + *en*, will be excluded. This excludes sentences such as *John was interested/engaged in investigating the question*.

II

With the *in -ing* complement clause pattern defined in section I, it is possible in this section to proceed to the task of collecting verbs governing the pattern in present-day English. Each verb considered is illustrated with at least one example, in order to make sure that it selects the pattern in question. For the most part, decisions here can be made with a fair degree of confidence, and the alternatives used in the taxonomies of verbs in this book will be limited to either including or excluding a given verb. Admittedly, there are verbs for which intuitions are less secure or even conflicting among informants, and a binary description no doubt sometimes glosses over gray areas or complexities of analysis. The comments offered in the discussion of individual verbs are meant at least partly to alleviate problems that may inhere in a binary procedure. Thus such comments—for instance, the labeling of verbs as "acceptable only with hesitation"—should be kept in mind throughout the discussion, even if they are not repeated in the taxonomies or in subsequent discussion.

In this chapter, as in most other chapters in this book, verbs are principally considered first on the basis of the two corpora, next on the basis of Poutsma's works, especially the grammars, then on the basis of Bridgeman et al. (1965), and finally on the basis of other sources. This general order is not an absolute precept, nor an end in itself in this treatment, but it is suited to take account of the relatively recent date of usage recorded in the corpora and therefore recommends itself as a general procedure for heuristic purposes. It should be noted, however, that when a verb is being considered on the basis of exemplification found in the corpora, it is fairly often advisable or necessary to supplement such exemplification from other sources of recorded usage. Further, acceptability judgments must be a constant and overriding concern throughout.

Verbs considered on the basis of the Brown and LOB corpora:

Verbs	Illustrations and Comments
aid	WHAT IT DOES: *Aids in reducing the incidence and severity of bloat in beef or dairy cattle on legume pasture* (Brown E27 1420-1430, from *Successful Farming* 59: 12).[2] An illustration of the verb from Poutsma (1905, 654, from Spencer, *Education*, chap. 1, 226) may also be cited: *Daily are men induced to aid in carrying out interventions which a mere tyro in science could show to be futile.* There is no doubt that the verb should be included. (See also the discussion of *help* below.)
assist	*Firstly, what does it cost a motor trader to assist in filling up an OH.P. form and posting it?* (LOB B10 170-171, from *Financial Times* 8/25). (See also the discussion of *help* below.)
believe	*Nevertheless, most of the teen-agers I interviewed believed in maintaining their Jewish identity and even envisioned joining a synagogue or temple* [Brown F25 0240-0260, from D. Boroff, "Jewish Teen-Age Culture" (*Annals of the American Academy of Political and Social Science* 338)].
concentrate	*When we had passed the chamois, I wanted to tell my mother something of my defeat over the Day of Atonement or the parable of the mustard seed, but she did not pay attention as her whole mind now focused on the Edelweiss, Gentian, or Christ's Thorn we had come to. So I too concentrated in forgetting my troubles in the flowers* [LOB G26 69-74, from E. Wakeford, *A Prize for Art* (Macmillan)]. The instance is found in the corpus. However, *concentrate in . . . -ing* is unacceptable to most

speakers of English, who prefer *concentrate on* quite definitely. (Stars or question marks will not be assigned to unmodified instances of recorded usage in this book, even when these are judged to be ill formed.) For this reason, it is best to drop the verb from further consideration in the present context.

consist *The other line of argument consists in putting forward a theory that tries to show how art in general and serious art in particular functions in man's attempt to achieve the good life* (LOB G47 81-83, from *Athene* 10: 2). Apart from *in -ing*, *consist* governs *of -ing* (with a somewhat similar meaning), as in *The other line of argument consists of putting forward a theory that*... The meanings of the two constructions are not really equivalent, for *consist in -ing* may be glossed as 'have as the chief/only element', and *consist of -ing* may be glossed as 'be made up of'. (The glosses are from the ALD for *consist in* and *consist of*.)

cooperate *Marine dealers and even some manufacturers who sell direct in non-dealer areas cooperate in enabling you to launch now and pay later* [Brown E06 0910-0930, from J. Choate, "The American Boating Scene" (*Rudder* 77: 1)].

delight *There are plenty of people—both sexes—who delight in showing their knowledge* [LOB F03 97-98, from C. Warrell, *Help Yourself to Good Speaking* (George G. Harrap)].

excel *On the other hand, Mr. Pearson excels in meeting people informally, but many still regard him "as some sort of cross between an egghead and a missionary"* (LOB A03 121-124, from *The Times* 1/10).

experiment *Beginning in* Cloth of the Tempest *(1943) he experimented in merging poetry and visual art, using drawings to carry long narrative segments of a story, as in* Sleepers Awake, *and constructing elaborate "poems-in-drawing-and-type" in which it is impossible to distinguish between the "art" and the poetry* [Brown G73 0620-0670, from C. See, "The Jazz Musician as Patchen's Hero" (*The Arizona Quarterly* 17:2)]. (Regarding *experiment*, see also chaps. 5 and 7.)

fail   *And to write his best both Forster and Georgina knew that Dickens needed a quiet mind; freedom from care and worry; an efficiently-functioning household; emotional and aesthetic satisfactions and companionships—all that poor Catharine, in her miserable inadequacy, had failed in providing* [LOB G27 25-30, from C. Du Cann, *The Love-Lives of Charles Dickens* (Frederick Muller)]. This example is pointed out in Granath (1994, 182). This construal, though attested, is not entirely acceptable to all speakers. To provide a broader perspective for considering the verb here, it is perhaps best to refer at some length to Poutsma (1929, 901 f.). Here are four examples from this source, grouped by Poutsma under 1 and 2: 1. *This rather saucy assumption failed in being offensive* (from Hardy, *Far from the Madding Crowd*, chap. 3, 19). *I have failed in attempting to trace how far his scheme of symbolism may have extended* (from W. M. Rossetti, *Shelley's Adonais* Notes, 4); 2. *He was quite bewildered by the diversion, and for the first time failed in finding a prompter in Field* (from Disraeli, *Sybil*, 6, chap. 10, 413). *Medina Sidonia failed in bringing his pursuers to a close engagement* (from Green, *A Short History of the English People*, 7, par. 6, 419). Poutsma makes the following comment: "As the above examples are intended to show, *to fail* when construed with *in* + gerund (-clause) is used in two meanings; viz.: 1) that of *not to have (the desired) effect of,* 2) that of *to be unsuccessful in.* The first meaning may also be expressed by *to fail* when followed by *of* + gerund (-clause), the second meaning by *to fail* when followed by an infinitive (-clause), the ordinary construction" (1929, 901 f.).

This treatment of *fail* from Poutsma (1929, 901 f.) has merit, for instance, in its sensitivity to semantic distinctions that are certainly relevant to the analysis of *fail*. Even so, one or two parts of it should be commented on and clarified from the point of view of present-day English. First, although the *of -ing* construction is attested, it is too dated to be acceptable to speakers today, as, for instance, consider ??*This rather saucy assumption failed of being offensive.* Therefore it does not merit further consideration in the present context. Further, it is desirable, where possible, to exclude adverbial constructions. Thus the *in* *-ing* construal in the second example cited from Poutsma, with *I have failed in attempting*..., seems adverbial in character, its meaning being along the lines of 'I have attempted... and failed', or even 'I have failed when attempting...'. Once adverbial construals are excluded, it seems safe to say, from the vantage point of today, that the infinitival construal is the ordinary construction for *fail* in the meaning of 'not to have the desired effect of'. As for the second meaning suggested by Poutsma, that of 'be unsuccessful in', there is no doubt that Poutsma is correct in calling the infinitival construal "the ordinary construction." Reactions to it by native speakers are clearly and uniformly favorable, as in this further example: *The Great Powers failed to prevent civil war in Ruritania,* which is indeterminate or ambiguous in meaning between 'did not prevent... ' and 'made an effort but did not succeed in preventing...'. As far as the *in -ing* construal is concerned, reactions to *The Great Powers failed in preventing civil war in Ruritania* are much more varied. Many speakers reject the sentence out of hand (on the complement clause interpretation), sometimes with vehemence, correcting it to the infinitival construction. On the other hand, there are speakers who find it acceptable. For the latter class of speakers, the meaning of the verb (on the complement clause interpretation) is along the lines of 'make an effort but not succeed in...'. This "processual feel" also extends to the sentences cited above from Poutsma under 2, which are likewise more or less acceptable to this class of speakers. Further, it seems relevant to the example from LOB, cited at the beginning of this discussion, where the subordinate clause is undoubtedly a complement clause. (The extraction criterion cited above may be recalled here.) The example is of recent occurrence, but in spite of this many speakers again prefer the infinitival construal, ... *all that poor Catherine, in her miserable inadequacy, had failed to provide.*

Intuitions seem divided on the acceptability of the *fail in -ing* construction (on a complement clause interpretation). Some speakers find it acceptable, especially with a "processual feel," but other speakers prefer the infinitival variant even in this case, sometimes very strongly. It is not easy to come to a fully satisfactory decision regarding this verb. The verb certainly deserves further consideration and analysis, but on the basis of the informant judgments available for the present study, it seems that most speakers are hesitant about, or negative toward, the construction. For this reason the verb will not be included, but the decision is a somewhat marginal one.

help	*The Government will help in transferring companies and workers into new lines, where modernization doesn't seem feasible* (Brown A43 1670-1690, from *U.S. News and World Report* 5/22). *Help* also selects the *to* infinitive construction, as in *We have helped to populate other countries* [Poutsma (1929, 902, from Morris, *News from Nowhere*, chap. 10, 81]. (For *help* and *at -ing*, see Chapter 5.)

Poutsma suggests that "in the infinitive-construction after the verbs *to help, to aid,* and *to assist* the idea of assisting is sometimes more or less obscured, approaching to that of joining or contributing" (1929, 902 f.). Setting aside *aid* and *assist*—they seem perceptibly less good with the infinitive today, as in *The whole family helped/?aided/?assisted to clear the snow from the driveway*—Poutsma's observation is insightful, especially if inanimate NP₁s that do not have an instrumental meaning are considered, as witness *In the countryside poverty helped to exacerbate social tensions/?In the countryside poverty helped in exacerbating social tensions*. From a slightly different angle, Granath's (1994, 184) comment (on a group of verbs that *help* is a prominent member of) that "an infinitive signifies a more active role of the subject, and the prep-phrase implies an action of some duration" also seems helpful, especially perhaps in cases where either construal is about equally acceptable, as in these sentences devised by Ian Gurney (personal communication): *The Government will help in establishing new industries in development areas* and *The Government will help to establish new industries in development areas*. (See also section III below.)

join	*Mrs. Molvar asked again that the board join in taking a stand in keeping with Jack Lowe's program* (Brown A10 0650-0660, from *The Oregonian* 10/24). A second example, freely invented, may be worth adducing, to confirm the inclusion of the verb: *John declined to join in paying the housekeeping expenses.*
lie	*If our national interest lies in being able to fight and win a war rather than committing national suicide, then we must take a much more penetrating look at ballistic missiles* [Brown E03 0300-0320, from D. Martin, "Will Aircraft or Missiles Win Wars?" (*Flying* 68: 2)].

participate	*I believe that the industrial countries are ready to participate actively in supplementing the efforts of the developing nations to achieve progress* [Brown G35 0470-0480, from D. Eisenhower, *Peace with Justice* (Columbia University Press)].
persist	*And yet Mr. Kennedy persists in trying to mollify the intransigents of the right with apologies and promises of "tightening up" and "economizing"* (Brown B22 1440-1460, from *Commonweal* 11/10).
rejoice	*He isn't at all Swiftian about women: he doesn't, getting close, rejoice in recoiling from their enlarged pores* (LOB C07 50-51, from *The Observer* 2/12).
result	*Whereas the maintenance rotary fund had in the past sustained losses considerably beyond expectations, the introduction of the cost-billing system plus other control refinements has resulted in keeping the fund on a proper working basis* (Brown H04 1260-1290, from Rhode Island Legislative Council. Research Report No. 1).
revel	*Australia revels in being Robinson* [LOB R01 113, from L. Gibb, *The Higher Jones* (Frederick Muller)]. A further example, freely invented, confirms the inclusion of the verb: *He absolutely reveled in giving the keynote address.*
share	*This prevents them at present from sharing in reading the literature of the same race from Greenland and Labrador because in those lands this syllabic system is not used* (LOB F36 74-76, from *The Lady* 1/26). The example is attested, but the construction does not seem to be very common. (Construals with nonsentential complements, such as *share in the spoils of victory*, are of course common enough.) The verb is retained with some hesitation.
specialize	*When Richard's parents told him they wanted to take him to an orthodontist—a dentist who specializes in realigning teeth and jaws—their young son was interested* [Brown F11 0080-0100, from L. Pompian, "Tooth-Straightening Today" (*Family Circle Magazine*, March, The Family Circle)].

succeed   *Finally, after a trial lasting seventeen days, he succeeded in getting the Eastbourne doctor acquitted* (LOB F13 165-167, from *Today* 3/18). To judge by the evidence of the two corpora considered, this is by far the most common verb in the pattern.

Verbs considered on the basis of Poutsma's grammars (1905, 652 f.; 1929, 897 ff.) come next:

agree   *Widely as Henry's ministers differed from each other, they all agreed in sharing and fostering the culture around them* [Poutsma (1929, 900), from Green, *A Short History of the English People*, chap. 4, sec. 4, 313]. A second example, freely invented (by Ian Gurney) may help to clarify the status of *agree* as a verb governing *in -ing* complement clauses: *They agreed in thinking that John was a nuisance.*

Poutsma compares the *in -ing* construction with the *to* infinitive construction, as in *It is much more probable that the Powers will agree to let the Moroccans fight it out by themselves* (cited by Poutsma from *The Review of Reviews*), and suggests that the former "describes an agreement concerning a sentiment," and the latter "an agreement concerning a course of action to be adopted" (1929, 900). Poutsma's point is insightful and seems especially relevant to the invented example and the example cited of *agree* and the *to* infinitive. It is perhaps possible to add that when *agree* combines with the *to* infinitive, it implies a decision on a future course of action arrived at jointly, whereas *agree in -ing*, which may be glossed as 'be of the same mind', implies that views run in parallel with what is expressed by S_2 even without a joint decision.

It might be added that *agree about -ing, agree on -ing*, and *agree over -ing* are possible as well, for most speakers, as in *They all agreed about fostering the culture around them, They all agreed on fostering the culture around them*, and *They all agreed over fostering the culture around them*. However, these seem further from the *in -ing* pattern than the *to* infinitive construal, for they imply a joint decision on the part of entities referred to by NP_1 and also express less commitment to what is expressed by the lower clause than does the *agree in -ing* construction.

be	*His greatest pleasure was in doing good* [Poutsma (1929, 898), from Goldsmith, *The Vicar of Wakefield*, chap. 31, 476]. Poutsma (1905, 653) observes that this verb "is sometimes used in the sense of *to consist*." The construction, even in the example quoted, is not quite readily acceptable to all speakers today, but the verb can perhaps still be retained, although with some hesitation.
concur	*I concurred with our incumbent in getting up a petition against the Reform Bill* [Poutsma (1929, 901), from G. Eliot, *Felix Holt*, 36 (OED, 3.a)]. An example without a *with* phrase (and with a plural NP_1) is well formed, as in *Both parties concurred in putting the proposal into effect*, and consequently the verb should be included. Intuitions on the precise meaning of the verb in a sentence such as the one just cited are sometimes slightly uncertain with respect to whether the sense is that of 'cooperate' or is limited to that of mental accord, in which sense the verb may be glossed as 'be of the same mind'. The latter meaning seems to predominate for most speakers today.
glory	*I glory in saying that every one of my young friends around me has a father, brother, or dear relative or friend, who is connected in a similar way with our glorious enterprise* [Poutsma (1905, 655), from Thackeray, *Samuel Titmarsh*, chap. 2, 14].
persevere	*She persevered in requiring an explanation of his two motives* [Poutsma (1905, 652), from *Pride and Prejudice*, chap. 11, 59].
unite	*Judge and prosecutor united in declaring that there could be no question as to the excellency of my motives* [Poutsma (1929, 898), from *The Review of Reviews*, No. 195, 308a]. In the example, NP_1 is plural, which seems typical of *unite* when it governs *in -ing*.
vie	*Journalists of the most violently opposed political creeds vied with each other in doing honour to their English guests* [Poutsma (1929, 903), from *The Review of Reviews*, No. 207, 239b]. In the example, there is a *with* phrase be-

tween Verb₁ and *in*, but *vie* occurs in the pattern of 1 without a *with* phrase, as in *They vied in singing his praises,* and should therefore be included.

We now consider verbs on the basis of Bridgeman et al. (1965, 30 f.), illustrated with invented examples:

acquiesce	*He acquiesced in granting the petition.*
collaborate	*They collaborated in putting the new regulations into effect.*
compete	*They competed in singing his praises.*
engage	*He engaged in denigrating his opponents.* (I am indebted to Ian Gurney for this example.)
indulge	*He indulged in denigrating his opponents.*
luxuriate	*He luxuriated in sampling the French wines available.*

One or two verbs that have suggested themselves or that have been suggested to me are listed next, illustrated with invented examples:

culminate	*The ultimatum culminated in threatening severe sanctions.*
dabble	*He dabbled in trading on the stock exchange.*
interfere	*I do not want to interfere in arranging your holiday.* I am indebted to Ian Gurney for suggesting this sentence and the possibility of including *interfere*.
wallow	*John wallowed in denigrating his opponent.*

III

The following classification may be proposed for the matrix verbs listed above as relevant. The classification is based on meanings and approximate paraphrases of the verbs in question.

1. Verb₁ is equative, NP₁ is equated with Verb₂*ing*: *be, consist, lie.*
2. Verb₁ has the approximate meaning 'feel joy or pleasure in', NP₁ feels joy or pleasure in Verb₂*ing*: *delight, glory, luxuriate, rejoice, revel, wallow.*

3. Verb₁ has the approximate meaning 'perform the act of' or 'carry out the activity of', NP₁ performs/carries out the act/activity of Verb₂*ing* or engages in Verb₂*ing*: *engage, indulge, persevere, persist, specialize.*
'do so with others': *aid, assist, collaborate, cooperate, help, join, participate, share.*
'do so as an uninvited participant': *interfere.*
'do so in a competitive fashion': *compete, vie.*
'do so successfully': *succeed.*
'do so in a preeminent fashion': *excel.*
'do so in a dilettante fashion': *dabble.*
'do so by way of experimenting': *experiment.*

4. Verb₁ has the approximate meaning 'agree in', NP₁ agrees in Verb₂*ing*: *acquiesce, agree, concur.*

5. Others: *believe, culminate, result, unite.*

The classification and the glosses should not be taken to mean that the verbs of each class are synonymous with each other. Rather, the idea underpinning the taxonomy is that the verbs of each class, except those of class 5, share a semantic property. The paraphrases are offered as approximations of such shared ingredients of meaning. Classes 1, 2, and 4 are relatively small in terms of the numbers of verbs belonging to them, and though their members are not synonymous, they display such a degree of semantic homogeneity that it does not seem profitable to divide them into smaller subclasses. A considerably larger number of verbs belongs to class 3. Further, to judge by the evidence of the two corpora considered, the overwhelming majority of instances of verbs governing *in -ing* in present-day English are verbs that belong to class 3. The verbs of this large class are held together by the paraphrase 'perform the act of (Verb₂*ing*)' or 'carry out the activity of (Verb₂*ing*)'. Here a number of subclasses do suggest themselves, as listed above. (The list does not mean that other or additional subclasses could not be distinguished. For instance, *persevere* and *persist* might form a subclass of 'do so by way of continuation'.) The verb *engage* seems fairly close to expressing the central meaning of verbs of this class, and it is offered here as a core verb of the class. Admittedly, it is not perfect as a core verb, for a number of reasons. First, it is slightly formal in flavor, whereas other verbs of the class are not necessarily marked in this way. Second, it tends to imply an activity or a series of actions and does not sound entirely felicitous when the lower clause expresses a single act. This property is shared by a number of other verbs of the class, including *persevere, persist,* and *specialize,* but not by all of them. *Succeed* is a case in point. It is entirely natural to say *John succeeded in scoring a goal,* but *?John engaged in scoring a goal* is less likely (unless one were perhaps to appeal to a "broad" sense of *engage*). Also, whereas *engage* is entirely grammatical and idiomatic with *in -ing,* it does not occur very frequently in the pattern. (It is perhaps more common with simple, nonsentential NPs, as in *engage in business, politics,* etc.) It is certainly not the most common verb with the *in -ing* construal. (To judge by the corpora used, this honor clearly goes to *succeed.*) Further, *engage* seems to be more common with lower predicates that express something in some way disreputable or unpleasant, as in *John engaged in denigrating his opponents* or *John engaged in disrupting meetings of his opponents,* which are impeccable. The verb is capable of occurring with lower predicates that do not express anything disreputable, but it is not very often used in this way, and when it is, it may still at times carry a suggestion of selfish, or even duplicitous, motives, as in *John engaged in flattering/helping/?praising his colleagues.* On the other hand, such imputations of ulterior motives do not always surface; see, for example, *John engaged in studying the history of his family* and *John engaged in writing short stories for magazines.* (I am indebted to Christopher Hall for the first sentence.) In spite of some hesitation, then, it seems possible to adopt *engage* as a core verb, and even as *the* core verb, of class 3 and to use it as shorthand for 'perform the act of' or 'carry out the activity of'. What does recommend *engage* in the present context is that we may discern the relation of entailment between statements such as A and B:

A. John persisted in denigrating his opponent.
B. John engaged in denigrating his opponent.

Of the two statements, A entails B, for if A is true, so is B, and if B is false, so is A. On the other hand, B does not entail A.

It seems possible to construct analogous statements pairing off *engage,* on the one hand, and other verbs of class 3, on the other. Even verbs of the subclasses appear fairly amenable to this treatment. (Of course, *engage* does not carry the specific ingredients of meaning of the subclasses, such as that of 'along with others' of the *help* class.) For instance, we may consider statements C and D:

C. John participated in spreading false rumors.
D. John engaged in spreading false rumors.

Again, C entails D in much the same way as A entails B. On the other hand, D does not entail C.

From a slightly different angle, it also seems possible to invoke what in the literature has been called the troponymy relation between *engage* and a number of other verbs of the class. As Miller and Fellbaum put it, the "troponymy relation between two verbs can be expressed by the formula *To V_1 is to V_2 in some manner*" [Miller and Fellbaum (1991, 216); see also Fellbaum and Miller (1990, 566 ff.)]. For instance, the troponymy relation seems to hold for the pair *engage* and *dabble*, for *to dabble (in selling stocks)* might be glossed as 'to engage (in selling stocks) in some manner', where the manner adverbial might be spelled out along the lines of 'in an unskillful manner'. While troponymy is not as easily established between *engage* and one or two other verbs of the class, it seems clear that *engage* is the most promising superordinate term with which verbs of the class may enter into a troponymy relation.

The classification is not exhaustive. No doubt other verbs can be found that take *in -ing* complement clauses. Also, it may be the case that verbs that occur in the pattern are susceptible of a more adequate and a more coherent semantic characterization than the one given above. (For instance, having *concur* only in class 4 is a cautious choice and does not do full justice to all senses of the verb for all speakers, and there might be a case for additionally including it in the 'do so with others' subclass of class 3. The same subclass might be extended to accommodate *unite*, now in class 5.) However, it may be hoped that the classification given is at least a reasonable first approximation, and the balance of this chapter will be devoted to pointing out and examining a number of conclusions suggested by the taxonomy.

In section I we paid attention to an important difference between *delight* and *persist*: the former cannot omit the *in -ing* clause (or a following nonsentential NP; see below) with the meaning of Verb$_1$ remaining at least approximately constant, whereas the latter may. The classes of verbs that have been compiled afford us an opportunity to consider the generality of the *delight* pattern and the *persist* pattern. There are some complexities to the task of assigning verbs to one of the patterns. For instance, whereas *They vied in singing his praises* does not easily reduce to *??They vied*, *They vied with each other in singing his praises* reduces to *They vied with each other* much more easily. This illustrates the difficulty of classifying verbs on the basis of the omissibility of the *in -ing* construction, but setting *vie* aside, the following verbs tend to pattern like *delight* in not normally omitting the *in -ing* clause (without an appreciable change of meaning): *be, consist, lie, delight, glory, luxuriate, revel, wallow, engage, indulge, aid, dabble. Believe* and *result* should probably be cited as members of the *delight* class as well. To be sure, sentences such as *John believes* and *Trouble resulted* are possible, but the senses of the verbs in such sentences seem appreciably different from their senses when they take *in -ing* clauses. The sense of *believe* in *John believes* is approximately 'be a believer'; when the verb is combined with *in -ing*, as in *John believes in keeping his promises*, its sense is approximately 'stand by the principle of'. (I am indebted to Nicholas Royle for this paraphrase.) The sense of *result* in *Trouble resulted* is approximately 'be the result', 'ensue'; when the verb is combined with *in -ing*, as in *The action resulted in weakening the opposition*, its sense is approximately 'have the consequence of', 'lead to'. (I am indebted to Ian Gurney for these paraphrases.) As for *join*, it might likewise be included here: *John joined* is possible, but has the approximate meaning 'John joined some group or scheme', the understood argument being nonsentential.

The class of *persist* includes *rejoice, experiment, persevere, persist, specialize, assist, help, collaborate, cooperate, participate, interfere, compete, succeed, excel, acquiesce, agree, concur, culminate, unite*. Admittedly, not all of these are equally likely to occur without a complement. For instance, *They helped*, reduced from *They helped in* Verb$_2$*ing* seems more likely than *They assisted*, reduced from *They assisted in* Verb$_2$*ing*, though it would be too harsh to mark the latter with a star or even with a question mark. [For instance, consider this sequence devised by Robert MacGilleon (personal communication): *The service was led by the Reverend Bloggs. Clutterbuck assisted.*] *Assist*, in turn, is much more likely than *aid* without *in -ing*, as compare *We should assist whenever possible*, reduced from *We should assist in* Verb$_2$*ing . . . whenever possible*, with ??*The new technique should aid*, reduced from *The new technique should aid in* Verb$_2$*ing*. (*Share* has been omitted from both groups because it is so rare or marginal in the pattern that evaluating the omission of the *in -ing* clause is difficult.)

Each group, then, includes a fair number of verbs. More significantly, it is difficult to find a very clear-cut semantic breakdown in terms of the taxonomy. For instance, *delight*, like most verbs of its class, is not good alone, but *rejoice*, of the same class, is. *Help*, like most verbs of its 'engage in with others' subclass, may omit the *in -ing* clause, but *aid*, of the same subclass, does not omit it, at least not as easily. One semantic regularity that does appear to hold is that verbs of the class of equatives (class 1) do not omit the *in -ing* clause.

It was observed above that *where* questions and *where . . . in* pseudocleft sentences are possible for *succeed*. The taxonomy, with its lists of verbs, affords an opportunity to consider the incidence of such questions and of such pseudocleft sentences in a slightly more systematic way. It seems that the permissibility of these two constructions is related to the dichotomy of the *delight* and *persist* patterns: verbs of the *delight* pattern tend not to permit the two *where* constructions, whereas several verbs of the *persist* pattern, perhaps most of them, tend to be more permissive. For instance, we may consider *believe* of the *delight* pattern. Neither *Q. *Where does John believe?* A. *He believes in helping himself* nor **Where John believes is in helping himself* is good. (*Aid* of the *delight* pattern is perhaps an exception, though given *They aided in nursing the sick*, neither ?Q. *Where did they aid?* A. *In nursing the sick* nor ?Q. *What did they aid in?* A. *Nursing the sick* is particularly likely.) Of the verbs of the *persist* pattern, a fair number seem possible in such *where* constructions (though not all of them are; for instance, *rejoice* is not). These include *assist, help, cooperate, succeed, excel,* and perhaps *acquiesce, agree, concur, culminate,* and *specialize*. For instance, given *He acquiesced in signing the petition*, a question-and-answer pair such as ?Q. *Where did he acquiesce?* A. *He acquiesced in signing the petition* and the pseudocleft *?Where he acquiesced was in signing the petition* seem at least marginally possible (though intuitions are sometimes somewhat hazy with regard to their status), alongside of Q. *What did he acquiesce in?* A. *He acquiesced in signing the petition* and *What he acquiesced in was signing the petition*. The latter seem to be the preferred variants for many speakers. It may, then, be observed that on the whole, the two *where* constructions tend to be limited to a subset of the *persist* pattern.

The taxonomy relates to a pattern of sentential complementation in that *in* precedes a sentence. However, it is also of interest from the point of view of the nonsentential pattern NP Verb$_1$ *in* NP, as in such sentences as *John delighted in his success* and *The bid resulted in a disaster for the company*. It seems that all the verbs listed above as occurring in the sentential pattern are capable of occurring in the nonsentential pattern. However, the converse is clearly not true, for there are verbs that may take nonsentential NPs in the pattern but that are difficult or impossible to combine with an *in* and an *-ing* clause. *Abound* is one such verb. It takes *in*, as in *abound in misprints*, but there is a contrast between 11a and 11b:

(11) a. John believes in maintaining a strong commitment.
b. *The book abounds in containing misprints.

Other verbs similar to *abound* in taking *in* with a nonsentential NP only include *confide*, as in *John confided in his friend/*John confided in telling his friend;* *invest*, as in *John invested in a stamp collection/??John invested in buying a stamp collection;* *major*, as in *John majored in French/??John majored in studying French;* and perhaps *end* [pace Poutsma (MS)], as in *The scheme ended in a disaster/?They ended in dividing the Church* [the example modeled after one in Poutsma (MS)] and *trust*, as in *John trusts in his wits/?John trusts in maintaining a strong commitment*. (Admittedly, there are some speakers who accept *end* and *trust* even in sentential construals of the kind illustrated.)

The classification also exposes intriguing differences in the interpretation of PRO. In this respect, the verbs of class 1 differ from the others in a major way. We may consider 12a–d:

(12) a. The process consists in matching the text words against a list of affixes.
 b. John delighted in frustrating his opponents.
 c. John succeeded in pronouncing the name.
 d. John acquiesced in signing the petition.

Sentences 12a and 12b–d each have PRO as the subject of the lower predicate, but the PROs are interpreted differently. In 12a the reference of PRO is not that of NP_1: the process does not do any matching. Rather, an unspecified person or unspecified persons are understood to do the matching. In line with fairly recent terminology, it is possible to say that in 12a, PRO is not controlled, or not bound, or that it "is arbitrary in reference" (Chomsky 1981, 24). The term "arbitrary" has established itself in the literature for the reference of this kind of PRO that lacks an antecedent [cf. Chomsky (1981, 24)] and has, by extension, been applied to the kind of PRO itself. The choice of the term is perhaps not completely felicitous, insofar as the reference of such a PRO, as in 12a, may not always be completely arbitrary in its context. Felicitous or not, "arbitrary" is the standard term and it will be used here, for to introduce another term might only create terminological profusion and confusion. An arbitrary PRO is "indefinite in interpretation, lacking specific reference" [Chomsky (1981, 191)]. In a typical case, as in 12a, it may be taken to designate 'people in general' or 'a certain subset of people in general that is relevant in the world of the discourse in question'. By contrast, in 12b–d, PRO is controlled, or bound, by NP_1, *John*. The type of control in question is "local," to use a term from Chomsky (1986b, 124 ff.). Local control is control by the subject or object of the head on which the complement clause depends. In the examples here, the head in question is of course $Verb_1$.[3]

Verbs of class 1, then, stand apart from those of other classes in that they govern clauses whose PROs may have arbitrary reference. To be sure, this statement should be modified in two directions, but the modifications do not seriously affect the substantive difference between verbs of class 1, on the one hand, and verbs of the other classes, on the other. First, whereas PRO in 12b–d is controlled by the subject NP_1 and by that NP only, some other verbs of the pattern involve a pattern of control that includes control by NP_1 but in addition, control by another unspecified NP. Thus, consider 13:

(13) John helped in repairing the damage.

It is clear in 13 that in some sense PRO is controlled by NP_1, but it is equally clear that it is in addition controlled by an unexpressed but understood NP, for the sentence means that there is more than one person repairing the damage. It should be emphasized that this presupposes that the subordinate clause of 13 is read as a complement clause. The point is worth making, because *help*, and a number of verbs similar in meaning to *help*, such as *assist, cooperate,* and *participate,* co-occur with adverbial clauses that are introduced by *by* or *in*. In the latter case, there is a deceptive resemblance to complement clauses. Indeed, it seems possible to interpret 13 as containing either a complement clause or an adverbial clause. A question-and-answer sequence such as Q. *What did John help in?* A. *He helped in repairing the damage* is possible, but so is a *how* question with an adverbial interpretation, as in Q. *How did John help?* A. *He helped in repairing the damage.* (Even though a pause is often possible before an adverbial *in -ing* clause, as in 2a–b and in 13 when these sentences are considered in isolation, it is hardly possible in such a question-and-answer sequence, not even in an adverbial reading.) As for pseudocleft sentences, *What John helped in was repairing the damage* seems possible, as does *How/where John helped was in repairing the damage.* (A double *in in* the pseudocleft sentence is possible as well: *What John helped in was in repairing the damage.*) However, even here it is profitable to keep complement clauses and adverbial clauses separate from each other. Apart from the looseness of the connection—in the case of adverbial clauses—between the matrix verb and *in,* the interpretation of PRO provides a striking difference between adverbial and complement clause constructions here. In the adverbial construal, as in *John helped(,) in/by repairing the damage,* PRO is interpreted as referring to *John* only. That is, the sentence means that John, and John alone, repaired the damage. In this case the matrix sentence has an understood constituent along the lines of sentence 9—recall the last of the four criteria discussed above—and the whole sentence has the approximate meaning 'John helped (in some larger operation) (,) by repairing the damage'. This adverbial reading will be set aside in the following.

The broader and more inclusive type of control that is relevant to the interpretation of PRO in 13 under the complement clause construal of the *in -ing* clause may be termed "NP_1 plus" control. Correspondingly, the more narrow and restrictive type of control displayed by *succeed*, as in 12b, may be termed "NP_1 only" control.

Patterns of control are often susceptible to investigation by means of reflexive Verb$_2$s. The antecedent of the reflexive pronoun in the construction here is PRO, and the admissibility or inadmissibility of reflexive pronouns exposes and makes explicit control properties of PRO. We may compare 14a–b and 15a–b:

(14) a. John succeeded in rescuing himself from the hole he was in.
 b. John succeeded in behaving himself on that day.
(15) a. ? John helped in rescuing himself from the hole he was in.
 b. *John helped in behaving himself on that day.

Sentences 14a–b are perfect, but 15a–b are less than perfect. There are speakers who regard 15a as acceptable, but others are by no means happy with it. Reactions to 15b are overwhelmingly negative. (The difference in acceptability between 15a and 15b is perhaps related to the choice of Verb$_2$.) The problem with 15a–b arises because of a conflict: *himself* and PRO are coreferential, but *help*, which involves "NP_1 plus" control, implies that the controller of PRO is not solely the subject of the higher sentence. Consequently, PRO receives features that are partly contradictory. No such conflict arises in 14a–b, where *succeed* involves "NP_1 only" control.

The "NP_1 plus" control pattern seems relevant to *aid, assist, collaborate, cooperate, help, participate,* and *share,* that is, in general to verbs of class 3 meaning 'engage in with others'. The "NP_1 only" control pattern seems relevant to virtually all other verbs of classes 2 to 5. One slight quibble that should be raised here concerns *believe*. Sentences such as *John believes in keeping faith with friends* mean that 'John believes in NP_1 keeping faith with friends', but over and above this they carry the meaning 'John believes in NP$_{\text{unspecified (people in general, for instance)}}$ keeping faith with friends', with an arbitrary PRO. To be sure, with a reflexive lower clause, as in *John believes in defending himself*, *believe* may involve the pattern of "NP$_1$ only" control and nothing else, but the control properties of *believe* are not entirely identical with those of *succeed* and other verbs involving "NP$_1$ only" control even in sentences with reflexives. We may consider 16a–b:

(16) a. John succeeded in behaving himself/*oneself on that day.
 b. John believes in behaving himself/?oneself at social functions.

In 16a *oneself* is quite inconceivable. In 16b, *oneself* is not entirely acceptable to all speakers by any means, but it is much less inconceivable than in 16a, and there are speakers who accept it in 16b. This is a reflex of a difference between *believe*, on the one hand, and verbs such as *succeed*, on the other. It also seems impossible to lump *believe* together with verbs of the *help* class, because 16b is perfectly good with *himself*, whereas 15a–b are doubtful. In effect, then, verbs of classes 2 to 5, even as a first approximation, display three types of control properties: the type of *succeed*, which may be characterized as straightforward subject control and seems relevant to most verbs of these classes; the type of *help*, which is NP$_1$ plus control; and the type of *believe*, which may have NP$_1$ control but may also permit PRO to be arbitrary. This diversity should be recognized, and no doubt it merits further investigation.[4] Even so, the three types of verbs, setting aside arbitrary PRO with *believe*, display variants of NP$_1$ control and therefore have different control properties from those of verbs of class 1.

It would also be a mistake to claim that a PRO in a clause governed by a matrix verb of class 1 always has arbitrary reference. Consider 17a–b:

(17) a. Our policy consists in rejecting new ideas.
 b. Our friends' policy consisted in warning us against the idea.

In 17a–b the reference of PRO is not arbitrary. Rather, PRO is controlled. In 17a it is controlled by the possessive pronoun *our*, and in 17b by the possessive NP *our friends'*. These patterns of control are highlighted if a suitable reflexive verb is chosen as Verb$_2$, as in 18a–b:

(18) a. Our policy consists in not perjuring ourselves/*themselves at the trial.

b. Our friends' policy consists in not perjuring themselves/*ourselves at the trial.

In each of 17a–b and 18a–b, PRO is controlled, not by NP_1, but by the possessive within NP_1, which may be viewed as the subject of NP_1.

Further, even in cases where NP_1 lacks a possessive (and a subject), it may still be possible to recover a controller—or at least a plausible controller—for PRO from elsewhere in the sentence, or indeed from the surrounding context. Thus consider 19a–b:

(19) a. The policy we have adopted consists in rejecting new ideas.
b. We have adopted a new policy. It consists in rejecting new ideas.

In each of 19a–b the controller of PRO may be understood as *we*.

The PROs in each of 17a–b, 18a–b, and 19a–b are controlled. However, it would be a mistake to suggest that they are controlled in the same way as the PROs in 12b–d and in similar sentences. The term "local control" was used for the latter cases, where PRO is controlled by the subject or object of the head of the complement clause. The type of control encountered in 17a–b, 18a–b, and 19a–b is not by the subject of $Verb_1$. (Nor, of course, is object control relevant here.) It emanates from a more remote controller, the subject of the subject of $Verb_1$ in 17a–b and 18a–b and from outside of the sentence of $Verb_1$ in 19a–b. The term "remote control" may perhaps be used to designate the type of control in such cases.[5] This discussion thus suggests a general distinction between verbs of class 1, on the one hand, and those of classes 2 to 5, on the other, along these lines: for the former, PRO may be arbitrary or controlled by a remote antecedent, whereas for the latter PRO is typically subject to local control emanating from the subject of the matrix verb.

With respect to selectional restrictions, verbs of class 1 take NP_1s that are +abstract, NPs such as *the suggestion, the solution, the plan*, etc. It is hard to imagine them taking +animate NP_1s. Verbs of class 2 take NP_1s that are properly +animate: *John/*the plan delighted in advancing the common cause*. All verbs of class 3 may also take +animate NP_1s, especially since collective nouns are included in the class of +animate noun phrases [cf. Quirk et al. (1985, 314 ff.)]. Such collective NPs are often found with verbs of class 3, as in *The committee specialized in holding unproductive meetings. Help, succeed, aid,* and perhaps *assist* of class 3—though *assist* is more doubtful here—also take a variety of

+abstract subjects, as in *The action, the measure, the idea, the proposal, the policy helped/succeeded/aided/?assisted in quelling dissent*. In such sentences, NP_1 carries an instrumental idea: 'by means of the action, etc., $NP_{unspecified}$ helped, etc., in quelling dissent', and the sentences still express purposeful action. (When purposeful action is not implied, the meaning of *help* veers toward that of 'contribute', and the *to* infinitive construal seems preferable to *in -ing*, as observed in section II on the basis of a sentence such as *Poverty/circumstances helped to exacerbate/?helped in exacerbating social tensions*.) It is noteworthy that some verbs fairly similar in meaning to *help* do not allow such instrumental NP_1s, not even when purposeful action is implied, but rather require +animate NP_1s, as in **The action, etc., collaborated/cooperated/participated in quelling dissent*. In the case of *help, succeed,* and *aid,* the instrumental character of NP_1s selected by these three verbs of class 3 sets them apart from +abstract NP_1s selected by $Verb_1$s of class 1. Verbs of class 4 as $Verb_1$s generally co-occur with +animate NP_1s. (*Concur* seems capable of being construed with +abstract NP_1s as well, with a slightly different sense, approximately 'be in accord' or 'coincide', as in *Such factors concurred in hardening attitudes*.) With regard to $Verb_1$s of class 5, *believe* takes +animate NP_1s, whereas *result* takes +abstract NP_1s only. *Result* differs from *help* and *succeed,* because a sentence such as *The action resulted in strengthening the opposition* cannot be turned into one of the form of **By means of the action, $NP_{unspecified}$ resulted in strengthening the opposition*.

In view of the difference in the interpretation of PRO and in overall selectional restrictions governing the choice of NP_1 between verbs of class 1, on the one hand, and verbs of classes 2 through 4, on the other, it seems possible to establish a twofold division. When NP_1 is –animate, $Verb_1$ characteristically means 'be equated with' (or 'result in'). Setting instrumental construals of verbs like *help* aside, it is possible to say that when NP_1 is +animate, $Verb_1$ characteristically means 'feel joy or pleasure over', or 'engage in' (or 'agree' or 'believe in'). Verbs expressing emotions may be termed emotive, other verbs being –emotive. It is then possible to say that when NP_1 of the pattern is +animate, a –emotive $Verb_1$ characteristically means 'engage in' (or 'agree' or 'believe in').

It is rather striking that in all of the classes 1 to 5, not a single negative $Verb_1$ was found. What is meant by a negative $Verb_1$ here is a verb that is negative with respect to the realization of the content of S_2 [cf. Rudanko (1989, 24)]. An example may illustrate the point: compare *John intended paying the bill*, where *intend* is positive with respect to the realization of the content of S_2, with *John grudged/put off/avoided pay-*

ing the bill, where *grudge, put off*, and *avoid* are negative with respect to the realization of the content of S_2. Admittedly, one or two verbs of the present pattern are negative in some sense. (The partially negative associations of *engage* were remarked on above.) *Dabble*, which carries a meaning of lack of skill or professionalism, is such a verb. However, although the verb expresses a negative comment on the manner of the engagement, the point is that it is still positive with respect to the realization of the content of S_2. After all, the verb means neither 'not to engage in skillfully or professionally' nor 'not to engage in unskillfully or unprofessionally' but rather 'to engage in unskillfully or unprofessionally'.

In order to probe the incidence of negative $Verb_1$s in the pattern, it is of interest to consider one or two approximate antonyms of verbs listed above. *Fail,* an approximate antonym of *succeed,* very commonly occurs with *in* and a nonsentential NP, as in *John failed in his efforts (to help me)*, but, as illustrated in section II, for many speakers it does not without strain select *in -ing* complement clause construals in present-day English. *Desist,* an approximate antonym of *persist,* is likewise fully idiomatic with *in* and a following nonsentential NP, as in 20a, but does not happily take *in -ing* complement clauses, as witness 20b–c:

(20) a. John desisted in his attempt to denigrate his opponent.
 b. ?? John desisted in denigrating his opponent.
 c. John desisted from denigrating his opponent.

The present investigation is not exhaustive, and it would be very audacious to claim that no negative $Verb_1$ can be found that takes *in -ing* complement clauses without any strain. Even so, it may well be that if such verbs are found, they will be in a distinct minority in this pattern. If this speculation is correct, it may be that the contrasts observed with *desist* are significant and point to at least a partial explanation: the preposition *in* may be felt to be connected to a positive localistic meaning, whereas the preposition *from* is perhaps associated with a negative localistic meaning [cf. chap. 5 of Rudanko (1989)].

We might perhaps also glance at the verbs included in the classification (setting classes 1 and 5 aside) from the point of view of the implicative versus nonimplicative dichotomy, as set up by Karttunen (1971). To start with class 3, the largest class, and with *engage*, its core verb, we may observe that it is implicative, as witness 21a–c and 22. (The illustrations of the dichotomy presented in 21a–c do not provide an exhaustive account of its effects and reflexes, but they are sufficient in the present context.)

(21) a. John engaged in denigrating his opponent.
  b. John did not engage in denigrating his opponent.
  c. Did John engage in denigrating his opponent?
(22) John denigrated his opponent.

Example 21a implies 22 in the sense that a speaker asserting 21a thereby commits himself to 22 [cf. Karttunen (1971, 344), Austin (1975, 48 ff.)]. Example 21b implies the negation of 22, but an affirmative answer to 21c again implies 22. Most other verbs of the class seem similar to *engage* in being implicative. Admittedly, verbs of the 'do so with others' subclass (perhaps also *interfere*) require a slight extension of the concept, for a sentence such as *John helped in clearing the snow* implies that he did it with others. On the other hand, there are also one or two nonimplicative verbs in the class, in particular *excel, persevere,* and *persist,* though even these pass some tests of implicativeness. Of the three, the last two are factive. (*John did not persevere/persist in interrupting me* implies *John interrupted me.*)

As for verbs of class 2, consider 23a–c and 24:

(23) a. John delighted in denigrating his opponent.
  b. John did not delight in denigrating his opponent.
  c. Did John delight in denigrating his opponent?
(24) John denigrated his opponent.

Example 23a and an affirmative answer to 23c imply 24. As far as the relation of 23b and 24 is concerned, intuitions are slightly less definite than those in analogous cases above. However, because *John did not delight in denigrating his opponent, but he denigrated his opponent* is not a contradiction, it seems that *delight* is not an implicative verb. [We may compare **John did not engage in denigrating his opponent, but he denigrated his opponent,* which is a contradiction; for the criterion of *but* sentences, see Karttunen (1971, 343).] Similar judgments seem to hold for other verbs of class 2 as well. They seem to satisfy some criteria of implicative verbs but are not fully implicative.

With regard to the verbs of class 4, consider *The ruling parties agreed/concurred in regarding John as a menace* and *The British government acquiesced in recognizing the new administration.* (The second sentence is due to Ian Gurney.) These imply that they did indeed regard John as a menace and that the British government did recognize the new administration. Consequently, the verbs appear to be implicative.

As far as the implicative versus nonimplicative dichotomy is concerned, the finding that verbs of class 3 are implicative almost in their entirety seems most significant, given the size of the class and its status within the present scheme of taxonomy. In this context, it is worth recalling the patterns of NP_1 $Verb_1$ PRO to $Verb_2$, as in *John intended to leave early*, and NP_1 $Verb_1$ PRO $Verb_2ing$, as in *John intended leaving early*. These are similar to class 3 in that, with very few exceptions, NP_1 in them is +animate. In Rudanko (1989, 35 ff.; 47 ff.) it was observed that a small number of $Verb_1$s in these patterns are implicative, like *manage*, as in *John managed to leave early*, or negative implicative, like *eschew*, as in *John eschewed answering my question*, but that on the whole, $Verb_1$s in these patterns are overwhelmingly nonimplicative, like *intend* in the two sentences cited. The high incidence of implicative verbs, then, serves in this respect to set off the *in -ing* pattern against the other two, which are its potential rivals. No doubt, the difference in implicativeness is related to characteristic meanings of $Verb_1$s in the patterns in question. In the 1989 study [Rudanko (1989, 22 ff.; 44 ff.)] of the infinitival pattern and the *-ing* pattern, it was suggested that $Verb_1$s in them characteristically carry such meanings as desideration, or desideration and intention, or desideration, intention, and endeavor. In the case of verbs of class 3 of the *in -ing* pattern, more than desideration, intention, and endeavor is involved: there is actual engagement, and the engagement would seem to be almost invariably positive. In this respect, then, the *in -ing* pattern has a fairly well defined semantic function in present-day English. Admittedly, this conclusion rests primarily on verbs of class 3, but at the same time it may be borne in mind that most verbs of the pattern belong to this class.

Consideration of the implicative versus nonimplicative dichotomy, then, supports the conclusion that the *in -ing* pattern has a fairly well defined function in the system of sentential complementation of present-day English. The suggestion made earlier that the preposition *in* in the pattern possesses at least a trace of a meaning specific to it reinforces the point. (As far as verbs of class 1 are concerned, some additional support for the same conclusion may be gathered from control properties of verbs of this class as compared with those of copular constructions; see n. 5.) At the same time, it should be recalled that, as was shown in section II, there are some matrix verbs that govern *in -ing* and some other pattern of complementation as well. For instance, *consist*, of class 1, and *help*, of class 3, select *of -ing* and *to* infinitive construals, respectively. There are also some verbs of classes 2 and 3 that select *at -ing*, as will be shown in chapter 5. However, overall, the availability of such alternative construals for verbs governing *in -ing* seems severely restricted. For instance, *consist* seems to be the only verb of class 1 that allows a different construal, and most verbs of class 3, including *engage, indulge, persist, specialize, participate,* and *succeed,* likewise prefer the *in -ing* pattern for most speakers. It should be added that the substitution of a different pattern for *in -ing,* in cases where it is possible, is often accompanied by a more or less definite change of meaning. The alternative construals available for *consist* and *help,* illustrated in section II, are cases in point here. (See chapter 5 for a comparison of *in -ing* and *at -ing* patterns.) Both the overall lack of syntactic alternation available to verbs governing *in -ing* and the general semantic distinctiveness of *in -ing* constructions, even in those relatively rare cases where syntactic alternation is available, reinforce the impression that the *in -ing* pattern has a fairly well defined semantic function in present-day English. In view of this more or less readily identifiable semantic function, one may indulge in speculating that, even though the number of verbs in the pattern is not very large, the *in -ing* pattern is a solidly established one and is in little or no danger of being encroached upon, let alone of being supplanted, by its potential rivals.

3

Resorting to and *Turning to*: On Verbs Governing *to -ing*

I

Consider sentence 1, modeled on a sentence from the Brown corpus (see below) and 1', a partially bracketed structural representation of 1:

1. John resorted to borrowing money.
1.' [[John]$_{NP1}$ [resorted]$_{Verb1}$ [to]$_{Prep}$ [[PRO]$_{NP2}$ [[borrowing]$_{Verb2}$ money]$_{VP}$]$_{S2}$]$_{S1}$

In 1', S$_2$ is a complement clause governed by the matrix verb *resorted*. Or, slightly more accurately, the matrix verb is subcategorized as taking *to* and a following complement sentence. Following Quirk et al. (1985, 1178), it is advisable to consider the *to* of the pattern a preposition.

The present chapter is an inquiry into the pattern of 1 as partially bracketed in 1'. The first objective is to compile a reasonably comprehensive list of matrix verbs that govern the *to -ing* pattern. Such verbs will then be characterized as explicitly as possible, with a focus on their semantic properties. A further objective is to consider alternation between the *to -ing* pattern and other syntactic complementation patterns that are close to it from a syntactic or semantic point of view. Because of brute similarity, the very common *to* infinitival pattern of the type *John wanted to borrow money* is of special interest in this connection.

Different types of sources of data will be drawn on. First, the Brown and LOB corpora will be consulted. Additional verbs and illustrations are taken from Poutsma (1905, 1929, MS). Bridgeman et al. (1965) likewise provide a number of verbs. A second type of source is constituted by intuitions of native speakers of English, particularly insofar as they relate to acceptability.

As observed in chapters 1 and 2, complement clauses may sometimes resemble adverbial clauses. As far as the present pattern is concerned, the distinction seems fairly clear, and there do not seem to be many problematic constructions [cf. in this connection Curme (1931, 493 f.)]. Corresponding adverbial clauses seem more or less invariably to have the form *to* + infinitive. This might be illustrated with an adverbial clause of time, as in *John fell(,) to land on all fours*. *Fall* may take *to* *-ing*, as in *John fell to watching these creatures* (see below), but an adverbial clause cannot take this form: **John fell(,) to landing on all fours*.

It is also worth noting that S_2 is a nominal clause in the pattern. This view is supported by a number of criteria, in much the same way as was the nominal status of the *in -ing* pattern in the previous chapter. First, the complement clause in the pattern may be questioned by *what*, as in Q. *What did John resort to?* A. *Borrowing money*. Second, it may be replaced by the pronoun *it* or by the pronoun *that*, as in *John resorted to borrowing money but Max would not resort to it/that*. Third, it is possible to move it by right dislocation, as in *John resorted to it, borrowing money*. Fourth, it is possible to place the complement sentence in the focus position of a pseudocleft sentence, as in *What John resorted to was borrowing money*. In view of these considerations,[1] S_2 may be taken to be a nominal clause.

II

In the following, matrix verbs governing the pattern of 1' considered on the basis of the two corpora will be listed and illustrated.

Verbs	Illustrations
admit	*There were no "casualties," but the "guerillas" admitted to being "a little tired" when the leaders called a halt at 9 a.m. to enable out-of-town members to catch a plane* (Brown B25, 1860-1880, from *The Nation* 193: 16).
amount	*Our understanding of the solar system has taught us to replace our former elaborate rituals with the appropriate*

action which, in this case, amounts to doing nothing [Brown G11, 0930-0960, from F. Oppenheimer, "Science and Fear—A Discussion of Some Fruits of Scientific Understanding" (*The Centennial Review* 5: 4)].

come *Russia, whose technology is not quite primitive, is still in the dark ages when it comes to improving the outboard motor, for instance* [Brown E06, 0760-0780, from J. Choate, "The American Boating Scene" (*Rudder* 77: 1)]. This usage is, of course, current and common in present-day English, but the construction in question, which is *when it comes (came) to -ing*, is frozen and formulaic to a considerable degree. If we try, for instance, to replace the subject *it* by some other pronoun such as *this*, the result is ill formed: **Russia, whose technology is not quite primitive, is still in the dark ages when this comes to improving the outboard motor, for instance.* Because of the formulaic nature of the phrase, it seems best to omit it from further consideration.

come around *Or else the North really believes that all Southerners except a few quaint old characters have come around to realizing the errors of their past, and are now at heart sharers of the American Dream, like everybody else* [Brown G01, 1360-1390, from E. Lawton, "Northern Liberals and Southern Bourbons" (*The Georgia Review* 15)].

come down *It would come down to saying that Fromm paints with a broad brush, and that, after all, is not a conclusion one must work toward but an impression he has from the outset* [Brown J63, 0200-0240, from J. Schaar, *Escape from Authority: The Perspectives of Erich Fromm* (Basic Books)].

contribute *Do patriots everywhere know enough about how the persecution of the Jews in Germany and later in the occupied countries contributed to terrorizing the populations, splitting apart individuals and groups, arousing the meanest and most dishonest impulses, pulverizing trust and personal dignity, and finally forcing people to follow their masters into the abyss by making them partners in unspeakable crimes?* [Brown F14, 1470-1530, from H. Rosenberg, "The Trial and Eichmann" (*Commentary* 32: 5)].

extend	*His kindness extended to taking her out to dinner and to his house for a drink after and bringing her back* [LOB K08, 128-129, from S. Gillespie, *The Neighbour* (Geoffrey Bles)].
fall	*As Lily-yo fell to watching these creatures, she thought in her mind of the grand plan the Captives had hatched, she flicked it over in a series of vivid pictures* [LOB M06, 127-129, from B. Aldiss, "Hothouse" (*Magazine of Fantasy and Science Fiction*)].
get	*At the corroborees, when they get to dancing and sweating, you'll see them rubbing up against a man who's supposed to have a specially good smell* [Brown G04, 1610-1630, from E. Burdick, "The Invisible Aborigine" (*Harper's Magazine* 223: 1336)].
get around	*For those who "like poetry but never get around to reading it," the Library of Congress makes it possible for poets to be heard reading their own work* (Brown B13, 1140-1160, from *The Times-Picayune* 6/19).
get down	*Again, a technique for identifying chemicals was neglected for decades until a chemist who was also a lawyer got down to presenting it to the chemical world as if he were presenting a brief* (LOB G64, 73-76, from *Time and Tide* 8/24).
go back	*Stuart had been laid off at the produce company and had to go back to sitting in his father's office, taking what salary his father could hand out to him* [Brown P02, 0180-0200, from A. Ritner, *Seize a Nettle* (Fred B. Ritner, J. B. Lippincott Co.)].
hear	*Cousin Emma is alone in that big old house and won't hear to parting from it* [Brown P21, 1250-1260, from E. Spencer, "The White Azalea" (*The Texas Quarterly* 4: 4)]. The illustration is authentic, but the idiomatic combination is *hear of -ing*, as in *Cousin Emma . . . won't hear of parting from it*. Consequently, the verb will be dropped from further consideration.
lead	*It is probable that his recommendations will be informed and workable, and that they will not lead to involving the*

United States in an Asian morass (Brown B06, 1830-1850, from *St. Louis Post-Dispatch*, 10/27).

look forward   At the moment he was excited about his son's having received the Prix de Rome in archaeology and was looking forward to being present this summer at the excavation of an Etruscan tomb [Brown G06, 1500-1530, from *The American-German Review*, Oct.-Nov.)].

object   Anyone who objects "on principle" to charging the borrower must stop complaining about a charge on the rates (LOB G70, 134-135, from *The Economist*, 4/22).

react   One good indication of the two men's personalities is the way they reacted to meeting their own heroes [Brown A39, 1270-1280, from "Sports" (*Newsweek* 58: 7)].

resort   While he was handling the multi-million-dollar funding operations of the Government he had to resort to borrowing small sums from friends [Brown G07, 1290-1310, from R. Morris, "Seven Who Set Our Destiny" (*The New York Times Magazine* 2/19)].

return   CHARMIAN SCOTT, 18-year-old niece of the Duchess of Gloucester, returned to modelling yesterday for the first time since the car accident that put her in hospital four weeks ago (LOB A09, 31-33, from *Daily Express* 3/22).

run   My scanty dollars did not run to buying any of them, but looking was free [LOB G10, 82-83, from D. Black, *The Foot of the Rainbow: A Writer's Biography* (Geoffrey Bles)].

settle down   He and Linda settled down to being social leaders, and Linda managed to look a little more beautiful each year [Brown P17, 1010-1030, from A. Hine, *The Huntress* (*Saturday Evening Post* 2/4)].

shift   To make it clearer he shifted to acting out, but with no change of manner, the killing of Rose Mallory [Brown L11, 0050-0050, from H. Stone, *The Man Who Looked Death in the Eye* (Simon and Schuster)].

stick   Why, oh why, doesn't he stick to preaching the Gospel, instead of meddling in civic affairs, politics, economics, and social issues that are no concern of the Church? [Brown

48   Chapter 3

	K10, 1030-1050, from G. Barr, *The Master of Geneva* (Holt, Rinehart and Winston)].
take	*Even musicians themselves have taken to writing poetry* [Brown G73, 0110-0110, from C. See, "The Jazz Musician as Patchen's Hero" (*The Arizona Quarterly* 17: 2)].
turn	*What makes the current phenomenon unique is that so many science-fiction writers have reversed a trend and turned to writing works critical of the impact of science and technology on human life* [Brown G69, 1010-1040, from M. Hillegas, "Dystopian Science Fiction: New Index to the Human Situation" (*New Mexico Quarterly* 31: 3)].

Poutsma (1905, 665 ff.; 1929, 913 f., 924 f.) will be consulted next, along with Poutsma (MS). As may be seen below, not all the verbs for which Poutsma has attested examples are necessarily current in present-day English, but a consideration of his grammars does yield a significant number of additional verbs, with one or two coming from his dictionary. [Poutsma's (1905, 665 ff.) italics will be omitted in illustrations.]

Verbs	Illustrations and Comments
allude	*(He) alluded to landing, and to the change of motion and repose she would have in a carriage.* [Poutsma (1929, 913); from G. Eliot, *The Mill on the Floss*, 6, chap. 14, 438).
approach	*It (sc. Adonais) is the single one by this author which approaches to being 'popular'* [Poutsma (1929, 914); from W. M. Rossetti and A. O. Prickard, *Shelley's Adonais*, Preface]. This does not reflect current usage and the verb is better omitted.
attend	*That part of the officers and crew of a vessel who attend together to working her for an allotted time* [Poutsma (1905, 665); from *Webster's Dictionary*, s.v. *watch*].
confess	*I confess to being somewhat surprised that in your issue of to-day you permitted the insertion of the letter on the above subject.* [Poutsma (1905, 666), from *Times*].

depose	*Catherine Cussack, maid to the Countess, deposed to having heard Ryder's cry* [Poutsma (1905, 666); from *Sherlock Holmes, The Adventure of the Blue Carbuncle*]. The verb is not very common in the pattern, and there are educated speakers of English who do not find it current with *to -ing* in their speech. However, it is current for others. Apart from Poutsma's example, its admissibility in the pattern is also illustrated in *to depose "to having seen..."* (ALD, s.v. *depose*). It seems worth including the verb.
feel up	*He felt up to shooting a tiger* [Poutsma (1905, 666), from *A Life Interest*, 2, chap. 1, 9]. The example is certainly well formed, but the *to -ing* construal here seems to depend on the particle *up*, to an extent that a verb *feel up* would be dubious. A similar dependence of the *to -ing* construal on the particle *up* is observed with *be*, as in *He was up to shooting a tiger*, and in dictionaries, including Collins-Cobuild and the ALD, the usage is in general cited under *up* in both cases. A verb *feel up* will not be "invented" here.
go	*Count what goes / To making up a Pope* (Poutsma, MS, s.v., from Mrs. Browning, *Casa Guidi*, 62, OED, s.v., 41). Poutsma comments: "As compared with the infinitive-construction, the gerund construction appears to be rather unusual, apparently least so in connection with *far, a long way* or a similar phrase." An example of each of these other two constructions lends support to Poutsma's observation: *With a single glance we view an army, without attending to every soldier that goes to compose it* (OED, s.v. 41, from *Man* No. 26, 3), *That will go far to making secondary instruction what it was before* (Poutsma, MS, from *Manchester Guardian Weekly* 6, 8, 150a). Reactions to the *to -ing* construal with *go* in the absence of an adverb tend to be negative today. Since the pattern here does not necessarily include an adverb, it seems best to omit the verb from the present discussion.
look	*They looked to setting up Presbyterianism in England and Ireland as well as Scotland* [Poutsma (1929, 924), from *Story of Old Mortality*].

own	*He owned to having treated her very ill* [Poutsma (1905, 667), from *Henry Esmond*, 2, chap. 13, 264].
relate	*The proposal in question relates to granting permission to discharged servants and warrant-officers to retain their uniform after discharge* (Poutsma, MS, s.v., from *Daily Mail*). Intuitions are sometimes slightly hazy on this construal [cf. also Bridgeman et al. (1965, 41)], as in this invented example: *The doctrine related to safeguarding our security;* but on balance the verb can be included without too much hesitation.
submit	*It is possible that the population of the Ruhr may submit to working for the French* [Poutsma (1929, 925), from *Manchester Guardian*, 8, 17, 322b].
swear	*Nineteen can swear to having seen him coming out of her bedroom in the hotel about ten o'clock in the evening* (Poutsma, MS, s.v., from Galsworthy, *In Chancery*, 3, chap. 2, 685).
trust	*There was nothing left for it but to drive home again, or else to go in alone and trust to finding Roy afterwards* [Poutsma (1905, 667), from *A Hardy Norseman*, chap. 30, 266].
vouch	*I can vouch to having heard your Highness tell the story* [Poutsma (1905, 667), from *Rodney Stone*, 1, chap. 7, 175]. The verb is not very common in the pattern, for more usually it takes the preposition *for* and a nonsentential NP. However, most speakers seem to accept it even with *to -ing*, and the verb may be retained.

Below are the verbs culled from Bridgeman et al. (1965, 41 f.), with examples freely invented.

adapt	*John adapted to serving under a new chairman rather well.*
adjust	*John adjusted to being out of work rather well.*
adhere, cling	*John adhered/clung to observing the Sabbath.*
agree	*The organization agreed to negotiating directly with its adversary.*
assent	*The Cabinet assented to revising the bill.*

consent	*John consented to paying the bill.* Strictly speaking, Bridgeman et al. (1965, 41) mark *consent* with a P, which for them designates sentences such as *John consented to my/me paying the bill.* However, even though there may be some hesitation, most speakers are quite happy to accept *to -ing* with *consent*. It is worth noting that Quirk et al. (1985, 1178) cite *She consented to getting engaged* without any question mark. *Consent* will therefore be included.
own up	*John owned up to being a coward.*
refer	Bridgeman et al. (1965, 41) mark the verb with a P, and the usage in question may be illustrated with *John referred to my needing more money.* However, there are speakers who also accept *refer* in the pattern of the present chapter, as in *John referred to needing more money* and *The doctrine referred to safeguarding our security*, though some speakers are dubious about this usage, especially about the second sentence. The verb can perhaps be included, though with some hesitation.
testify	*John testified to being on drugs.*

Additionally, one or two verbs have suggested themselves to me:

convert	*The factory converted to producing tanks.* NP$_1$s with this verb are often +collective NPs such as *the factory, the firm, the business.* [On the notion of +collective, see Quirk et al. (1985, 316 f.).] NPs that are −animate or at a further remove from +animate seem worse in the pattern, as witness *??The building converted to housing recruits.* On the other hand, a sentence such as *John converted to drinking tea without sugar*, with *convert* carrying a more figurative sense, is quite conceivable.
descend	*John would not descend to denigrating his opponent.* Not all speakers are entirely happy with this construction. However, Collins-Cobuild provides the illustration *All too soon they will descend to spreading scandal and gossip*, and on balance the verb can be included without too much hesitation. By contrast, it might be mentioned at

this point that speakers are generally less happy with *ascend* selecting *to -ing*. This verb may, of course, occur in a nonsentential construal such as *ascend to great heights*, but is awkward for many speakers with a sentential complement, as in *??John never ascended to dining with his superiors*. *Ascend*, then, will not be included.

go over	*John went over to drinking tea without sugar*. NP₁ may also be +collective, as in *The factory went over to producing tanks*.
keep	*John kept to looking for suitable data*. The sense of the verb in this construal implies maintaining a course of action, possibly to the exclusion of some other course of action.
move over	*The factory moved over to producing tanks*. This is reminiscent of *convert* in that an NP₁ that is +collective is good with the verb. A +human NP₁ is not always very natural, as witness *?John moved over to drinking tea without sugar*.
revert	*John reverted to denigrating his opponent*.
stoop	*John would never stoop to denigrating his opponent*. Intuitions are sometimes slightly hazy on sentences of this type, but on balance it seems possible to include the verb without too much hesitation [pace Poutsma (MS, s.v.)]. (Cf. also the discussion of the verb below.)
switch	*The factory switched to producing tanks*.
switch over	*The factory switched over to producing tanks*.

Finally, as Robert Cooper (personal communication) has pointed out, *change over* may be included:

change over	*The factory changed over to producing tanks*. The verb and the example are reminiscent of *convert*, and much as in the case of *convert*, an inanimate NP₁ sounds strange in the pattern, but an NP₁ denoting a person is fine, as witness *?The building changed over to housing recruits* and *John changed over to drinking tea without sugar*.

III

In this section the task of characterizing semantically the verbs listed as relevant in section II will be undertaken. Here the animacy of NP_1 or the lack of it suggests itself as a first consideration. It seems that scarcely any verbs of the pattern are indifferent to this feature and accept either +animate or −animate NPs. *Contribute* is a clear exception here in that it accepts both types of NP_1s with equal ease, as witness *John contributed to raising morale immeasurably* and *The end-of-term party contributed to raising morale immeasurably*. In a much more limited way, *allude* and *refer* are perhaps also exceptions. (As noted above, not all speakers are entirely comfortable with *refer* in the pattern.) To the extent that they are found in the pattern, both verbs (and especially *allude*) probably tend to occur with animate NP_1s, and inanimate NP_1s with these verbs seem more or less limited to NPs expressing communication, as in *The document alluded/referred to safeguarding our security*. These three verbs seem to be virtually the only verbs of this kind.

A larger class of $Verb_1$s take typically −animate NP_1s. These include *amount, come down, extend, lead, relate,* and *run*. Of these verbs, the first two have the approximate meaning 'NP_1 is to be equated with S_2', whereas *extend* and *run* have the approximate meaning 'go as far as'.

A still larger class of $Verb_1$s take typically +animate NP_1s. Such verbs divide into a number of subclasses. Verbs of the largest of these subclasses have the approximate meaning 'turn to', 'NP_1 turning to $Verb_2ing$': *come around, fall,* etc. Further subclasses may perhaps be identified within this large class. Several verbs that often occur with +collective NP_1s, including *change over, move over,* and *convert,* may be grouped under the gloss 'change over', and *descend* and *stoop* may likewise be classed together. Outside of the 'turn to' class of verbs, a much smaller number of verbs with +animate subjects are held together by an ingredient of meaning that may be glossed as adherence, having the approximate sense 'keep to (doing something)'. Such verbs often imply that what is being adhered to is some kind of commitment or promise. Third, there is a sizable group of verbs that express communication. It has been recognized in earlier studies [for instance, Rudanko (1984, 1989)] that the class of verbs of communication is a very large one in English. Such verbs are often collocated with *that* clauses, especially when the verbs in question express fairly 'pure' communication. Such verbs of 'pure' communication include *mention, note, observe, say,* etc. By contrast, verbs of the *to -ing* pattern, in general, combine rather special shades of meaning with that of communication. First, *depose, testify,* and *vouch* carry legal, or possibly even legalistic, connotations. (Of the three verbs, *testify* is undoubtedly the most common in the pattern.) Second, *admit, confess,* and *own (up)* have a concessive meaning. Third, *agree, assent,* and *consent* express agreement. Disagreement is expressed by *object*. As for other verbs taking +animate subjects, *adapt, adjust,* and *submit* form a small subclass, and remaining verbs may be placed in a subclass of "Others." Of verbs of the class of Others, *attend*, with the approximate meaning 'apply oneself to' (OED, under I.4.b.), perhaps has some relation to the class 'keep to', but this link is fairly tenuous. Consequently, it is classed separately.

It may be helpful to number the classes:

I. NP_1 is either −animate or +animate: *contribute; allude, refer.*

II. NP_1 is typically −animate: *amount, come down, extend, lead, relate, run.*

III. NP_1 is typically +animate:
   a. $Verb_1$ has the approximate meaning 'turn to', NP_1 turns to $Verb_2ing$: *come around, fall, get, get around, get down, go back, resort, return, revert, settle down, shift, take, turn.*

   $Verb_1$ has the approximate meaning 'change over', NP_1 being often +collective: *change over, convert, go over, move over, switch, switch over.*

   $Verb_1$ has the approximate meaning 'descend': *descend, stoop.*

   b. $Verb_1$ has the approximate meaning 'keep to': *adhere, cling, keep, stick.*

   c. $Verb_1$ expresses communication:
      1. 'As in a court of law': *depose, swear, testify, vouch.*
      2. $Verb_1$ has a concessive meaning: *admit, confess, own, own up.*
      3. $Verb_1$ expresses agreement or disagreement: *agree, assent, consent; object.*

   d. $Verb_1$ has the approximate meaning 'adjust' or 'submit': *adapt, adjust, submit.*

   e. Others: *attend, look, look forward, react, trust.*

The classification outlined and the glosses provided can no doubt be improved upon. Also, it would be audacious to claim that the lists of verbs are exhaustive. Even with such caveats made, however, the taxonomy may serve as a first approximation. The balance of this chapter will therefore be devoted to examining such conclusions as emerge from it. In particular, it seems worthwhile to comment on four aspects of the pattern: the universally nominal character of the *-ing* clause of the present pattern, the extent and nature of variation between the *to -ing* pattern and the *to* infinitive pattern, the interpretation of PRO, and the overall semantic character of the present *to -ing* pattern. These four aspects are interrelated in varying degrees, but listing them helps to give structure to this discussion.

Above it was observed that in the case of *resort*, the sentence that follows is nominal. It is noteworthy that the same holds for all the other verbs listed as well, independently of semantic class. It seems sufficient to illustrate the point with questions and answers and pseudocleft sentences, using verbs chosen at random and sentences that have been modeled on those above:

(2) a. What did the measures contribute to? A. Terrorizing populations./What the measures contributed to was terrorizing populations.

b. What does the action amount to? A. Doing nothing./What the action amounted to was doing nothing.

c. What have even musicians themselves taken to? A. Writing poetry./What even the musicians themselves have taken to is writing poetry.

Another reflection of the nominal character of *-ing* clauses of the pattern is their replaceability with nonsentential NPs. *Resort* and *agree*, chosen at random, may serve as examples. Both allow NPs with ease, as in *John resorted to his fists* and *John agreed to the proposal*. It may be added that *relate* and *refer*, included in the taxonomy with some hesitation, are quite readily possible with nonsentential NPs, as in *The doctrine relates to our security* and *John referred to his need for more money*.

At the same time, it should be observed that not all verbs taking the preposition *to* and a following NP allow the NP to be replaced with a sentential complement. Illustrations include sentences such as *John spoke to me*, where the NP designates something animate, but also verbs such as *accrue*, where the NP may be more abstract, as compare *A large amount of goodwill has accrued to our project* and ??*A large amount of goodwill has accrued to furthering our project.*

The classification also makes it possible to focus on the interpretation of PRO. Here a generalization suggests itself that sets verbs of class III apart from those of class II in a rather conspicuous fashion. It is helpful to start by considering a number of verbs of class III, as in 3a–c:

(3) a. John fell to dreaming of better times.
    b. John confessed to cheating.
    c. John objected to paying the full price.

It is clear that in 3a–c PRO is interpreted as coreferential with NP_1. (For an elaboration on control properties of such verbs of class III as *agree*, see below.) To use the terminology introduced in the previous chapter, in 3a–c PRO is controlled by the subject of $Verb_1$, which means that PRO is locally controlled.

Verbs of class II typically behave in a different fashion, as is apparent in 4a–b:

(4) a. The technique amounted to twisting the truth.
    b. Kindness should extend to inviting friends to dinner.

In 4a–b the reference of PRO is not that of NP_1. For instance, in 4a the technique does not twist the truth. Rather, an unidentified person or unidentified persons twist the truth, by using the technique. Analogously to the terminology of chapter 2, such a PRO may be said to be arbitrary in reference. Further, again in a manner reminiscent of the equative verbs (*consist*, etc.) of the *in -ing* pattern, PRO may also be controlled even in the case of verbs of class II of this chapter, as in 5a–b:

(5) a. His technique amounted to twisting the truth.
    b. His kindness extended to inviting friends to dinner.

The PROs in 5a–b are understood to be coreferential with the possessives: *his* is the understood subject of *twisting the truth* and of *inviting friends to dinner*.

Of course, in the interpretation of control sentences it is not necessary to rely on intuitions alone. The admissibility or inadmissibility of reflexives affords confirmation for the patterns of control that were suggested. Thus consider contrasts such as those in 6a–d.

(6) a. John confessed to misbehaving himself/*herself.
 b. Sue objected to perjuring herself/*himself.
 c. John's technique amounted to not perjuring himself/*herself.
 d. Sue's kindness extended to sacrificing herself/*himself to everyone else's convenience.

Where NP_1 does not have a possessive, PRO may still be controlled by some other NP in the sentence, or indeed in the surrounding context, as in 7a–b. In a manner again reminiscent of equative verbs of the *in -ing* pattern, the concept of remote control may be invoked here:

(7) a. The technique adopted by John amounted to twisting the truth/perjuring himself/*herself.
 b. The generous attitude adopted by Sue extended to inviting friends to dinner/sacrificing herself/*himself to everyone else's convenience.
 c. John adopted a new technique. It amounted to twisting the truth/perjuring himself/*herself when required.

Further, when the head noun of NP_1 has an indirect object complement, these verbs may shift the control of PRO to this indirect object complement. (This seems to diverge from the pattern of the equative verbs of the *in -ing* pattern; see chapter 2, n. 5.) This is perhaps less possible for *extend*, even if the lexical meaning of the sentence favors such a reading:

(8) a. Their demand to us amounted to giving back the territory.
 b. ??Their demand to us extended to giving back the territory.

Example 8a is modeled on a sentence from Poutsma: *These demands amount to giving back to the Boers practically everything they want* [Poutsma (1905, 665), from *Times*]. In 8a it is we who are understood to be giving back territory, it being understood that we as the recipient of the demand have at our disposal what is being demanded of us. Such a reading of PRO seems less possible for *extend*, as in 8b. Analogous sentences with reflexives are not always very good, as witness *John's advice to me amounted to perjuring *himself/?myself*, but in the sentence *myself* seems more readily possible than *himself*, confirming the interpretation of Poutsma's sentence.

Such niceties aside, there is a difference in kind between verbs of class II and class III. In the case of the former, the reference of PRO is often arbitrary. Even when it is controlled, as in 6c–d, 7a–c and 8a–b, control is not by NP$_1$ and is thus not local but remote. In the case of verbs of class III, on the other hand, the reference of PRO is typically controlled and the control relation is local, the subject of the head of the complement acting as the controller.

At times in English, there is variation between -*ing* and *to* infinitive constructions. Such alternation occurs in a number of complementation patterns, and it has been observed and commented on by Ellinger (1910), Budde (1956) and Wood (1956), among others, but in the specific context of the investigation of the *to* -*ing* pattern under review here and the *to* infinitival construction in variation with it, Poutsma's (1905, 1929) work merits special attention. There is little doubt that his treatment remains unrivaled even today in its incisiveness and comprehensiveness of systematic coverage and documentation. My discussion of alternation between the two constructions here may perhaps be offered as a contribution to one part of a research task pioneered by Poutsma.

A first example of alternation, admittedly from outside of the scope of the present book, is afforded by the adjective *accustomed* [Curme (1931, 493)], which allows both construals [cf. also Budde (1956, 108)], as in 9a–b [from Curme (1931, 493); cf. also Jespersen ([1940] 1965, 245)].

(9) a. I am accustomed to doing it this way.
  b. I am accustomed to do it this way.

To some speakers the infinitive with *accustomed* sounds slightly old-fashioned but generally not to the extent of being obsolete, and the sentences of 9a–b are both well formed. At first sight the two constructions may look rather similar, apart from the form of the lower verb, and their meanings may not seem very different either. However, on closer inspection it is observed that *accustomed* illustrates a matrix predicate that permits two construals that are not entirely equivalent from a semantic point of view. Poutsma's (1929, 927) explanation that "mere recurrency of an action or state" favors the infinitive and that the "notion of a habit or custom" favors the -*ing* form with this matrix predicate is succinct, insightful, and hard to improve upon even today. [Cp. also Sweet (1903, 120) on the possibility of associating the -*ing* form with habit more generally.] In a broader perspective, the semantic difference illustrates the need to be sensitive to potential meaning contrasts where alternation is found.

There are also important syntactic differences between the two constructions. It was observed at the beginning of the chapter that the *to* of the *to -ing* pattern is a preposition. This category assignment fits in well with the point made above about the nominal character of the lower clause in the pattern. By contrast, the *to* in the infinitival pattern is not a preposition, but rather an infinitive marker, to adopt a term from Quirk et al. (1985, 1178). The difference with regard to the category status of *to* may be substantiated, for instance, by the consideration that what follows *to* can be questioned by means of *what* in the case of 9a but not in the case of 9b, as witness the following contrasts:

(9') a. Q. What am I accustomed to? A. Doing it this way.
b. Q. What am I accustomed to? A. *Do it this way.

The well-formedness of 9'a follows naturally from the nominal character of the lower clause in the *to -ing* pattern. By contrast, what follows the infinitive marker, as in 9b, is not nominal, and the ill-formedness of 9'b is therefore not unexpected.

In the present context, reference might also be made to Right Dislocation. If what follows *to* is nominal in 9a but not in 9b, the expectation is that the sequence in question can undergo Right Dislocation in the former but not in the latter. This expectation is borne out by the contrast between *I am accustomed to it, doing it this way* and **I am accustomed to it, do it this way.*

If the analysis of the two patterns presented here is on the right lines, there is also a point to be made about the position of *to* with respect to PRO in the order of constituents in the two patterns. Given that *to* is a preposition preceding a nominal clause in the pattern of 9a, it follows that it precedes PRO. (This was taken for granted at the beginning of the chapter.) By contrast, in the infinitival construction of 9b, the order of constituents in the subordinate clause is PRO *to* VP [cf. Rudanko (1989, 8)].

The two patterns are sharply different from a syntactic point of view. Even so, the preposition *to* and the infinitive marker *to* have the same realization, and there is a superficial similarity between the two patterns. The extent and the character of alternation should therefore be examined. The listing and classification of verbs taking *to -ing* afford us a useful opportunity for examining the extent of such alternation from the perspective of the present pattern. The result is surprising in a way, for the scope of alternation is fairly restricted. *Contribute* of class I is restricted to the *to*

-ing construal, as witness *John/the news contributed to raising/*raise morale immeasurably.* (So are *allude* and *refer,* as in *John alluded/referred to needing/*need more money.*) The same seems true of verbs of class II. For instance, *amount* does not allow the infinitive, as witness *What he said amounts to denying/*deny the obvious.* As far as *lead* is concerned, Poutsma (1929, 923) suggests that the "gerund-construction appears to be distinctly unusual" in comparison with the *to* infinitive construal. However, Poutsma's examples of the *to* infinitive—sentences such as *She is almost beautiful, and not in any way what you have been led to fancy* [Poutsma (1929, 923), from Meredith, *The Ordeal of Richard Feverel,* chap. 2, 155]—are all of a transitive pattern, in the terminology used here, of NP_1 $Verb_1$ NP_0 *to* $Verb_2$, and they are therefore not necessarily relevant. (For discussion of the transitive *-ing* pattern, that of NP_1 $Verb_1$ NP_0 *to* $Verb_2ing$, see chapter 4.) When the intransitive pattern is considered, it is observed that there is a marked preference in present-day English for *to -ing* over the *to* infinitive construal. Poutsma's one example of the intransitive pattern is a case in point: *The postponement of the measure led to bringing to the front other bills comparatively less distasteful* [Poutsma (1929, 923), from *The Graphic*], for it does not permit **The postponement of the measure led to bring to the front other bills...*

Class IIIa is a large class in terms of the number of verbs belonging to it, but these verbs do not in general allow the *to* infinitive construal. *Resort,* as in *John resorted to borrowing/*borrow money,* is a case in point. Poutsma has examples of *fall* selecting the *to* infinitive, as in *Upon this they fell again to rummage the will* [Poutsma (1929, 922), from Swift, *Tale of a Tub,* sec. II, 63b], but speakers today in general prefer to change this to *Upon this they fell again to rummaging the will.* Poutsma's comment that "there can be little doubt that the infinitive-construction is unusual in the latest English" [Poutsma (1929, 922)] is to the point and can be made more categorical, to the effect that the *to -ing* construal is the only option available to *fall.* Similarly, *take* rather clearly prefers *to -ing* over the infinitival construal in present-day English, as in *He took to writing poetry,* rather than **He took to write poetry.* [Admittedly, Poutsma, MS, s.v., cites *She has taken to like him,* from Meredith, *One of our Conquerors* (?), 3, chap. 11, 233 (OED), as an "indubitable instance" of an infinitival construction with *take,* but even here the *to -ing* construal, *She has taken to liking him,* seems preferable to most speakers today.] As for *turn,* as in *Of late the Press has turned from defending public interest to making inroads upon private life* [Poutsma (1929, 925), from R. Ashe King, *Oliver Goldsmith,* chap. 22, 254], the same statement seems to hold. [To be sure, Poutsma adduces *Let us turn for a moment to view those agencies at work* [Poutsma (1929, 925), from *Good Words*], but the verb here suggests the meaning 'step aside', and the construction appears to be adverbial.] On the other hand, *get* does allow the infinitive, for both 10a and 10b are possible. [The sentences are modeled on an authentic sentence in Poutsma (1929, 923).]

(10) a. They got to talking about business.
b. They got to talk about business.

However, there is a perceptible difference in meaning between 10a and 10b. The meaning of the matrix verb in the former might be paraphrased 'got around to' or 'almost accidentally drifted into'—the latter gloss due to Ian Gurney—while 10b might be glossed 'they got an opportunity to talk about business'. (There is also a third version possible, *They got talking about business*, which is again different, implying deliberate engagement in the activity.)

Verbs of the 'change over' subclass do not in general allow infinitival complements, as witness *John went over to drinking/*drink tea without sugar*. (The infinitival construction here is well formed, of course, on an adverbial interpretation.) As far as *descend* and *stoop* are concerned, in a sentence such as *John descended/stooped to denigrating his opponent,* the *-ing* clause expresses a pattern of behavior or a line of activity and a *to* infinitive does not sound very likely here to most speakers, except perhaps on an adverbial interpretation. (Admittedly, as observed above, not all speakers are entirely happy with *descend* in the *-ing* construal either.) However, when an isolated event, or a series of isolated events, is being talked about, an infinitive is much more readily possible, and perhaps even the preferred variant, especially with *stoop,* as in *I will not stoop to answer that allegation*. This kind of difference reminds us of the comment made above on the adjective *accustomed,* where the *-ing* form was connected with a pattern of behavior. However, too much should not be made of this finding, for neither *stoop* nor *descend* is common in the *-ing* pattern—neither was found selecting the pattern in the corpora—and speakers' reactions to construals involving the verbs are sometimes hazy.

As far as verbs of class IIIb are concerned, infinitival construals do not easily come to mind, as witness *John clung to demanding/*demand his share*. The same holds for IIIc1, as witness *John testified to being/*be on drugs,* and for IIIc2, as witness *John confessed to being/*be on drugs*. Poutsma does have an example of the infinitive construction with *own:*

What the chief commanders... owned to have reserved for each of themselves [Poutsma (1929, 924), from C. Johnstone, *Chrysal*, 3, 70 (OED, 5, a, c)]. He terms it "rare" [Poutsma (1929, 924)] or "unusual" (Poutsma, MS, s.v.), and with *own* in a concessive meaning, speakers today generally reject the *to* infinitive, preferring *to* -*ing*. On the other hand, class IIIc3 is different from those considered so far in that its verbs are much more readily and more systematically compatible with the *to* infinitive. Or, more precisely, the verbs expressing agreement are compatible with it, for *object* is not. Regarding *object*, Poutsma does have examples of *object* combined with the *to* infinitive, as in *We object to join with men who do not wear our badges and utter our shibboleths* [Poutsma (1929, 924), from *Good Words*], going as far as suggesting that "one construction may be as frequent as another," but in present-day English there is a robust preference for *to* -*ing*, as in *We object to joining*, to the extent that the *to* infinitive variant can be excluded. With regard to the verbs expressing agreement, consider 11a–c and 12a–c:

(11) a. The Cabinet agreed to revising the bill.
 b. The Cabinet assented to revising the bill.
 c. Sue consented to marrying John.

(12) a. The Cabinet agreed to revise the bill.
 b. The Cabinet assented to revise the bill.
 c. Sue consented to marry John.

There are some speakers who have somewhat hazy intuitions about one or two of the six sentences, especially perhaps about 12b, but, on the whole, speakers are reasonably happy with them. [Regarding *agree*, see also Budde (1956, 109).] At the same time, there is a systematic difference between the two types of construal. Characterizing the difference is not very easy, but it is possible to say that the *to* infinitive variants are more direct, and the *to* -*ing* forms suggest more distance between the matrix subject and the matrix verb, on the one hand, and the lower predicate, on the other. In the latter case it is as if the action or activity expressed by the lower clause were at a further remove from the constituents of the matrix clause. The difference with respect to directness and distance may be reflected in the interpretation of PRO. In the case of the *to* infinitives, it is clear that PRO is controlled by NP_1. For instance, to take 12a as a case in point, the sentence means clearly that it is the Cabinet that is going to revise the bill. On the other hand, in 11a this is less definite, and there is more scope for thinking that some entity other than the Cabinet (though quite conceivably in the Cabinet's charge) is going to revise the bill. Such a difference does not always surface in exactly the same way. Thus 11c is about Sue marrying John, not about somebody other than Sue, not even about somebody in her charge, marrying him. However, even here the idea of distance plays a role, for 11c means something like 'Sue consented to the idea of marrying John', while 12c, as it were, implies a more straightforward prospect of marriage.

As far as verbs of class IIId are concerned, there is little or no alternation, systematic or otherwise, between the two patterns, for verbs of the class do not generally allow *to* infinitives on complement clause interpretations. For instance, *adjust* does not allow them, as consider *John adjusted to losing/*lose his income*. Recorded usage also again needs to be handled with care if present-day English is to be the yardstick. Poutsma has several recorded instances of *submit* with the *to* infinitive, such as *Could he ever submit to give up Sibyl to any other?* [Poutsma (1929, 925), from Mrs. Alexander, *For His Sake*, 2, chap. 2, 30] and *They will not submit to be treated as inferior races* [Poutsma (1929, 925), from *The Westminster Gazette*. No. 8663, 5a]; and he goes so far as to say that "the gerund-construction appears to be unfrequent" [Poutsma (1929, 925)]. However, speakers today have in general a definite preference for the *to -ing* construal with *submit*, as in *submit to giving up Sibyl* and *They will never submit to being treated...*, to the extent that the *to* infinitive construal should be excluded as a complement clause construction. At the same time, there perhaps remains the possibility of an adverbial interpretation of the infinitive, even in Poutsma's sentences. On that reading, the lower clause does not necessarily specify what NP_1 submits to, and for Poutsma's sentences, paraphrases such as *Could he ever submit and give up Sibyl* and *They will never submit and be treated...* might be suggested. (I am indebted to Robert MacGilleon for drawing my attention to the possibility of an adverbial interpretation with *submit*.)

As for the remaining verbs with typically +animate subjects, grouped in IIIe, it is not easy to discern systematic alternation between the two construals. Some of these verbs, including *look forward*, do not allow *to* infinitives at all, as witness *John looked forward to getting/*get back to work*. On the other hand, *look* and *trust* do allow *to* infinitives on complement clause interpretations, as in 14a–b. [The sentences in 13a–b and

14a–b are modeled on sentences cited from Poutsma (1929) above.]

(13) a. They looked to setting up Presbyterianism in England.
b. She had to trust to finding Roy afterwards.

(14) a. They looked to set up Presbyterianism in England.
b. She had to trust to find him afterwards.

Not all of 13a–b and 14a–b are equally common, but the two types of constructions again feel different, at least up to a point. Here the differences seem less systematic and more connected with the particular matrix verbs in question than in the case of 11a–c and 12a–c. Thus with regard to *look*, 13a has an echo of 'look forward', whereas *look* in 14a carries a slight suggestion of 'seek'. On the other hand, *trust* in 13b seems stronger than in 14b. In the former it has a suggestion of 'rely on', whereas in the latter it has the flavor of 'strongly hope'. This sentence from the ALD (s.v. *trust*) is of interest here: *We trust to receive a cheque from you in settlement of this account.*

The present survey of the alternation between the *to -ing* and the *to* infinitive patterns has identified some verbs which do allow either construal. However, for the great majority of verbs selecting *to -ing*, a *to* infinitive construction is not possible. Indeed, from the vantage point of present-day English, it seems as if the *to -ing* pattern has supplanted the *to* infinitive construal with some verbs, such as *object*. From a different perspective, it is also worth emphasizing that when both construals are possible with a verb, the survey shows that there is often a difference in meaning, of a more or less robust nature, between the two constructions. In most cases such differences seem connected with the matrix verb in question, especially when only a small minority of a class of the taxonomy allows an alternative construal. The class of IIIc3 is an exception here, for its verbs allow the *to* infinitive construal much more systematically. However, a semantic difference was again observed between the two construals, and the fact that verbs of the class allow either construction more systematically only serves to make the contrast in meaning more systematic and consistent in nature.

Lest the conclusion about lack of free variation be accepted too hastily, we might avail ourselves of the opportunity to double-check by approaching the question from the opposite angle. The opportunity is afforded by the collections of verbs taking the *to* infinitive pattern that are presented in Rudanko (1984, 1989). These collections comprise over one hundred verbs that are current in present-day English. An examination of the lists yields little or nothing by way of verbs selecting both patterns. For instance, *want, intend, contrive, manage,* and *neglect* all take the *to* infinitive pattern but do not take the *to* *-ing* pattern: *John wanted, intended, contrived, managed, neglected to do/*doing his duty.*

The taxonomies and semantic analyses of Rudanko (1984, 1989) also afford an opportunity to compare meanings that are characteristically carried by verbs selecting *to* infinitives with those carried by verbs of the present pattern. Such a comparison does not reveal much semantic overlap. The sort of meanings that were identified as typical of major classes of verbs of the *to* infinitive pattern in these earlier studies—those of desideration, intention, and endeavor—do not, with very few exceptions, carry over to verbs of the present pattern.

The *to -ing* and *to* infinitive patterns are similar in that both are control patterns, often involving control of PRO by NP_1. Very specifically, the patterns are similar in that both have the element *to*. Setting the grammatical analysis of *to* aside, we might well expect considerable distributional and semantic overlap between the two patterns. Indeed, one might expect confusion. However, the present discussion suggests that overall there is surprisingly little variation between the two patterns and that there is even less variation between them that is unconnected with differences in meaning. Where systematic distributional alternation is encountered, its description is facilitated by the taxonomy proposed, in that the verbs affected are brought together by it. It also seems possible to pair such systematic distributional alternation with systematic differences in meaning. This discussion of alternation between the two patterns suggests the overall conclusion that the two construals are fairly sharply distinguished in present-day English.

As far as distributional alternation and semantic overlap are concerned, the *to* infinitive pattern is the obvious object of comparison. However, setting this aside now, we might consider some other construals that suggest themselves in this connection. To start with the pattern of NP_1 $Verb_1$ $Verb_2 ing$, as in *John avoided making a mistake*, it seems that much the same finding, that there is little or no overlap, holds true here. *Avoid* is a case in point, for **John avoided to making a mistake* is inconceivable. Going through the lists of verbs collected in Rudanko (1985; 1989, 44 ff.), we observe that virtually the only area of distributional and semantic overlap is a subgroup of verbs of communication: in both patterns there are matrix verbs expressing communication that are concessive. From a distributional point of view, the two sets of verbs include one or two identical members, such as *admit* and *confess*. [On these two verbs, see Dixon (1991, 273).] Apart from this one subgroup, there is virtually no overlap. It is also observed that the meanings that were identified as typical of the other pattern—such as those of negative desideration, negative intention, and negative endeavor—are even further from the types of meaning associated in the taxonomy with the present pattern of complementation.

One or two verbs of class II of the present pattern (*amount, come down*) are semantically similar to verbs of a subclass of verbs taking the *in* -*ing* pattern of complementation, as discussed in the previous chapter. The most prominent member of this subclass of the *in* -*ing* pattern is probably *consist*, as in *His technique consisted in twisting the truth*. However, verbs of class II of the present pattern do not in general take *in* -*ing*: **His technique amounted in twisting the truth*. Nor do the corresponding verbs of the *in* -*ing* pattern—such as *consist in*—in general take *to* -*ing*: **His technique consisted to twisting the truth*. The semantic similarity, then, does not carry over to distributional overlap, at least not to any great extent.

There is also a degree of semantic similarity between class III of the present pattern, especially its subclasses IIIa and IIIb, on the one hand, and the central class of verbs expressing engagement of the *in* -*ing* pattern, on the other. (It will be recalled that in the latter case, Verb$_1$ was glossed 'perform the act of' or 'carry out the activity of'.) Thus from *John resorted to borrowing money*, for instance, it follows that he performed the act of borrowing money (at least once). At the same time, it may be pointed out that verbs of classes IIIa and IIIb of the present pattern tend to focus on NP$_1$'s orientation or movement toward engagement, on NP$_1$'s changing or maintaining his or her orientation, more than do verbs expressing engagement that select *in* -*ing* (Ian Gurney, personal communication). Admittedly, some verbs of the latter class, including *persevere* and *persist*, likewise involve an element of orientation, but perhaps of a "milder" sort than corresponding verbs of class IIIb, such as *adhere* and *cling*. In any case, it is important again to notice how little distributional overlap there is between the *to* -*ing* and *in* -*ing* patterns. For instance, neither *persevere* nor *persist* permit *to* -*ing*, as witness the ill-formedness of **John persevered/persisted to coming to class*. Nor do *adhere* and *cling* allow *in* -*ing*, as witness the ill-formedness of **John adhered/clung in coming to class*. The same lack of distributional overlap holds of verbs such as *engage* and *indulge* of the *in* -*ing* pattern, as witness **John engaged/indulged to borrowing money*, and of verbs such as *resort* and *turn* of the *to -ing* pattern, as witness the ill-formedness of **John resorted/turned in borrowing money*. Sentences such as these are felt to be quite inconceivable, and this lack of distributional overlap between the two construals suggests that speakers do not feel that they are close to each other.

There is more distributional overlap between the present pattern and the *that* clause construction, for class IIIc of the former is a sizable one. Matrix verbs that combine with *that* clauses characteristically express communication. As observed above, the meanings of verbs of IIIc are rather more specialized. This demarcates the two patterns to some extent, but not completely, for most of the verbs of IIIc may also co-occur with *that* clauses. A more interesting difference of a fairly systematic nature is that when these verbs occur with *that* clauses, the *that* clause variants tend to carry meanings that are often subtly different from those carried by the *-ing* variants. For instance, if sentences such as *John testified that he took drugs* and *John testified to taking drugs* are compared, the *that* clause version tends to be closer to being a paraphrase of what was actually said. [In this connection, cf. Bresnan (1972, 69 ff., especially 76) and Rudanko (1989, 80 ff.).] Because of this difference, the overlap between the present pattern and the *that* clause construal is perhaps more apparent than real.

Overall, it may be observed that at times there is a degree of distributional or semantic overlap between one or two subclasses of the present pattern and those of other patterns. Because of obvious similarity on the surface level, the *to* infinitive pattern may be felt to be especially close to the *to -ing* pattern. However, it is argued here that the degree of distributional overlap between these two patterns is relatively limited. The same finding holds for other alternative construals. Further, where distributional overlap is encountered, it is often the case that semantic distinctions, sometimes subtle, sometimes less subtle, separate the *to -ing* patterns from alternative construals.

There is one other consideration that bears on this discussion of the position of the *to -ing* pattern vis-à-vis alternative construals in the system of complementation of present-day English. It is not possible to claim that the class of verbs selecting *to -ing* is completely homogeneous semantically. However, it is still possible to discern core classes. If the numbers of verbs that belong to the classes of the taxonomy are considered, and if some account is taken of the probability of occurrence of relevant verbs in actual usage, as reflected in the corpora, it is hard to escape the conclusion that class IIIa, of verbs meaning approximately 'turn to', is a core class—or even *the* core class—of the *to -ing* pattern. It is striking that there is comparatively little overlap between this class and classes of other patterns. The reason for this relative absence of overlap is perhaps not far to seek, as least as far as the superficially so similar *to* infinitive pattern is concerned. Although it may be suggested that the *to* of the *to* infinitive pattern may still retain a touch of the localistic meaning of *to* [cf. Rudanko (1989, 34 f.)], in the case of IIIa the localistic meaning of *to* may be felt even more strongly. Of course, as far as verbs of IIIa are concerned, the meaning of *to* is at some remove from a concrete meaning of the preposition. However, it seems much closer to it than in the case of the *to* of the *to* infinitive pattern. It may be added that the localistic meaning of *to* also involves a focus on movement that sets verbs in IIIa off against the class of verbs selecting *in -ing* that express engagement. Overall, the core class of IIIa gives the pattern a fairly distinctive and well-defined semantic domain. I have argued elsewhere (Rudanko 1989, 152) that when two syntactic patterns of complementation have very similar semantic domains, this may lead to a decline of one of them. In the present case, there is little similarity. We may speculate, then, that even though the number of verbs selecting *to -ing* is not very large, the pattern is nevertheless a healthy one with a distinctive semantic function in the system of complementation of present-day English. This conclusion is reinforced by the consideration that not many verbs taking *to -ing* take other patterns of complementation.

4

Reducing Someone to Groveling:
On Verbs Governing NP *to -ing*

I

Consider sentence 1 and structure 1', which is a partially bracketed representation of 1:

(1) The rebuff reduced John to groveling before his idol.
(1') [[The rebuff]$_{NP1}$ reduced [John]$_{NP0}$ [to]$_{Prep}$ [[PRO]$_{NP2}$ [[groveling]$_{Verb2}$ before his idol]$_{VP}$]$_{S2}$]$_{S1}$

   In 1', the lower clause is a complement clause, which means that there is a close syntactic connection between it and the matrix predicate, with the latter subcategorized as co-occurring with the former. The empty NP$_2$, PRO, is interpreted as coreferential with, or is controlled by, the direct object of the matrix verb. The *to* in the structure, preceding the *-ing* form, is classed as a preposition, along the lines of Quirk et al. (1985, 1178 f.).
   S$_2$ in the pattern of 1 is a nominal clause. This may be substantiated with the help of considerations used earlier in this book. Thus the following question and answer sequence is possible: Q. *What did the rebuff reduce John to?* A. *Groveling before his idol.* Replacement of the lower clause by *that* is likewise possible, though replacement with *it* does not sound emphatic enough, as consider *The rebuff reduced John to groveling*

before his idol but it did not reduce me to that/?it. A right dislocation construction is not very likely, but still seems within the bounds of possibility, as in *?The rebuff (finally) reduced John to it, groveling before his idol.* Finally, pseudocleft sentences such as *What the rebuff reduced John to was groveling before his idol* are well formed. The criteria, then, on the whole, coincide in demonstrating that S_2 is a nominal clause in the pattern in question.

In this chapter we will examine some basic properties of the pattern of 1. The first task is to compile a reasonable list of matrix verbs that occur in the pattern. Next, a semantic characterization of such verbs will be attempted. The taxonomy will be used further to comment on the syntactic analysis of matrix verbs in the pattern, including the nominal character of the lower clause. A further important task is to compare the pattern of 1 with alternative construals, especially with that of 2, which may be represented as in 2':

(2)   The news forced John to reevaluate his position.
(2') [[The news]$_{NP}$ [forced]$_{Verb1}$ [John]$_{NP0}$ [[PRO]$_{NP2}$ to [[reevaluate]$_{Verb2}$ his position]$_{VP}$]$_{S2}$]$_{S1}$

The infinitival pattern of 2 bears some similarities to the *-ing* pattern of 1. For instance, in 2, as in 1, PRO is interpreted as coreferential with NP_0, that is, with a direct object in either case. However, there are also differences, one of these relating to the status of the element *to:* in 2' *to* is not a preposition but rather an infinitive marker, to revert to the terminology of Quirk et al. (1985, 1178). It may also be pointed out that the patterns are not interchangeable, at least not in the case of 1 and 2. Thus 3a–b are bad:

(3)   a. *The rebuff reduced John to grovel before his idol.
      b. *The news forced John to reevaluating his position.

To accomplish such tasks, it is advisable to draw on different types of data. Intuitions of native speakers are relevant, especially insofar as they relate to acceptability, and as far as recorded usage is concerned, the Brown corpus and the LOB corpus again recommend themselves as sources of data. Earlier grammarians of English that are worth consulting include Quirk et al. (1985). However, the pride of place here again undoubtedly belongs to Poutsma [(1905, 1929); the latter is more comprehensive in covering the pattern, and references to Poutsma will be mostly to that edition]. The present treatment is indebted to his work not only for data but also for a research perspective, his sensitivity to variation and to limits to variation. To this day, his discussion of the alternation between what in the terminology employed in the present investigation are NP_1 $Verb_1$ (NP_0) *to* PRO $Verb_2 ing$ and NP_1 $Verb_1$ (NP_0) PRO *to* $Verb_2$ constructions—the discussion of the present chapter relating to structures where NP_0 is present—remains unrivaled and a standard of excellence, on account of its incisiveness and its breadth of systematic documentation. Much as in chapter 3, the segment of the present discussion that deals with this issue may perhaps be offered as a contribution to one part of a research task pioneered by Poutsma.

II

Starting with the task of compiling a list of relevant matrix verbs, the following verbs will be considered on the basis of the two corpora, with most illustrations quoted from, or modeled on, the same sources.

Verb	Illustrations and Comments
commit	*If we accept our equation (4.1) as a basic structural relation, then we are virtually committed to accepting the view that the level of 'excess demand' for labour had a significant effect on wage rate changes in that period* [LOB J44 179-182, from L. Klein et al., *An Econometric Model of the United Kingdom* (Basil Blackwell)]. This is a common way of construing *commit*, but the verb also allows an active sentence such as *By what you just said you have committed us to changing our policy*—the example devised by Ian Gurney—which provides clearer motivation for including the verb in the present discussion.
confine	*Nevertheless, we do not consider that the work of the After Care Council should be confined to assisting those who are statutorily placed under its supervision* [LOB H08 82-84, from *The Extension of Compulsory After-Care to Additional Categories of Inmates and Prisoners* (Her Britannic Majesty's Stationary Office)]. An additional example, modified from the above, may again clarify the inclusion of the verb: *We should not confine the Council to assisting people under its supervision.*

Chapter 4

dedicate A report by the Rockefeller Brothers' Fund (News Chronicle, June 25, 1958) arraigns 'the public lassitude that has accepted without question an educational system dedicated mainly to turning out good little conformist Americans who, as Stringfellow Barr puts it, even when they have graduated from college (famous institutions) are unfamiliar with the ideas that are the stock-in-trade of Western Culture' [LOB G55 93-99, from T. Pear, *The Moulding of Modern Man* (G. Allen and Unwin)]. The verb also allows *We should dedicate our educational system to turning out good citizens* and should be included.

devote Most examples of this verb in the corpora are of the following type: *It is estimated that more than 600 stations (of a total of 3,400) do a significant amount of programming for the Negro. At least 60 stations devote all of their time to reaching this audience in about half of the 50 states* (Brown C12 0160-0190, from *The Christian Science Monitor* 10/17). Strictly speaking, this is not the pattern of 1', since the understood controller of PRO is not NP_0. After all, *all of their time* does not reach this audience. Rather it is NP_1, *at least 60 stations*, that controls PRO. For its part, the direct object expresses a resource at the disposal of NP_1. However, the verb may occur in the pattern of 1', as in *We will devote our special branch to investigating internal abuse of power*, where *our special branch*, though again expressing something at the disposal of, or in the charge of, NP_1, is the understood controller of PRO. For this reason, the verb may be retained.

drive For years he wore hand-me-down suits and homemade paper collars, was even driven to scrounging for cigarette butts in Vienna's gutters [Brown B24 1730-1750, "Reviews" (*Time* magazine 77:3)].

gear Has your company developed selection and training processes that are geared to providing the caliber of salesmen you will need in the next 10 yr.? [Brown E28 1630-1650, from J. Sargent, "Where to Aim Your Planning for Bigger Profits in '60s" (*Food Engineering* 33: 2)]. Active sentences such as *The company geared its training pro-*

cesses to providing top class salesmen* and *The experience geared me to coping with stress*—the last example due to Ian Gurney—are also possible.

give over   THE DEMAND *for food is so great in the world that little arable land can be given over to growing the nonfood crops* [Brown F34 0360-0380, from F. Senti and D. Maclay, "Age-Old Uses of Seeds and Some New Ones" (*Seeds*, U. S. Department of Agriculture)].

inure   *Of course, in this small way of forcing the people to watch as tiny and innocent and dependent creatures die because we're afraid to feed them and afraid to protest and say "How come? What's your motive? WHO wants this deed done"?—in this small way do the leaders of a city, or of a nation, iniure the masses to watching, or even inflicting, torture and death, upon even their fellow men* (Brown B19 1360-1420, from *The Philadelphia Inquirer* 11/5). In the source the verb is spelled as *iniure*, but the normal spelling is without the second *i*.

limit   *I have limited myself to proving completeness, but, at least in certain cases, much more can be proved* [LOB J20 54-55, from J. McLeod, "Eigenfunction Expansions Associated with a Complex Differential Operator of the Second Order (*Quarterly Journal of Mathematics* 12)]. A nonreflexive example, where the control relations are clearer, would be *Shortage of money limited the agency to helping a few families only*.

move   *Linda Evans felt more wretched than she had ever dreamed Bobbie's death could move her to feeling* [Brown P17 1110-1110, from A. Hine, "The Huntress" (*Saturday Evening Post* 2/4)].

put back   *He should put the police back to patrolling and walking the streets at night* (Brown B18 1510-1520, from *The Detroit News* 11/17).

reduce   *The centres, after one or two tentative thrusts early on when the ground was not cut up, soon found they were reduced to kicking. This they did all too often straight to the opposition* (LOB A08 23-25, from *Daily Telegraph* 2/3).

regiment   *We are slowly being regimented to having everything packaged, whether we want it or not* (Brown B16 0670-0680, *Chicago Daily Tribune* 8/12). The instance is genuine, but speakers generally prefer *We are slowly being regimented into having* to the *to -ing* pattern to such an extent that it seems best to drop the verb. (The author is indebted to an anonymous reader for drawing attention to the availability of, and the preference for, the *into -ing* construction with *regiment*.)

set   *The building shook, setting the lantern to swaying, and the buckskin to pitching again* [Brown N12 1380-1380, from E. Booth, *Outlaw Town* (Ballantine Books)]. The instance is genuine, but there are many speakers today, especially perhaps of British English, who are dubious about this construction, at least in this instance. Virtually all speakers accept *setting the lantern swaying,* and this is the preferred variant for many speakers, at least in comparison with the *to -ing* form. Reactions to the infinitive variant *setting the lantern to sway* are generally less favorable, but there are speakers who accept it and some who even prefer it to the *to -ing* form. Some hesitation may be felt about *set* in the present pattern, but on balance it seems best to include it. (For further discussion of the verb, see below.)

start   *JUST WHEN IT SEEMS baseball might be losing its grip on the masses up pops heroics to start millions of tongues to wagging* (Brown A13 1010-1020, from *Rocky Mountain News* 5/2). Again, this is not a universally accepted construction. Virtually all speakers accept *start millions of tongues wagging,* and this is the preferred variant for many speakers, especially perhaps of British English. Reactions to the infinitive variant *start millions of tongues to wag* are again often less favorable, though there are some speakers who not only accept it but prefer it to the *to -ing* construction. The verb is included in the *to -ing* pattern only with some hesitation.

switch   *One of the more remarkable of the new cooling systems is one that can be switched to heating* [Brown E20 0860-0870, from Anon., "What You Should Know about Air

Conditioning for New Homes" (*How-to-Do-It-Encyclopedia*, Golden Press)].

A few more verbs may be gathered from the list of verbs in Quirk et al. (1985, 1211) that occur in their pattern of D2b. This is the pattern of *warn* in *Mary warned John of the danger*, where the constituent after the preposition is nonsentential. Quirk et al. (1985, 1211) have a list of verbs taking the preposition *to* with a following NP but do not single out sentential constructions for treatment. They list six verbs in their nonsentential pattern with the preposition *to*: *confine to, introduce to, refer to, sentence to, subject to* and *treat to*. *Confine* was included above. Nominal noun phrases are perhaps more common with the rest. However, *John introduced Mary to taking the waters at a resort nearby*, *The judge in effect sentenced the prisoner to rotting in jail* (the example due to Ian Gurney), and *John subjected his guests to eating their meals without proper wines* are possible and motivate the inclusion of these three verbs. On the other hand, *??John referred Mary to consulting the timetable* seems pleonastic and doubtful in comparison with *John referred Mary to the timetable;* and *?John treated Mary to dining at a good restaurant* likewise seems slightly dubious in comparison with *John treated Mary to dinner at a good restaurant*, and these verbs will not be included.

A largish number of other additional verbs may be gleaned from Bridgeman et al. (1965, 43 ff.). There are no illustrations of usage in this source, except for *adapt*, and the examples of usage below, apart from *adapt*, have been freely devised.

abandon	*John abandoned Mary to fending for herself.* There are speakers who find this construction slightly strained, and the verb can be included only with some hesitation.
accustom	*John accustomed Mary to being punctual.*
adapt	*We'll adapt it to making steel at lower temperatures.*
bind	*The promise that he had made bound John to finishing the job.*
condemn	*The judge condemned the prisoner to rotting in jail.*
condition	*His poverty conditioned John to accepting handouts.*
convert	*Mary converted her husband to drinking tea without sugar.* (The example is due to Ian Gurney.) The verb may also

	have a +collective NP_0, as in *The management converted the plant to producing tanks*.
delegate	*John delegated his assistant to doing menial tasks.*
demote	*John demoted his assistant to cleaning floors.*
hold	*John held Mary to keeping her word.*
pin down	*John pinned Mary down to answering the question.*
put up	*John put Mary up to devising a new plan.*
reconcile	*John reconciled Mary to accepting her circumstances.* On *reconcile* in this pattern, see also Budde (1956, 108).
relegate	*John relegated his assistant to cleaning floors.*

One or two more verbs can perhaps be added. On the analogy of verbs such as *devote*, *allocate* might be included, as witness *We should allocate/devote/dedicate/give over our special branch to investigating internal abuse of power*. *Attract* [cf. Sager (1981, 349)] also seems possible in the pattern, as in *The prospect of getting rich quickly attracted John to running for office*. In addition, there are speakers who find *rouse* acceptable in a sentence such as *The news roused the tribunes to pressing their case*; but this verb can be included only with considerable hesitation, for many speakers find the construction strained. Further, *change over*, *move over*, and *switch over* might be included, as in *The management changed/moved/switched the factory over to producing tanks*. With these, NP_0 often seems +collective, something like *a firm*, *an enterprise*, etc. A −collective NP_0 seems less likely, and many speakers object to sentences such as *Mary changed her husband over to drinking tea without sugar* and in *Mary gradually moved her husband over to drinking tea without sugar*, though others find them possible. Finally, as pointed out by Ian Gurney, *assign* and *resign* may be included, as witness the admissibility of *They assigned John to translating secret documents* and *Circumstances resigned John to accepting his fate*.

III

It would be foolhardy to claim that the lists of verbs given and illustrated in section II are exhaustive. No doubt in a larger survey other verbs that occur in the pattern of 1′ would be found. However, the verbs listed are perhaps sufficiently numerous to provide at least an approximation and to permit a first discussion of properties of the pattern. An initial task here is to attempt a characterization of meanings that are typical of matrix verbs in the pattern. One way to approach this task is to consider the nature of NP_1, the subject of the matrix clause, and of NP_0, the object of the matrix clause and the controller of PRO. It seems on the basis of the illustrations above that for most verbs in the pattern, NP_1 characteristically designates a +animate entity. Or if it does not, as in 1, it often has at least an instrumental force: the rebuff was the means by which John was reduced to groveling before his idol and the rebuff presumably came from an animate entity. (For one or two verbs, such as *condition*, as in the example above, NP_1 generally expresses an abstract cause.) As for NP_0, it typically designates the entity that is acted upon by NP_1 and which then undertakes the action expressed by $Verb_2$.

The following semantic characterization of verbs in the pattern then suggests itself:

1. $Verb_1$ has the approximate meaning 'act on', 'influence', or 'move', NP_1 moves NP_0 to realize (or realizing) S_2: *abandon, accustom, adapt, assign, attract, bind, commit, condition, delegate, demote, drive, gear, hold, introduce, inure, move, pin down, put back, put up, reconcile, relegate, resign, rouse, set, start, subject.*

    $Verb_1$ has the approximate meaning 'change over', NP_1 changes NP_0, often +collective, over to $Verb_2 ing$: *change over, convert, move over, switch, switch over.*

    $Verb_1$ is judicial or quasi-judicial: *condemn, sentence.*

2. $Verb_1$ has the approximate meaning 'limit', NP_1 limits NP_0 to realizing S_2: *confine, limit, reduce.*

3. $Verb_1$ has the approximate meaning 'give over', with NP_0 often +collective: *allocate, devote, dedicate, give over.*

It bears emphasizing that such semantic groupings are not meant to imply that all—or even any two—verbs in any one of the groups are synonymous. The point is rather that the verbs of each group share an ingredient of meaning. Teasing out that ingredient of meaning is not always easy. In the ideal case there is a verb in the class that comes close to expressing the ingredient of meaning in question. The larger the class, the more difficult it generally is to find such a verb. In the present classification, *limit* seems appropriate enough at the top of class 2, but the class is very small. Similarly, *give over* seems a possible choice at the head of class 3, but this is another small class. Far more verbs belong to the first class. *Move* is not the perfect verb to be at the head of the class (see below), but the gloss provided that makes use of it is meant to convey the idea that (the entity or abstract object designated by) NP_1 influences, or acts upon (the entity designated by) NP_0, NP_0 then undertaking the action expressed by the lower clause.

The taxonomy suggests that matrix verbs of this pattern have the typical meaning 'act on', 'move', or 'influence NP_0 to'. Indeed, it may be possible to view both class 2 and class 3 as subgroups of class 1, with the proviso that for verbs of class 2, the lower clause characteristically designates something that NP_0 finds unfulfilling or undesirable, and for verbs of class 3, NP_0 expresses something at the disposal of NP_1, such as a resource that NP_1 can control at will. In any event, as far as verbs of class 2 (such as *reduce* in *Circumstances reduced John to writing hack stories*) are concerned, they mean that NP_1 acts upon or influences NP_0, moving the latter to do whatever is expressed by the lower clause. An analogous analysis seems possible for verbs of class 3; for instance, consider *devote*, as in *They devoted the special branch to investigating internal abuse of power*.

This discussion of the semantics of verbs of the three classes—if they are still kept separate—invites a reference to what has been called the *order/permit* type in the control literature. As Sag and Pollard put it, "verbs of the *order/permit* type all submit to a semantic analysis involving STATES OF AFFAIRS (SOAs) where a certain participant (the referent of the object) is influenced by another participant (the referent of the subject) to perform an action (characterized in terms of the SOA denoted by the . . . complement)" [Sag and Pollard (1991, 66)]. Sag and Pollard's discussion focuses on infinitival complements, and the verbs that they list as of the *order/permit* type are almost entirely different from the verbs listed in the three classes above. However, the easy applicability of the notion of influencing in the context of verbs of the three classes confirms the status of the *order/permit* type in the analysis of object control. In the light of the present discussion it is clear that its scope is not restricted to the analysis of control verbs selecting infinitival complements but extends to that of control verbs selecting *to -ing* complement sentences.

Combining the three classes into one is a possibility. At the same time, there are perhaps also some subgroups discernible within class 1 as it is currently constituted. As Ian Gurney (personal communication) has pointed out, some verbs of the class, including *accustom, adapt, condition, gear, inure, reconcile,* and *resign,* express or may express a gradual process of influencing or of bringing NP_0 around to $Verb_2 ing$, while several other verbs, including *assign, commit, dedicate, demote, devote, condemn,* and *sentence,* imply that NP_1 has a position of authority over NP_0. (In the case of the verbs of the 'change over' subclass, NP_1 is viewed as having more or less complete power over NP_0.) This distinction is substantiated by the consideration that NP_1s denoting +abstract causes—NPs such as *circumstances,* etc.—tend to occur with, or even be limited to, verbs of the process class, while subjects of verbs implying a sense of authority are typically restricted to +animate NPs.

The lists of verbs also make it easy to see that NP_0 is mostly +animate in the pattern. From the point of view of the semantic characterization of the major class, this does not seem altogether unexpected, for NP_0 needs to be something that can be acted upon and influenced, and such NPs are typically animate. However, there are some verbs in class 1 that take inanimate NPs. These include *adapt, gear, set, switch,* and *start* (insofar as *set* and *start* are allowed in the pattern). Even with these verbs, the character of NP_0 often bears some link to animacy in a more extended sense, for, as pointed out by Ian Gurney (personal communication), the NPs in question, such as *a machine, a system,* etc., can typically be conceived of as exhibiting behavior. Beyond class 1, the tendency for NP_0 to be typically +animate carries over to verbs of classes 2 and 3. Regarding the latter, examples such as *The agency dedicated/ devoted their special branch to investigating internal abuse of power* may be cited as illustrations.

It was previously remarked that *devote* often occurs in sentences such as *John devoted a great deal of his time to studying the problem.* This pattern is outside this discussion, since the controller of PRO is NP_1 and not NP_0. It may be observed in passing, though, that other verbs of the 'give over' class likewise occur in this non–object control pattern, as in *He allocated/ gave over all his time to reading newspapers.* As for verbs of the other two major classes, those of class 1 do not normally occur in this kind of non–object control construal, as witness the ill-formedness, for instance, of **He conditioned/converted his attention to finding a scapegoat.* (*Switch* and *switch over* seem exceptions, for *He switched his attention (over) to finding a scapegoat* is possible.) On the other hand, verbs of class 2 may occur in this non–object control pattern in a regular fashion, as in *They confined/ limited/reduced their efforts to dropping supplies from the air,* where it is they who are dropping supplies. The subject control pattern seems generally to need a direct object that is +abstract, such as *time, effort, endeavor*. If the object is +animate, as in *They confined the air force to dropping supplies from the air*, the pattern is one of object control.

With the taxonomy in place, it is possible to utilize it for further analytic discussion of the pattern. From a syntactic point of view, there are two aspects of the taxonomy in particular that deserve attention. First, it appears that the present pattern duplicates the finding in chapters 2 and 3 that all verbs listed as occurring in the sentential pattern may also occur in a nonsentential pattern, where the sentential complement following the preposition is replaced by an appropriate NP. *Condition* and *drive* may serve as examples. They are possible not only in construals with sentential complements, illustrated above, but also with nominal complements, as in *Intimidation conditioned the population to a resigned acceptance of their fate* and *The collapse of his project drove John to despair*. From another point of view, the nominal status of S_2 with verbs of the present taxonomy can be substantiated by considering syntactic constructions adduced at the beginning of the chapter. *Confine* might serve as a case in point here, and all of the following sentences, modeled on the authentic example given above, are possible, or at least tolerably so: Q. *What should the After Care Council be confined to?* A. *Assisting those placed under its supervision; The After Care Council should be confined to assisting those under its supervision, but the Family Care Council should not be confined to that/?it;* ?*The After Care Council should be confined to it, assisting those placed under its supervision; What the After Care Council should be confined to is assisting those under its supervision.* On the other hand, just as in chapters 2 and 3, the converse is not true. As was seen above, there are verbs such as *refer* that take nonsentential NPs as complements of prepositions but are more difficult to combine with sentential complements. Consequently, it is possible to consider the set of verbs governing the present sentential pattern of complementation as a subset of verbs governing the corresponding pattern with nonsentential NP complements.

Second, this taxonomy is of interest from the point of view of what in the literature has come to be called Bach's generalization [see Bach (1980, 304)]. This generalization has been motivated on the basis of data such as the sentences in 4a–d, from Rizzi (1986, 503):

(4) a. This leads people [PRO to conclude what follows].
    b. *This leads [PRO to conclude what follows].
    c. This leads people to the following conclusion.
    d. This leads to the following conclusion.

Example 4a is an object control construction, with the NP *people*, the direct object of the matrix clause and NP_0 in the terminology of this book, controlling PRO, the understood subject of *conclude what follows*. The generalization, then, relates to the nonomissibility of the direct object of the matrix clause in an object control construction and has been phrased as follows: "In object control structures the object NP must be structurally represented" [Rizzi (1986, 503)].

The generalization is offered as an explanation for the ill-formedness of 4b. However, the generalization cannot be taken to mean that verbs whose direct objects are subject to Bach's generalization are necessarily excluded from having uses without direct objects, with the meaning of the verb remaining at least approximately constant (apart from control). *Lead* is a case in point, since 4d is well formed.

Lead is not a verb that belongs to the present pattern of complementation, since **The news leads people to concluding what follows* is ill formed, and a full discussion of the verb cannot be undertaken here. Even so, one additional observation suggests itself. In sentence 4d there is no structurally represented object. However, it may be suggested from a semantic perspective that in this sentence there is still an understood or suppressed direct object, with a meaning such as 'people in general' or 'the subset of people relevant in the discourse in question'. The sense of the verb in 4d is approximately 'enable/cause to arrive at', and the idea of an understood object in 4d might be motivated by the semantic consideration that only an +animate NP can arrive at a conclusion. [It may be mentioned here that Lehrer (1970, 252) cites *lead* as an object-deletion verb in her classification. She does not have an illustration, though, and it is not possible to be sure if she had the same sense of the verb in mind.] The case for an understood object in 4d must remain somewhat speculative here. However, it is a robust fact about English that where no understood object NP can be hypothesized from a semantic point of view, an ill-formed sentence results with *lead*, as in 5a–b:

(5) a. *People lead to conclude what follows.
 b. *People lead to the following conclusion.

Example 5a is formed by turning NP_0 of an object control construction, as in 4a, into the subject of a subject control construal. This is clearly out of the question for *lead*.

As far as can be ascertained, Bach's generalization has not been discussed in the literature with reference to the present pattern of complementation. When this is done, there emerge at least two types of verbs that are each different from the use of *lead* illustrated in 4a–d and in 5a–b. *Convert* may serve as an example of one type. Thus consider 6a–d:

(6) a. The management converted the plant to making steel.
 b. The plant converted to making steel.
 c. The management converted the plant to the requirements of the free market.
 d. The plant converted to the requirements of the free market.

Convert is an object control verb in 6a, where PRO is controlled by NP_0. However, 6b, where analogously to 5a, NP_0 of the object control construction is turned into the subject of a subject control construal, is quite well formed, showing that *convert* is also a subject control verb. It bears emphasizing that in 6b there is no feeling of an understood or suppressed object. 6d is an illustration of how *convert* may be used intransitively with the preposition *to* taking a nonsentential complement. The well-formedness of 6d comes as no surprise, since it was argued above that sentential complements of the preposition *to* can regularly be replaced with nonsentential NPs in the present pattern. At the same time, it is important to notice that just as in 6b (but unlike sentence 4d), there is in 6d no sense of an understood or suppressed object. From a semantic point of view, there also seems to be a fairly well defined shift in meaning correlated with the shift from object to subject control: the former involves causation, with NP_1 bringing about a new state of affairs by acting on, or doing something to, NP_0. The latter does not involve causation, and the plant, or the collective body of people working at the plant, does the converting under its own steam, so to speak.

Limit may be taken as an example of another type. Thus consider 7a–d:

(7) a. Shortage of money limited the agency to helping a few families only.
 b. *Shortage of money limited to helping a few families only./*The agency limited to helping a few families only.
 c. Shortage of money limited the agency to a minor role.
 d. *Shortage of money limited to a minor role./*The agency limited to a minor role.

The examples cited suggest that the type of patterning exemplified by *limit* is more restrictive than either the type of *lead* or that of *convert*, in that it is less readily capable of being used without an expressed direct object. When a direct object is preserved, the verb does allow a nonsentential complement, as in 7c, which is as expected, but it permits neither subject control constructions, as witness the sentences of 7b, nor intransitive uses with nonsentential complements, as witness the sentences of 7d.

Three different types of constructions have been established, illustrated with *lead, convert,* and *limit.* To facilitate discussion in this chapter and also to look forward to discussion of other object control patterns in later chapters, it is proposed here that Bach's generalization be split into two versions. They will be called the strong form and the weak form of the generalization, with the stronger form being more restrictive and the weaker form less so. At the same time, the generalization is renamed B's generalization, because its splitting up entails its redefinition.

> Strong form of B's generalization: In object control structures, the object NP must be structurally represented, and matrix verbs that select such structures do not have intransitive uses.

> Weak form of B's generalization: In object control structures, the object NP must be structurally represented, but matrix verbs that select such structures may have intransitive uses.

The strong form of B's generalization holds for *limit* and captures the data of 7a–d. It does not hold for either *lead* or *convert.* For these the weak form of the generalization is operative. The weak form, therefore, encompasses object control verbs of two types: verbs such as *lead* that can be used intransitively in noncontrol structures with nonsentential complements, and verbs such as *convert* that can be used intransitively in both noncontrol constructions with nonsentential complements, and in subject control constructions with sentential complements. Verbs of the former type are less clearly intransitive, for they involve understood direct objects even when none is structurally represented. Verbs of the latter type do not, and consequently they are more clearly intransitive. Another reflex of the difference is that with the former type, NP_0 of the transitive construal does not become a subject in an intransitive use, whereas with the latter type it typically does.

With the two versions of B's generalization defined, the verbs of the taxonomy may be examined to see which form is the prevalent one. For the overwhelming majority of verbs of the pattern, it is possible to maintain the strong form of the generalization, because they do not have uses without expressed direct objects. *Delegate* and *confine* are further examples of such verbs, for neither *John delegated his assistant to doing menial tasks* nor *Shortage of money confined the agency to helping a few families only* allows omission of NP_0, as witness the ill-formedness of resulting sentential complements, as in **John delegated to doing menial tasks only*, and **Shortage of money confined to helping a few families only*, and of nonsentential complements, as in **John delegated to menial tasks* and **Shortage of money confined to a few families only*. However, there are some verbs of the present pattern—though they are definitely a minority—for which it is not possible to maintain the strong form of B's generalization. *Switch* is another case in point. Not only is *We will switch the plant to making steel* possible, with an object control construal, but so is *The plant switched to producing steel*, with a subject control construal. (As expected, a nonsentential complement is likewise possible, as in *The plant switched to a new line of products*.) Similar possibilities for both object control and subject control exist for one or two other verbs of the pattern, including *change over*, *move over*, and *switch over*. (These verbs were illustrated in subject control constructions in chapter 3.) The kind of change in meaning observed above with *convert* as connected with the switch from object to subject control seems to extend to these verbs, in that in the object control construal the verb has a causative element, along the lines of NP_1 bringing it about that NP_0 does $Verb_2$ by acting on, or doing something to, NP_0, whereas in the subject control construal NP_0 does $Verb_2$ under its own steam. Verbs that permit this switch also seem to exhibit some semantic cohesion or regularity. Such verbs tend to cluster in or around the subclass of verbs meaning 'change over', and they are typically capable of occurring with NP_0s that are +collective. A verb such as *convert*, as in *Mary converted her husband to drinking tea without sugar*, may not take +collective NP_0s as often or as necessarily as *change over* and *move over*, but in the object control construal the same kind of meaning of NP_1 moving NP_0 from one state to another seems operative, and correspondingly, in the subject control construal, as in *John converted to drinking tea without sugar*, the meaning of NP_0 moving from one state to another under its own steam is observed.

    To sum up, most verbs of the present pattern are subject to the strong form of B's generalization, but for a minority, the weak form of B's generalization is needed. Verbs of the latter type exhibit some semantic cohesion or regularity. At the same time, the discussion suggests the broader point that redefining Bach's generalization as the strong and weak forms of B's generalization provides a helpful framework for the syntactic and semantic description of verbs of the object control pattern.

The taxonomy also offers a convenient framework for comparing this pattern of complementation with the infinitival pattern of NP_1 $Verb_1$ NP_0 PRO *to* $Verb_2$, where PRO is again controlled by NP_0, but where, as observed above, *to* is not a preposition, as in the *to -ing* pattern, but rather an infinitive marker [cf. Quirk et al. (1985, 1178 f.)]. Poutsma's (1929, 921 ff.) discussion of the alternation between gerund and infinitive clauses provides a suitable starting point here, for the pattern of 1 is a focal point of Poutsma's discussion. (The other focal point is the intransitive pattern of the type *John got to doing something* as opposed to *John got to do something*, but this was discussed in the previous chapter and will be set aside in the present context.)

Changing Poutsma's [(1929, 921 ff.); all examples in this section attributed to Poutsma are from this part of Poutsma's work] order of presentation slightly, we may consider the following:

Accustom, from class 1 of the classification. Poutsma only has an example of an infinitive: *I should be sorry to accustom Philammon to suppose that [etc.]* (Kingsley, *Hypatia*, chap. 15, 74a). He suggests that the infinitive is "regular" with the verb *accustom*. Here the *-ing* form is not impossible, nor indeed the dispreferred variant, though there are informants who are not too happy with either of them in *accustom somebody to suppose/supposing that*... It bears repeating here (see chap. 3) that with the adjective *accustomed*, infinitives may be found more freely, along with *-ing* forms, as in *John was accustomed to get/getting up early*, and *John was accustomed to think/thinking that*... Poutsma's (1929, 927) explanation that "mere recurrency of an action or state" goes with the infinitive and that the "notion of a habit or custom" goes with the *-ing* form will likewise be recalled from chapter 3.

Confine, from class 2. Here is an example each of an *-ing* form and of an infinitive given by Poutsma: *He did not confine himself to writing the Examiner* (D. Laing Purves, *Life of Swift*, 17), *If they do not confine themselves altogether to eat either 'Bread or the Herb of the Field'* [Wesley, *Primitive Physic* (OED)]. Poutsma's comment is worth quoting: "Although the OED does not give a single instance with the gerund-construction, it is no doubt far more frequent than the infinitive-construction" (1929, 921). Here Poutsma was leaning in the right direction, from the point of view of present-day English, for the infinitive can now be safely starred.

Devote, from class 3. Most of Poutsma's examples are of the subject control variety. Here is an example of each construction: *The young man devoted much of his time to reading* (Macaulay, *Lord Clive*, 500 a), *He devoted every energy of his mind to save shillings and pence wherever shillings and pence might be saved* (Trollope, *The Small House at Allington*, chap. 16, 191). Poutsma's comment that "the gerund-construction has been more frequently met with than the infinitive-construction" is again helpful. It can safely be made more categorical, to the effect that in this complement clause pattern the gerund construction is the only possibility today.

Drive, from class 1. Here are a few illustrations from Poutsma: *She would be driven to supporting life upon such birds as she could catch* (Rider Haggard, *Mr. Meeson's Will*, chap. 11, 110); *You will drive me to be a priest* (Reade, *Cloister*, chap. 9, 49); *Henry was driven to conclude peace* (Green, *A Short History of the English People*, chap. 4, par. 4, 312); *A man who lies to avoid lending, won't be driven to lend* (Reade, *It is Never too Late to Mend*, 1, chap. 1, 17). "The gerund construction," Poutsma (1929, 922) comments, "appears to be unusual. The O.E.D. registers none." Here it seems that either form is potentially possible and that the character of the subordinate clause plays a role. More specifically, there is perhaps often a semantic difference between infinitive and *-ing* clauses governed by *drive*. The difference is not always easy to pin down, but the *-ing* form seems to imply generality, or a pattern of repetition or of repeated instances of some action or activity, whereas the infinitive focuses on a single instance or perhaps on single isolated instances that do not form a general pattern. (I am indebted to Ian Gurney for commenting on the distinction.) Indeed, Poutsma's comment on the adjective *accustomed*, referred to above, seems to express the difference succinctly: the *-ing* form suggests "a habit," whereas the infinitive implies "mere recurrency of an action" [Poutsma (1929, 927), discussing *accustomed*]. The account also captures the difference between *John was driven to beg* and *John was driven to begging*.

Reduce, from class 2. Here is an example of each from Poutsma: *This reduced her to laying her other hand almost timidly over his* (Mrs. Alexander, *A Life Interest*, chap. 10, 178); *Why, you have been reduced to wrap yourself in a shawl* (Mrs. Alexander, *For His Sake*, 2, chap. 1, 24). Poutsma (1929, 924) observes that there are four illustrations of the infinitive construction in the OED but none of the gerund, and he adds: "The latter, however, appears to be common enough." Again, Poutsma's comment can be taken a step further, and it seems appropriate to exclude the infinitive with *reduce* in present-day English, on account of overwhelmingly negative reactions to the construal by native speakers. By contrast, the *to -ing* construction is quite idiomatic with *reduce* today.

Set, from class 1. Here Poutsma has examples with or without an NP object. Here are examples of the former: *So now we must set ourselves seriously to finding this gentleman* (Conan Doyle, *Sherlock Holmes, The Adventure of the Blue Carbuncle*); *Mr Wyndham has declared that no Irish M.P. ... has been set to do laundry work* (*Punch*). "The two constructions," Poutsma (1929, 925) observes, "may be of equal frequency." Above, an illustration of *set* was provided from the Brown Corpus: *The building shook, setting the lantern to swaying*, and it was suggested that the construction in question is not entirely acceptable to all speakers. In this sentence, it may be noted, NP_0 is inanimate. Poutsma's example of the *-ing* form, where NP_0 is animate, points to a slightly different usage, though the sense of the verb remains within the range of glosses provided for verbs of class 1. The *-ing* form in Poutsma's sentence with *find* carries the implication of a process or task of finding, and the construction sounds quite good to many speakers with this implication, as witness the sentence from Conan Doyle and also *John set the children to peeling potatoes*. (This sentence was devised by Jane Hill, personal communication.) Here the infinitive construction, *John set the children to peel potatoes*, is also possible for most speakers and may even be felt by native speakers to be more common than the *-ing* form. With regard to the meanings of the two forms, the infinitive variant may perhaps carry the implication of a more specific event and the *-ing* form of a more general line of activity, but the difference between the two should not be exaggerated in this case. [Beyond the range of usages discussed, the infinitive in a sentence such as *He set the alarm clock to wake up his guest at dawn*, where an *-ing* form appears to be excluded, seems to be adverbial in character—cf. also Granath (1994, 213)—allowing a paraphrase along the lines of 'he set the alarm clock so that it might wake up his guest at dawn'.]

Put up, from class 1. Poutsma has only one example of each: *It's that damned traitor, Thady Glynn, that put you up to measuring it (sc. the pier)* (Birmingham, *The Adventures of Dr. Whitty*, chap. 2, 40); *He put me up to try to get into Harris's secrets* (*Good Words*, Sept., 1892, 584, 1: OED, 53, 9, b). Poutsma (1929, 926) surmises that "the two constructions may be of equal frequency," but in present-day English the *-ing* form seems generally preferable, as witness *Who put you up to attempting such a thing?* as compared to ?*Who put you up to attempt such a thing?*

The foregoing discussion demonstrates how acute and well directed Poutsma's intuitions were in most cases. (The present discussion cannot do justice to his breadth of documentation.) In a broader sense, later grammarians owe a debt to him for having painstakingly formulated and documented a research problem that needs careful attention. I might perhaps append a few remarks to the topic here, addressing myself to verbs that did not come up in this review of Poutsma (1929, 921 ff.).

Of the first group of verbs of class 1, *bind*, *condition*, and *rouse*, among others, in addition to *drive* and *set*, just discussed, and *start*, discussed above, permit the infinitive variant. With regard to *bind*, both *The promise bound John to finish the job* and . . . *to finishing the job* seem possible. In the passive *John was bound by his oath to observe/observing the laws of the land*, the infinitive is as possible as the *-ing* form, or indeed it may be felt to be the preferable form. As for *condition*, both *The authorities conditioned the population to lower their expectations* and . . . *to lowering their expectations* seem possible. There may be a subtle difference between the two variants. If so, the infinitive seems to focus on the end result and the *-ing* form on the process of conditioning. (I am indebted to Ian Gurney for this point.) *Rouse* likewise allows an infinitive, as in *The news roused John to act*, with many speakers even preferring this to *?The news roused John to acting*.

Move is of particular interest because of the gloss that was given of class 1. It takes the infinitive without any strain whatsoever. An example, freely invented, is *Her husband's death moved Mary to sell their house*, which is certainly as possible as *Her husband's death moved Mary to selling their house*. Indeed, there are speakers who prefer the infinitive form and hesitate about the acceptability of the *-ing* construction with *move* in the first place. However, if both constructions are allowed, there seems to be a subtle difference between the two, at least with this lower clause predicate, with the *-ing* form emphasizing the extent of the movement, along the lines of 'moved her to the extent that she sold the house', whereas the infinitive is more neutral in this respect. This rather special shade of meaning carried by the *move* + *-ing* construction is shared by some verbs of class 1, including *condition*, *drive*, and *reconcile*, but not necessarily by all of them. Consequently, it is not entirely felicitous automatically to associate the sense of the verb in the gloss of the class with the use of the verb when it takes the *-ing* construction. Almost paradoxically, the sense of the verb when used with the infinitive, being more neutral, seems sometimes to capture the common ingredient of meaning of verbs of class 1 better than the sense of the verb when it is combined with the *-ing* form.

It should be added that the meaning of the lower clause may also play a role. *Selling their house* is a predicate that expresses a single event.

Move may also combine with predicates that express a recurrent activity. For instance, the *-ing* construction in *His poverty moved John to painting portraits* is possible, at least for many speakers, as is the infinitive in *His poverty moved John to paint portraits.* Here the *-ing* form tends to focus not so much on the extent of the movement as on John's pattern or habit of behavior, whereas the infinitive highlights John's decision or "mere recurrency of an action," to hark back to Poutsma's comment on the adjective *accustomed*, referred to above. (I am indebted to Ian Gurney for commenting on *move.*) The *-ing* form, then, again tends to go with habitual behavior, especially when the verb in question, like *move*, is also acceptable with the infinitive. However, there are verbs of class 1, especially verbs that are not acceptable with the infinitive, that do not necessarily share this property. (For instance, consider *pin down* in *Her promise pinned Mary down to answering the question.*) Consequently, although *move* is probably the best that one can do with regard to finding a verb taking an *-ing* form to head class 1, it is perhaps also necessary to retain the double gloss 'NP_1 moves NP_0 to realize (or realizing) S_2', and it is not possible to restrict the gloss to the *-ing* form.

Of other verbs of class 1, *abandon* may perhaps allow the infinitive, especially in the passive, as in *Mary was abandoned by John to fend for herself*, which seems as good as, or perhaps even better than, *Mary was abandoned by John to fending for herself.* Also, both of the judicial or quasi-judicial verbs allow the infinitive easily, as in *The judge condemned/sentenced the prisoner to serve ten years in a jail.* The infinitive may perhaps be felt to be pleonastic here, but if it is allowed, there seems to be a subtle semantic difference between it and the *-ing* form. The former suggests literality, an approximation of what the judge said, whereas an *-ing* form is appropriate where the lower clause is less literal, more a description of effect than of communication, as in *The judge in effect condemned/sentenced the prisoner to rotting in jail for years.* (I am indebted to Ian Gurney for pointing out this distinction.)

Assign, delegate, and *demote,* also of class 1, merit a comment. In the case of *assign* and *delegate,* infinitives are often possible and sometimes preferable to *-ing* construals. The choice of construction seems to correlate with the meaning of the lower clause. When something specific or particular is being talked about, the infinitive is generally the preferred variant for most speakers, as in *They assigned John to shred the incriminating document* and *John delegated his assistant to take care of the visitor,* as compared with *?They assigned John to shredding the incriminating document* and *??John delegated his assistant to taking care of the visitor.*

However, in a manner slightly reminiscent of *drive*, discussed above, when a habitual practice or line of action is being talked about, the *-ing* form tends to sound better and is acceptable—or at times even the preferred variant—for many speakers, as in *They assigned John to shredding documents* and *John delegated his assistant to taking care of visitors.* As for *demote*, the *-ing* form is definitely preferred by most speakers, as in *John demoted his assistant to doing menial tasks only.* The contrast between specific action and habitual or general action or activity may likewise be invoked here, for the meaning of *demote* is along the lines of 'to lower in rank', and this seems to imply that a lower clause governed by this verb expresses something more general or habitual than need be the case with *assign* or *delegate*.

Verbs of class 3, the 'give over' class, seem immune to infinitival variants, as do verbs of the small class 2. However, overall infinitival variants are rather widespread. The 'move' class of verbs is the core class of the pattern, at least in terms of the number of verbs belonging to it. Even here the number is not very large, about twenty. Of these, approximately one-third have infinitival variants. And even of the rest, three verbs are complex, *put back*, *put up* and *pin down*, where the choice of the *-ing* form may be related to the particle following the main verb. At any rate, it is interesting to observe that the verb *put* itself almost prefers the infinitive, at least for some speakers, as in *The city council put the police to patrol the streets*, as opposed to *The city council put the police to patrolling the streets.* Nor perhaps is it perhaps without interest to consider the verb *direct* in the present context. It is fine in sentences such as *They directed their efforts to dropping supplies from their air*, but this is an example of NP_1 control, first observed with *devote* above. (Recall *John devoted a great deal of time to studying the problem.*) It is notable that *direct* is capable of NP_0 control, but then it has a different sense, that of 'command' [see Poutsma (1929, 915)], and takes the infinitive rather than the *-ing* form, as in *John directed Sue to work on the problem*, as opposed to **John directed Sue to working on the problem.*

Considering the semantics of the core class of verbs of this pattern, it is not altogether surprising that there should be vacillation with the infinitive form, for, as was argued in Rudanko (1989, 113 f.), the core class of the corresponding infinitival pattern is very similar with regard to the characteristic meanings of matrix verbs in that pattern. (The notion of NP_1 moving NP_0 toward or away from realizing S_2 was used there to characterize matrix verbs in the infinitival pattern, with virtually all verbs of the pattern carrying the positive meaning of 'move NP_0 toward'.)

What is also noteworthy are sheer numbers. Over one hundred verbs were listed in the infinitival pattern in Rudanko (1989, 112 f.). Those lists afford a handy way of checking whether additional verbs in these lists might be found that also accept the *-ing* form and that might have been overlooked above. That search yields little or nothing. For instance, if we take *coerce* and *persuade* from class 2.3.2 of Rudanko (1989, 113), it will be observed that they are possible with the infinitive form but not with *to -ing*: *John coerced/persuaded Mary to come along*, not *... to coming along*. The verbs that were found to vacillate between the infinitive and the *-ing* form are included for the most part in the lists of the infinitive pattern in Rudanko (1989, 113). However, the effect is quite different from what it is in the case of the *-ing* pattern. There are about sixty verbs in the infinitival pattern corresponding to class 1 of the *-ing* pattern, and the vacillation of a handful of verbs does not threaten the overall cohesion of the class, since it affects such a small portion of the total number. In addition to the class of about sixty verbs corresponding to class 1, there is in Rudanko (1989, 113) a class of about fifty verbs where NP_1 moves NP_0 toward realizing S_2, but where the matrix verb also expresses communication. *Condemn* and *sentence* are accommodated here, but they seem the only ones of the approximately fifty verbs that take *-ing* form variants. (As was pointed out above, the idea of communication is not necessarily prominent in the *-ing* construal with these two verbs.) Again the impression is one of solid cohesion in the case of the infinitival pattern.

As noted elsewhere [see Rudanko (1989, 140, 152)], where two syntactic patterns serve similar or closely related semantic functions, one of them may come to dominate over the other one. The present investigation suggests that where a matrix clause has the basic meaning of 'NP_1 moves NP_0 toward realizing S_2', the infinitival pattern is the more homogeneous or cohesive one at present. The *-ing* pattern is not in any danger of imminent extinction. Also, as became clear in the discussion of individual verbs, it seems, at least to judge by comparing Poutsma's comments with current preferences, that with one or two verbs, including *confine* and *reduce*, the *-ing* pattern may have actually been gaining ground in relatively recent times. In spite of this, the present overall numbers are rather against the *-ing* construal, and from that point of view it is vulnerable and a candidate for losing the struggle for syntactic and semantic space, perhaps sooner than the intransitive *to -ing* pattern of the previous chapter. However, numbers alone cannot be decisive. Above, attempts were made to tease out several kinds of semantic differences between *-ing* and infinitival patterns, with matrix verbs that took both. Some of these differences may be idiosyncratic, but others seem at least potentially more general, including, in particular, the one relating to *drive* and *delegate,* among others, where the *-ing* form goes with habitual behavior and the infinitive with single or particular actions. Admittedly, when such differences are contemplated, it must be borne in mind that a slight majority of verbs taking *-ing* and the overwhelming majority of verbs taking infinitives take only *-ing* or only infinitives, quite irrespective of any potential semantic differences between the two constructions elsewhere. Even so, the mere existence of such semantic differences and especially of systematic patterns of differences, be they only partial, is of importance. They go some way toward separating the two construals, even in the face of the approximate similarity of the central 'move' classes of the two construals. Whether the differences and their patterns are substantive enough to keep the present *-ing* construal of the 'move' class of verbs alive alongside of the very powerful infinitival construal will bear watching. At any rate, the question will merit another look in fifty or a hundred years.

5

Balking at and *Working at*: On Verbs Governing *at -ing*

I

Consider sentence 1 and structure 1', which is a partially bracketed structural representation of 1:

(1) John balked at extending the deadline.
(1') [[John]$_{NP1}$ [balked]$_{Verb1}$ [at]$_{Prep}$ [[PRO]$_{NP2}$ [[extending]$_{Verb2}$ the deadline]$_{VP}$]$_{S2}$]$_{S1}$

The pattern of 1, as partially bracketed in 1', is the object of investigation in this chapter. In it S_2 is a complement sentence dependent on the preposition *at* governed by the matrix verb *balked*, and PRO is typically interpreted as coreferential with NP_1, the subject of the matrix clause. As in the case of other patterns discussed in this book, the key to the *at -ing* construction resides in the selection and properties of the matrix verb. These are the focus of my investigation. More concretely, the first task is to compile a list of verbs which govern the pattern in present-day English. Compiling such a list is by no means either a trivial or a mechanical task. To accomplish it, recourse will again be had to the Brown and LOB corpora, to Poutsma (1929) and Bridgeman et al. (1965). In addition to corpora and grammars of English, intuitions of native speakers will also be taken into account in the consideration of data.

A second step is to attempt a semantic characterization of matrix predicates that are found in the list. It may be hoped, on the basis of such previous work on other patterns as Rudanko (1989) and earlier chapters, that meanings of such matrix verbs do not show random variation and that it is possible to isolate and identify a relatively small number of meanings that cover a large number of the verbs on the list. The semantic characterization of verbs will also be used to point to some further syntactic properties of these verbs. Some comparison will also be made between verbs governing the *at -ing* pattern and other patterns that seem close to it syntactically or semantically.

In the pattern of 1, S_2 is a nominal clause, as can be shown by the criteria applied in previous chapters. To start with, the subordinate clause may be questioned by *what*, as in Q. *What did John balk at?* A. *Extending the deadline*. Further, it may be replaced by the pronoun *it* or the pronoun *that*, as in *John balked at extending the deadline but Sue did not balk at it/that*. Right dislocation of S_2 is likewise possible, as in *John balked at it, extending the deadline*. Finally, S_2 fits eminently in the focus position of a pseudocleft sentence, as in *What John balked at was extending the deadline*. Such tests confirm what is a traditional insight, namely, that S_2 in a sentence such as 1 is a nominal clause.

The conclusion that S_2 is a nominal clause in the pattern of 1 suggests that verbs selecting the *at -ing* pattern may also be combined with *at* and a nonsentential NP. This expectation is fulfilled in the case of *balk*, since *John balked at the new demand* is good, and it will be further checked below. However, it does not necessarily follow from the nominal status of S_2 in the *at -ing* pattern that all verbs selecting *at* NP automatically co-occur with the sentential *at -ing* pattern. In point of fact, there are verbs that select *at* NP but do not readily allow the NP to be sentential. For instance, verbs such as *grab, jump,* and *nibble* are cases in point. They select *at* NP, as in *John grabbed at Sue's sleeve* (the example due to Ian Gurney), *John jumped at the offer of a new job*, and *The fish nibbled at the bait*, but seem difficult to combine with *at -ing*, as witness **John grabbed at catching hold of Sue's sleeve*, ??*John jumped at accepting the offer of a new job*, and ??*The fish nibbled at eating the bait*. The impossibility of equating the class of verbs selecting *at* NP with the class of verbs selecting *at -ing*, in spite of the undoubted nominal category status of the *-ing* clause, serves to justify the focus of the present investigation and its limitation to the sentential pattern.

In the pattern of 1, the preposition *at* introduces a complement clause. This means that there is a close syntactic and semantic connection between it and the matrix predicate, in the sense that the latter must be subcategorized as selecting *at*. This is to be distinguished from adverbial clauses introduced by *at*. Such adverbial clauses are illustrated by 2a–c. [2a is due to Ian Gurney, 2b is modeled on a sentence from the LOB corpus (LOB K22, 155), and 2c is quoted from Poutsma (1929, 951, from Washington Irving, *The Sketch-Book of Geoffrey Crayon, Gent.*, 5, 46.]

(2) a. John simply left at finding another man in the house.
 b. He promised at parting to call the Council the following day.
 c. Rip's heart died away at hearing of these sad changes.

Undoubtedly the *at -ing* constructions of 2a–c are sentential, with PROs as their subjects. Further, the PROs are again interpreted as coreferential with the subjects of the matrix clauses. In spite of such properties, the *at -ing* clauses of 2a–b should be distinguished from *at -ing* clauses that are complements. The distinction is not a new insight. It was made in slightly different terms by traditional grammarians, including Poutsma (1929), who treated *-ing* clauses of the type of 1 under the heading "Gerund-clauses that answer to Subordinate Statements," and those of type 2a–c under the title of "Gerund-clauses that answer to Adverbial Adjuncts or Clauses" (1929, 829). With regard to his example, reproduced here as 2c, Poutsma (1929, 951) speaks of "*at*, which denotes a mixed relation of time and cause." Similar semantic characterizations seem appropriate likewise for 2a–b. In such sentences the preposition *on* is also generally possible, and often even preferable to *at*, especially when the emphasis is more or less exclusively on the relation of time, as in *John slipped on/??at reaching the top step*. *On* is also quite possible in 2a–c and for some speakers is even the preferred choice.

To motivate the distinction syntactically, Bridgeman et al. (1965, 9) point to the fact that in the case of what (in the terms used here) are adverbial clauses, it is generally easier to prepose the *at -ing* clause than in the case of what (in the terms used here) are complement clauses. Thus there is a difference between *??At extending the deadline, John balked*, which is rather strained, and *At finding another man in the house, John simply left*, which is more natural. From this perspective, it is interesting to observe that the original LOB sentence which was modified to 2b had the *at -ing* clause preposed: *At parting he promised to call the Council the following day*. The comparative ease with which adverbial *at -ing* clauses may be preposed and the comparative difficulty inhering in the preposing of complement *at -ing* clauses are reflexes of a difference in the nature of the connection between the matrix verb and the type of the *at -ing* clause in question: in the case of adverbial clauses the connection is looser, permitting preposing, whereas in the case of complement clauses, the connection is tighter, which acts as a brake on preposing.

There also tends to be a difference between complement *at -ing* clauses and adverbial *at -ing* clauses with regard to the syntactic tests cited above in support of the nominal character of the *-ing* clause in 1. In general, complement *at -ing* constructions allow the tests more easily, whereas adverbial *at -ing* clauses are more recalcitrant with regard to these tests. To compare the constructions, we might apply the tests to 1 and to 2a, as in 3a–d:

(3) a. Q. What did John balk at? A. Extending the deadline.—Q. *What did John simply leave at? A. Finding another man in the house.

b. John balked at extending the deadline, but Sue did not balk at it.—*John simply left at finding another man in the house, but Mack did not leave at it.

c. John balked at it, extending the deadline.—*John simply left at it, finding another man in the house.

d. What John balked at was extending the deadline.—*What John simply left at was finding another man in the house.

Further, analogous to the case of *in -ing* complement clauses (chap. 2), the extraction of a constituent out of a complement *at -ing* clause tends to be more readily possible than the extraction of a constituent out of an adverbial *at -ing* clause. Thus sentences such as 4a tend to be better than sentences such as 4b, even if *simply* of 4b is omitted and the object of *finding* in 4b is replaced by a more suitable NP:

(4) a. Q. What did John balk at extending? A. The deadline.
b. Q. *Who did John leave at finding in the house? A. Sue's lover.

On the other hand, an *at -ing* clause with adverbial force often admits a question beginning with *why, when,* or *how,* as in Q. *Why/when/how did John (simply) leave?* A. *At finding another man/Sue's lover in the house.*

The distinction between complement and adverbial clauses is clear enough in the case of 1 and 2a–c. This does not mean that it is always clear. With a number of verbs allowance should be made for a gray area between the two types of constructions. In such cases, it seems advisable to adopt a permissive attitude and to exclude from discussion only *at -ing* clauses that have a clearly adverbial force.

II

In the following, verbs occurring in the pattern of 1 considered on the basis of the corpora will be listed and illustrated.

Verbs	Illustrations and Comments
aim at	*The solitary learner should aim at mastering all four approaches* [LOB F01 41, from P. Meredith, *Learning, Remembering and Knowing* (Hodder and Stoughton)]. To judge by the two corpora used, this is by far the most common verb selecting the pattern.
hesitate at	*He told us that people seem to think nothing of spending £6 to light the way to their doorsteps, but will hesitate at spending the same amount for indoor lighting* (LOB E05 116-119, from *House and Garden*, April).
stop at	*Since it was August, widely advertised as the Adriatic's most benign month, we had not stopped at bringing no raincoats and no umbrellas: we had brought no coats and no sensible shoes either* [LOB K22 96-99, from D. Athill, "Never Speak to Strange Men" (*Flair*, May)].

A consideration of Poutsma (1929, 878 ff.) yields a considerable number of additional verbs and illustrations. He has two groups of verbs. (The groups are not limited to verbs but also include "adjectives or equivalent word-groups"; these, however, will be set aside here.) Members of the first group characteristically "express a state of mind or an action consequent on a state of mind brought about by an event" [Poutsma (1929, 878)]. Here are verbs of this group, with examples from Poutsma (1929, 879 f.):

blush at	*They only blush at being detected in doing good.* Goldsmith, *The Vicar of Wakefield,* chap. 15, 325.

cry at	He cried piteously at being unable to assist a wretched woman. Dickens, *A Christmas Carol*, 1, 24.
delight at	He delighted at being restored to the society of his own rank. Scott, *Waverley*, chap. 62, 154a.
exult at	Boys had jeered him because of his noble little sweetheart, and he had exulted at hearing her so called. Trollope, *Lady Anna*, 1, chap. 4, 46.
grieve at	In his heart he grieved at having left her in disgrace. *Story of the Abbot*, 15.
groan at	King Richard lay on his bed, feverish and restless, ... groaning at having to stay there. *Story of the Talisman*, 10.
grumble at	They grumbled perpetually at paying tithes. Ruskin, *The King of the Golden River*, chap. 1.
laugh at	Henry laughed at recognizing in the parlour the well-remembered old piece of Sir Peter Lely. Thackeray, *Henry Esmond*, 1, chap. 10, 96.
revolt at	My pride revolted at being obliged to plaster my hair with flour and candle-grease. Thackeray, *Barry Lyndon*, chap. 4, 66.
suffer at	No man would suffer more acutely at being tabooed in society. Gunnyon, *A Biographical Sketch of Burns*, 35.
triumph at	Adrian, generally patient of results, triumphed strongly at having evoked this view. Meredith, *The Ordeal of Richard Feverel*, chap. 13, 64.

Of these, *laugh at recognizing* seems to have adverbial force. Thus, to consider one or two of the criteria mentioned above, extraction out of the lower clause produces an ill-formed sentence, as witness **What did Henry laugh at recognizing in the parlour?* and preposing the *at* clause gives a fairly well formed result: *At recognizing in the parlour the well-remembered old piece of Sir Peter Lely, Henry laughed.* *Cry* may perhaps also be omitted, for similar reasons. (To consider the first test, extraction is still not possible: a sentence such as *He cried piteously at losing his friend* does not readily permit **Who did he cry piteously at* *losing?*) Some of the other verbs, including *blush*, likewise have a slightly adverbial feel to them, but they may perhaps nevertheless be retained, sometimes with some hesitation. For instance, with regard to *blush*, extraction in a sentence such as *He blushed at doing good* is certainly not perfect but still seems slightly better than in the case of *laugh* and *cry*, as witness *?What did he blush at doing?*

Additionally, Poutsma (1929, 879) includes the verbs *ache*, *rejoice*, *sicken*, and *stare* in this list of verbs of the first group. For these Poutsma only illustrates infinitival constructions, but observes that "it must not always be concluded that the alternative construction is non-existent or even unusual." The alternative construction here is that of *at -ing*, and three of these four verbs may be included in our survey, for sentences such as *John ached/rejoiced/sickened at seeing their circumstances* are well formed, though admittedly again slightly adverbial in flavor. [Regarding *rejoice*, cf. also Poutsma (MS).] On the other hand, the fourth, *stare at -ing*, seems too clearly adverbial to be included, as in *John stared at seeing her misery*.

As for his second group, Poutsma (1929, 883) observes that there are "but few" verbs "governing a prepositional object with *at*" that have "another meaning" than that of verbs of the first group. Poutsma's group includes *aim* and *hesitate*, illustrated above. It also includes *aspire* and *endeavor*. However, for these the *at -ing* construction, of the type *aspire/endeavor at doing something*, is obsolete, as compared with the infinitival construction, of the type *aspire/endeavor to do something*, which is current. [Poutsma (1929, 884) himself observes that with *aspire* the infinitive construction "is, no doubt, the ordinary one" and terms the *at -ing* construction with *endeavor* "obsolete."] It is therefore advisable to drop these two verbs. Here are the remaining verbs of the group, with examples from Poutsma (1929, 883 f.):

arrive at   *You will, perhaps, wonder how a country boy should arrive at possessing such elegant manners.* Thackeray, *Barry Lyndon*, chap. 1, 19.

excel at   *We do all other men excel / At wrestling . . . leaping, running well.* Hobbes, *Odyssey*, 86 (OED, 2). Poutsma suggests that this is "no doubt an unusual construction, the ordinary preposition being *in*," but the construction is not at all that unusual and most speakers are quite happy not only with sentences such as *John excels in lecturing* but also with *John excels at lecturing.* The verb should therefore be retained without any hesitation.

help at *Cooper he was and carpenter, and wrought / To make the boatmen fishing-nets or help'd / At lading and unlading the tall barks.* Tennyson, *Enoch Arden,* 812. Poutsma observes the availability of the infinitive construction, as in *helped to load,* and of the *in -ing* construction, as in *helped in loading.* He terms the infinitive construction "the ordinary one" and the *at -ing* construction "the least frequent." This seems correct, but even the *at -ing* construction is possible for many speakers, and the verb may be retained, though with some hesitation.

rebel at *Paul sat down at the end furthest from the master, inwardly rebelling at having thus education forced upon him.* Anstey, *Vice Versa,* chap. 6, 118. Poutsma observes the availability of *against -ing,* terming it the "ordinary construction." However, the *at -ing* construction is also possible today.

stick at *I'll not stick at giving myself trouble to put down such hypocritical cant.* G. Eliot, *Scenes of Clerical Life,* 3, chap. 1, 183.

stickle at *They have not stickled at avowing the high-church principles they learned at Waverly-Honour.* Scott, *Waverley,* chap. 32, 97a. Not all native speakers are sure that they "know" the verb, but insofar as they do, the construction is precisely the current one.

work at *He worked hard at clearing a path.* OED, s.v. *at,* 17.

Dabble may perhaps be added from Poutsma (MS):

dabble at *The man who dabbles at saving the world by science, education, hygeian and other economies.* G. Macdonald, *Paul Faber, Surgeon,* 3, chap. 1, 14 (OED, s.v. 3). Admittedly, reactions of native speakers to this particular example are not always entirely favorable. They are generally more favorable to *John dabbled at trading on the stock exchange,* and it seems possible to admit the verb.

Further relevant verbs are found in Bridgeman et al. (1965, 11 ff.), illustrated here with invented examples, except where noted otherwise.

balk at	*John balked at working on Sundays.*
boggle at	*John boggled at taking on extra responsibilities.*
bristle at	*John bristled at having to obey orders from the likes of that man.* (The example is due to Robert MacGilleon.)
chafe at	*John chafed at having to wait for his turn.*
fail at	*John failed at completing the task.* The *at -ing* construction with *fail* is subject to considerable idiolectal variation. Some speakers are fairly happy with it; others reject it out of hand, only allowing the infinitive construction, as in *He failed to complete the task.* At best, the verb can be included only with a great deal of hesitation.
marvel at	*John marveled at being made director of his uncle's company.*
play at	*John played at being the boss.*
rail at	*John railed at having to obtain a permit.* Here both *about* and *over* are alternatives.
sneer at	*John sneered at saluting officers.* *About* and *over* are again conceivable alternatives.
strain at	*John strained at explaining the sentence.* Here *over* is likewise possible.
succeed at	*John succeeded at completing the task.* There is again considerable idiolectal variation regarding the admissibility of the construction, for many (probably most) speakers insist on, or at least prefer, the *in -ing* construction, as in *John succeeded in completing the task.* However, on balance the verb can still be included. Dixon (1991, 181) mentions *succeed in/at* and cites *She succeeded at (playing) golf (well)*, noting that *playing* is optional.
toil at	*John toiled at writing a novel.* *Over* is a possible alternative here.

wink at	*The dean winked at admitting students with poor qualifications.* The sense of the verb is approximately 'acquiesce in'. By contrast, when the verb has a more concrete sense, the *at -ing* clause has an adverbial force, as in *John winked at hearing the mistake.* (I am indebted to Ian Gurney, personal communication, for discussion of *wink*.)

Additionally, I have noticed one or two other verbs that are relevant:

bridle at	*John bridled at accepting the proposal.*
connive at	*The chairman connived at lowering standards in the department.*
demur at	*John demurred at working on Sundays.* (The example is adapted from the ALD, s.v.)
experiment at	*The group experimented at performing modernist plays.*
jib at	*John jibbed at paying for repairs alone.*
keep at	*John kept at hammering away at inconsistencies in the proposal.* Undoubtedly, constructions with nonsentential complements are more common ways of construing *keep at*, as in *keep at a task* and *keep at it*, and there are speakers who do not find the sentential construal entirely natural. To the extent that it is admissible, *keep at -ing* focuses on unslackening effort on the part of NP_1. (I am indebted to Ian Gurney, personal communication, for commenting on *keep at -ing*.)
labor at	*John labored at getting his point across.*
look at	*John looked at giving up the plan.*
persevere at	*John persevered at looking for new data.* Some speakers are slightly hesitant about *at -ing* here, preferring *in -ing* instead. However, on the whole, *at -ing* seems acceptable enough.
scheme at	*John was scheming at undermining the chairman's authority.*
scruple at	*John did not scruple at stretching the truth.*

scoff at	*John scoffed at saluting his inferiors.*
wince at	*John winced at informing on his friend.*
writhe at	*John writhed at testifying against his friend in court.*

III

Considering the verbs listed in section II and their illustrations, it seems clear from a syntactic point of view that such verbs allow nonsentential *at* NP constructions virtually across the board. For instance, *exult* and *boggle* do, to take two examples, as in *John exulted at the news* and *John boggled at the new demand.*

From a semantic point of view, most of the verbs of the present pattern clearly select subjects that are +animate. Apart from this similarity, the verbs in question display semantic differences and necessitate the setting up of at least four separate classes.

1. $Verb_1$ has the approximate meaning 'show unwillingness (to do something)', 'hesitate', or 'hold oneself back (from doing something)': *balk, hesitate, jib, scruple, stick, stickle, stop.*

2. $Verb_1$ expresses an emotion toward the content of S_2:

    A. The emotion is negative vis-à-vis the content of S_2.

    NP_1 is critical of the content of S_2 and expresses criticism of the content of S_2: *demur, groan, grumble, rail.*

    NP_1 is critical of the content of S_2 but does not necessarily communicate his criticism of S_2: *boggle.*

    NP_1 is irritated or angry at the content of S_2: *bridle, bristle, chafe.*

    NP_1 is contemptuous of the content of S_2: *scoff, sneer.*

    NP_1 is disturbed by, or disgusted at, the content of S_2: *rebel, revolt, sicken, wince, writhe.*

    NP_1 feels pain or sorrow at the content of S_2: *ache, grieve, suffer.*

    NP_1 feels shame at the content of S_2: *blush.*

    B. The emotion is positive vis-à-vis the content of S_2.

    NP_1 feels delight at the content of S_2: *delight, exult, rejoice, triumph.*

    C. Others: *marvel.*

3. Verb$_1$ expresses intention, engagement, or effort, real or pretended, on the part of NP$_1$ with regard to the realization of S$_2$: *aim, dabble, experiment, help, keep, labor, persevere, play, scheme, strain, toil, work.* Verb$_1$ has the additional meaning that NP$_1$ succeeds or fails in the attempt at realizing S$_2$: *fail, succeed.*

Verb$_1$ expresses engagement in a preeminent fashion: *excel.*

4. Others: *arrive, connive, look, wink.*

The semantic classification and the glosses given are offered by way of providing a structured and systematically organized set of accounts of major or dominant senses of the verbs in question. Here, as in the taxonomies of other chapters, such accounts can no doubt be improved upon. Also, it bears emphasizing that they are not intended as a substitute for a dictionary and that they do not purport to furnish full descriptions of the semantics of individual verbs. Nor is it being claimed that the verbs of any class—or of any subclass—are synonymous with each other in all (or even in any) of their senses. (In some cases there may also be room for disagreement over what the dominant sense of a verb may be, or indeed over whether a verb has a dominant sense.) From another point of view, it would be presumptuous and misguided to claim that all verbs governing the *at -ing* pattern in present-day English are covered in the present survey. No doubt a larger-scale inquiry would unearth additional verbs. Such caveats must be made, but in spite of them the present survey and the taxonomy provided are perhaps sufficient to afford at least a first approximation to the range and types of verbs governing the *at -ing* pattern.

Verbs of class 1 carry the central meaning that (the referent of) NP$_1$ feels or shows (a degree of) unwillingness toward doing whatever is expressed by S$_2$. *Balk* and *hesitate* seem to be the most common verbs of the class, and they also probably come closest to expressing its prototypical meaning.

One or two verbs of class 1, *stick* and *stop* of the verbs listed, are unlikely in simple affirmative sentences, as witness *??John stuck/stopped at asking for a $5 top.* (I am indebted to Ian Gurney, personal communication, for drawing my attention to this subclass within class 1.) These verbs seem limited to nonassertive contexts. [For the notion of nonassertive contexts, see Quirk et al. (1985, 83 f.).] In such contexts, they are possible but carry a rather special meaning that sets them apart from the rest of the class from a semantic point of view as well. A descriptive account of the peculiarity must be sufficient here. The meaning of most verbs of the class in a negative sentence, as in *John did not balk at asking for a $5 tip*, may be glossed, approximately, as 'did not have scruples about' or 'did not hold himself back from'. This kind of meaning is expected and unremarkable. However, *stick* and *stop* behave differently, as in *John did not stick/stop at asking for a $5 tip*, for the meanings of these verbs here go beyond the expected paraphrase 'hold oneself back from', and require a gloss along the lines of 'did not restrict himself to'. (That is, both verbs imply that John asked for more than $5.) The same peculiarity, illustrated with negation, carries over to interrogative sentences. The expected meaning, relevant to most verbs of class 1, may be exemplified by *Why did John balk at asking for a $5 tip?* with the gloss 'why did John have scruples about asking for a $5 tip?' As for *stick* and *stop*, as in *Why did John stick/stop at asking for a $5 tip?* a more adequate paraphrase is again along the lines of 'why did John restrict himself to asking for a $5 tip?'

Verbs of class 2 express some emotion that NP_1 feels regarding the content of S_2. Such emotions range from negative feelings, such as criticism, contempt, irritation, anger, and disgust, to positive ones, such as delight. By and large class 2 of the present classification bears a correspondence with Poutsma's first class referred to above, for typically, the emotion felt by NP_1 and conveyed by $Verb_1$ is caused by what is expressed by S_2. Or, to use some of Poutsma's terms, NP_1's state of mind or action, as expressed by $Verb_1$, is brought about by the event expressed by the lower clause. (S_2 need not express an event, however, and consequently, a broader reference to the content of S_2 seems appropriate.) To put it another way, for verbs of this class, the content of S_2, or whatever S_2 expresses, provides the source of the emotion in question. As a consequence, as far as intransitive verbs of the class are concerned—and most verbs of the class are intransitive—it is often possible to form a sentence of the pattern "S_2 makes NP_1 $Verb_1$," or "S_2 causes NP_1 *to* $Verb_1$," as in *Leaving her in disgrace made him grieve in his heart* and *Paying tithes caused them to grumble perpetually*. (These examples are modeled on authentic ones quoted above.)

As far as the relation of classes 1 and 2 is concerned, it should be pointed out that unwillingness is an emotion. Not surprisingly, therefore, some verbs of class 2 may come rather close to those of class 1, from a semantic point of view. For instance, this holds for *bristle* and *chafe*. These verbs imply that NP_1 feels irritation or anger at the content of S_2. This may come close to meaning that since the person designated by NP_1

feels irritation or anger at the content of S_2, he or she feels reluctant to do whatever is expressed by S_2 (where the predicate of S_2 expresses an action that can be willfully undertaken by PRO, and by NP_1, since these are coreferential). However, it is worth comparing 1 with 5a–b:

(5) a. John bristled at extending the deadline.
    b. John chafed at working on Sundays.

The comparison reveals that verbs of class 1 are oriented toward focusing on NP_1 realizing S_2, whereas those of class 2 merely express an emotion on the content of S_2, whether or not this has to do with NP_1 realizing S_2. (Some verbs of class 2, including *grumble* and *rail*, go beyond expressing emotion and imply communication on the part of NP_1.) The verbs of class 1 might accordingly be called "active," and those of class 2 "reactive." Coming at it from another angle, verbs of class 1 imply a degree of controllability or control, or at least of potential controllability or control, on the part of NP_1 regarding the realization of S_2, whereas verbs of class 2 do not necessarily have this implication. Therefore, where the realization of S_2 is viewed as being outside of the control of NP_1—and of PRO, since NP_1 and PRO are coreferential—verbs of class 1 are slightly, or even clearly, strained or strange, whereas those of class 2, including *bristle* and *chafe*, tend to be more possible. For instance, 6a seems worse than 6b. (Care should be taken to interpret the *at -ing* clauses of 6a–b as complement clauses. This holds especially for 6a.)

(6) a. ??John balked/hesitated at being told to wait in line.
    b. John bristled/chafed at being told to wait in line.

A similar difference may be observed in 7a–b.

(7) a. ??John balked/hesitated at having to wait in line.
    b. John bristled/chafed at having to wait in line.

In view of sentences such as 6a–b and 7a–b, verbs of class 1 may be considered separate from those of class 2. While verbs of class 1 involve unwillingness, which is an emotion, they also express a degree of controllability or control, exerted by NP_1, regarding the realization of S_2, which is absent from verbs of class 2. The distinction is further reinforced when attention is focused on the choice of NP_2, that is, of the subject of the subordinate clause. In the pattern of 1 the subject in question is

PRO, but if this requirement is relaxed, it is noticeable how subjects in complement clauses dependent on verbs of class 1 are by and large restricted to PRO, whereas verbs of class 2 accept expressed (non-PRO) subjects more freely, as witness the contrasts in 8a–b:

(8) a. ?John balked/hesitated at Sue extending the deadline.
    b. John bristled/chafed/grumbled/marveled at Sue extending the deadline.

Classes 1 and 2, then, stand as separate entities. At the same time, the difference between them should not be exaggerated. In point of fact, one or two verbs seem sufficiently flexible, or polysemous, to be able to straddle the fence, having a foot in each camp. *Boggle* and *demur*, in particular, are cases in point here. They have 'reactive' uses, expressing an emotion regarding the content of S_2 in sentences analogous to 6b, 7b, and 8b, as witness 9a–c:

(9) a. John boggled/demurred at being told to wait in line.
    b. John boggled/demurred at having to wait in line.
    c. John boggled/demurred at Sue extending the deadline.

However, when the semantic properties of the lower predicate allow or imply control on the part of PRO (and, consequently, of NP_1), as in *John boggled/demurred at extending the deadline*, these verbs focus on NP_1 being reluctant to realize S_2 or raising difficulties about realizing S_2, rather than simply commenting on the content of S_2. That is, although these verbs were listed in class 2, they might also be listed in class 1, or, perhaps preferably, a separate class between classes 1 and 2 might be set up for them. Of course, the new class would not need to be limited to these two verbs. *Bridle*, in particular, would be another candidate for inclusion. Also, there are some speakers that allow 'noncontrol' readings (of the type of 9a–c) for *jib* (from class 1), which would then be another candidate for inclusion in the intermediate class for such speakers. This emphasizes the closeness of classes 1 and 2 but does not undercut the scheme of classification. On the contrary, the classification makes possible a principled account of verbs such as *boggle* and *demur*, which are more flexible than most verbs of classes 1 and 2, and this lends credibility to the present taxonomy.

For their part, verbs of class 3 stand further apart from those of classes 1 and 2 than those of the latter two do from each other. To be sure, *aim*, accommodated in class 3, though somewhat exceptional for this class, expresses something in the mind and is in this respect reminiscent of verbs of class 1 and of many of those of class 2 (except for verbs of communication). At the same time, the *make* or *cause* construals are out of the question for *aim*: *John aimed at finishing the job quickly* does not permit **Finishing the job quickly made John aim*. Some other verbs of class 3 are more possible in the *make* or *cause* construction, but the result is still not a very likely sentence, as in *?Repairing the puncture made John labor*, etc.

Setting the *make* or *cause* construals aside, the outstanding characteristic of verbs of class 3 is that, apart from *aim*, they express something more, or something other than, matters of the mind. They imply that NP_1 engages in some activity or expends some effort, though the effort may be futile or even playful and may not lead to completing the act or action denoted by S_2. Further, the element of controllability and of control exerted by NP_1 over S_2 suggested above for verbs of class 1 is in general also relevant to verbs of class 3. Thus 10a–b seem strange:

(10) a. John ?aimed/??labored/??toiled/??worked at being told to wait in line.
 b. John ?aimed/??labored/??toiled/??worked at having to wait in line.

To be sure, sentences such as *John aimed/labored/toiled/worked at being elected* are acceptable enough, but they do not constitute counterexamples, for in such constructions there is a tendency for the subject of the lower clause to be interpreted agentively, along the lines of 'John labored/toiled/worked to get himself elected' [cf. Rudanko (1989, 95 ff.)].

Further, the restriction that the subject of the subordinate clause should be PRO, and PRO only, seems applicable to verbs of class 3, for sentences such as *John ?aimed/??labored/??toiled/??worked at Sue repairing the puncture* are not likely.

Verbs of class 4 are rather disparate. Some of them bear undoubted relations to each other or to one of the classes 1 to 3. For instance, the meanings of *connive* and *wink* are clearly related. However, the meanings of verbs of class 4 seem difficult to generalize and they are left as a separate class here.

The present classification suggests that classes 1, 2, and 3 represent the major semantic groupings of verbs governing the *at -ing* pattern in present-day English. Looking at these three classes from the point of view of *at*, specifically, it is perhaps possible to discern three fairly distinct ranges of meaning of the preposition when it occurs in the *at -ing* pattern, corresponding to the three classes. Here Wesche's [(1986/87); see also Bennett (1975, 65 ff.) and Shumaker (1977, 88 ff.)] view of the meaning of *at* as basically or prototypically locative seems helpful, even though she does not consider *at -ing* constructions in her article. The three ranges of meaning proposed here may perhaps all be considered extensions of a basic locative sense of the preposition. As far as verbs of class 1 are concerned, the preposition, it may be suggested, expresses an abstract location, or, more precisely, a boundary or a line: NP_1 is willing to go, or has been willing to go, some way in the direction of S_2, but is hesitant about going as far as what S_2 expresses. To put it another way, NP_1 draws the line at what S_2 expresses. As far as verbs of class 2 are concerned, *at* does not express a boundary, but rather a cause or a source, the cause or the source of the emotion conveyed by the higher verb [cf. Wesche's (1986/87, 392) causal concept of *at*]. And as far as verbs of class 3 are concerned, a concept of intentional location might be invoked, though it must be admitted that the sense of *at* here is at a further remove from Wesche's (1986/87, 389) examples such as *The children are at school* and *Tom and Jerry are at the zoo*. Intention is involved, but more specifically, when selected by verbs of class 3, *at* designates a task that NP_1 contemplates or expends some effort in undertaking or a field of activity in which the effort is expended or to which it is directed.

A necessary part of the consideration of virtually any pattern of complementation in English syntax consists in investigating the position of the pattern in the system of English verb syntax by comparing it with others that suggest themselves for this purpose, on the basis of syntactic or semantic similarity. The three classes of verbs and their ranges of meaning, as well as the ranges of meaning of *at* associated with the classes and identified as those of 'boundary', 'cause', and 'field of activity' are useful here, for they give structure to the comparison, in that different objects of comparison suggest themselves for each. As far as verbs of class 1 are concerned, the pattern of NP_1 $Verb_1$ *from* $Verb_2 ing$, as in *John abstained from voting* and in *You will refrain from smoking cigarettes during class* [this sentence from Bridgeman et al. (1965, 25)], is close semantically, in its implication of the meaning 'hold oneself back from doing something'. However, verbs of class 1 do not in general allow *from -ing*, as witness 11:

(11) John ??balked/*hesitated/*scrupled/*stickled from extending the deadline.

Coming at it from the other end, a look at verbs such as *abstain* and *refrain* occurring as matrix verbs in the pattern of Verb$_1$ *from* Verb$_2$*ing* shows that these do not necessarily allow *at -ing* as an alternative construction, for *John *abstained/*refrained at extending the deadline* is clearly ill formed. One or two other verbs of the *from -ing* pattern that are relevant here from a semantic point of view are more conceivable (or even possible for some speakers) with *at -ing*, as witness *John ?flinched/ ?recoiled/?shrank at extending the deadline*, as compared with *John recoiled/flinched/shrank from extending the deadline*. [*Shrink at -ing* sounds even better with a negative, as in *John did not shrink at imposing a deadline;* cf. also Poutsma (MS, s.v.).] However, in general, verbs of the *from -ing* pattern do not occur in the *at -ing* pattern, at least if one makes a judgment on the basis of the list of Bridgeman et al. (1965, 25). Apart from *abstain* and *refrain*, *desist* and *shy away* might be cited as examples from Bridgeman et al. Both are impossible with *at -ing*: *John desisted/shied away from extending the deadline* is good, but **John desisted/shied away at extending the deadline* is not. (*Shy at -ing* seems much more readily possible, at least for some speakers, as in *John shied at extending the deadline.*)

This survey, then, suggests that there is not much distributional overlap between the two constructions. This lack of overlap is also emphasized by a semantic dissimilarity at a more delicate level. In general, verbs of class 1 of the present pattern seem less specific, or less definitely negative implicative, with regard to the realization of what is expressed by S$_2$. For instance, *John hesitated at extending the deadline* leaves some room for doubt as to whether he did or did not extend the deadline, whereas *John abstained/refrained from extending the deadline* implies more definitely that he did not extend it. This intuition can be made explicit by noting that *John hesitated at extending the deadline, but he did extend it in the end* is less of a contradiction than are corresponding sentences with *abstain* and *refrain*, as in *??John abstained/refrained from extending the deadline, but he did extend it in the end.*

Overall, class 1 of the present classification seems fairly discrete and homogeneous when compared with the *from -ing* pattern. As far as distributional overlap with other patterns is concerned, verbs of the class may sometimes also be found with one or two other prepositions: for instance, *about* and *over* seem possible with *hesitate*, as in *John hesitated about/over extending the deadline*. [With regard to *hesitate about*, see also the ALD, s.v.; with regard to *hesitate over*, see Dixon (1991, 243); Dixon (1991, 243) also mentions *hesitate with*, but reactions to sentences such as *?John hesitated with extending the deadline* seem more negative, and this construal will be set aside in the present investigation.] Further, *hesitate*, of course, occurs with the infinitive, as in *John hesitated to extend the deadline*, and there is little doubt that this is more common than the *at -ing* construal. There may also be felt to be a perceptible difference between the infinitive and the *at -ing* patterns here, for the latter is felt to imply that NP_1 has undertaken a series of actions or steps somewhat similar to, but less extreme than, what is expressed by S_2, but is hesitant about (or when it comes to) undertaking the extra step expressed by S_2. On the other hand, when *hesitate* occurs with the infinitive pattern (or indeed with *about* or *over*), no such progression of steps is necessarily implied, in that the action expressed by S_2 may be the only one in question. This difference is at least partly captured by the meaning ingredient 'boundary' set up above for *at* when selected by verbs of class 1.

As far as other verbs of class 1 are concerned, the infinitive is occasionally also found with *stickle* [see Poutsma, (MS), s.v.] and with *scruple*, though speakers may be hesitant about such constructions, especially with *scruple* [cf. Rudanko (1989, 17)]. *At -ing* construals seem more common and more generally acceptable for these verbs, but the rarity of the infinitival construction makes it difficult to say whether there is a semantic difference connected with the selection of complement type.

In general, verbs of class 2 seem more permissive in allowing other patterns than do those of class 1. Sometimes more than one alternative prepositional pattern is possible, as in the case of *rail*, for which the OED mentions not only *at* but also *against* and *upon*, to which *about* might be added. A full survey of alternative prepositional patterns is beyond the confines of this investigation, but one or two tendencies might be observed. For instance, alternation with *in -ing* seems rather narrowly limited to one subclass, that of verbs expressing a positive emotion, such as *delight, exult,* and *rejoice* (cf. the class of verbs with the gloss 'feel joy or pleasure over' in chap. 2). A comparison of the two patterns, as in *John rejoiced at/in helping others,* reveals, at least in the case of *rejoice* in this sentence, that *at -ing* may suggest a single event ('John helped others once'), whereas *in -ing* may suggest a pattern or a habit ('John helped others several times'). As for the preposition *about*, it is often possible when the verb in question (of class 2) expresses communication, as in *John grumbled/railed about having to work on Sundays.* At the same time, the *about -ing* pattern may focus on NP_1 communicating the emotion in question. For instance, *John triumphed about winning the first prize,* to the extent that it is possible, suggests the meaning 'spoke triumphantly about'. To the extent that such comparable patterns carry identifiable shades of meaning that are different from that carried by the *at -ing* pattern, they do not threaten the homogeneity of class 2. However, in other cases, such extra shades of meaning are more difficult to tease apart. Construals with *over*, in particular, which are possible for several verbs of class 2, as in *John grumbled/groaned over not getting another chance,* deserve further study in this connection. [See Brugman (1988, 49 ff.) on how to separate *over* and *at* constructions with nonsentential complements.]

From another perspective, it seems, especially as far as verbs of class 2 are concerned, that the difference between interpreting S_2 as a complement clause as opposed to an adverbial clause of reason or cause (or of time) may sometimes be a slight one (cf. section I and the discussion of some of the data in section II). Even in the case of some of the sentences cited in the paragraph above, adverbial construals such as *John grumbled/ groaned because of not getting another chance* are not very far semantically from the complement clause interpretations of the *at -ing* (or *over -ing*) versions of these sentences. This is perhaps no surprise, for as noted above, the lower clause with verbs of class 2 is often causative in nature.

As far as verbs of class 3 are concerned, the meaning 'engage in an activity' suggests the *in -ing* pattern of chapter 2 as a possible object of comparison, because a core group of verbs of that pattern express the meaning 'perform the act of' or 'carry out the activity of'. However, in spite of the similarity of meaning between this class and class 3 now being discussed, there is only a limited amount of distributional overlap. To be sure, *dabble, excel, experiment, help, persevere,* and *succeed* figure in both lists of matrix verbs. Of these, *excel* and *experiment* seem possible in either pattern. As for *dabble,* the *in -ing* construal seems more common, whereas *dabble at -ing* perhaps carries a meaning ingredient of 'trying' or 'trying one's hand at', as *He dabbled at trading on the stock exchange.* (As observed above, not all speakers are entirely comfortable with *dabble at -ing* in the first place.) A somewhat similar meaning ingredient relating to the idea of trying on the part of NP_1 or to an activity that requires an effort from NP_1 may be relevant, in a relatively prominent way, to *persevere at -ing,* as in *He persevered at looking for new data,* distinguishing it from *persevere in -ing,* at least up to a point, as in *He persevered in looking for new data,* where the complement simply names the area of activity where he persevered. (I am indebted to Robert MacGilleon and Ian Gurney for comments on *dabble* and *persevere.*)

Further, as observed above, *succeed* quite definitely prefers the *in -ing* pattern, for most speakers. As for *help*, some speakers again prefer *in -ing* to *at -ing*, but even the latter is reasonably acceptable to most speakers, as in *John helped at/in clearing a path through the thicket*. However, here there is a slight semantic difference, in that the *help in -ing* construction implies that the contribution of NP_1 is relatively important to realizing S_2, whereas the meaning of *help at -ing* veers toward 'be occupied with' or 'be busy with', with less focus on NP_1's role in realizing S_2. (The point is due to Ian Gurney, personal communication.) As far as other verbs of the 'perform the act of' class selecting *in -ing* are concerned, few, if any, of them select *at -ing* without strain. For instance, *persist*, which is of course fine with *in -ing*, as in *She persists in wearing that old-fashioned hat* (ALD, s.v.), does not in general combine with *at -ing*, as witness *??She persists at wearing that old-fashioned hat*. In the context of *persevere* and *persist*, it is an interesting finding, emphasizing the lack of distributional overlap, that *keep*, of the present taxonomy, which is somewhat similar in meaning to these two verbs, takes *at -ing* but not *in -ing*: *John kept at hammering away at inconsistencies in the proposal*, *in -ing* being impossible: **John kept in hammering away at inconsistencies in the proposal*. (*Keep to -ing* is of course possible but slightly different in sense from *keep at -ing*; cf. the glosses in chap. 3 and in section II of the present chapter.) Further, it bears noting that such common verbs of the *in -ing* class as *engage*, *indulge*, and *specialize* do not occur with *at -ing*, since sentences such as *John *engaged/*indulged/ *specialized at writing pamphlets* are inconceivable. A comparison of class 3 of the present pattern with the 'perform the act of' class of the *in -ing* pattern, therefore, uncovers some distributional overlap, but the overlap is limited in scope.

On the other hand, there is again considerably more overlap with the infinitival pattern. Several verbs of class 3 allow it, including *aim*, *labor*, *toil*, and *work*. (*Fail* definitely prefers it for many speakers, as noted above.) As far as *aim* is concerned, we might compare 12a–b:

(12) a. John aimed at clearing a path through the thicket.
b. John aimed to clear a path through the thicket.

Example 12a suggests that clearing a path through the thicket was John's plan or the target that he was aiming at, whereas 12b suggests his intention more directly. There is thus perhaps a slight difference regarding his degree of commitment to the task: in the case of straightforward intention, as in 12b, the degree of commitment and determination seems more definite or specific and therefore perhaps higher. However, the difference seems rather subtle, at least in 12a–b, and should not be exaggerated.

As for other verbs, we may consider 13a–b:

(13) a. John labored/toiled/worked at clearing a path through the thicket.
b. John labored/toiled/worked to clear a path through the thicket.

The infinitive after a verb such as *labor* is not always easy to keep apart from an adverbial infinitive of purpose. Referring to such verbs, Visser writes: "there is the possibility that the infinitive after some of these verbs . . . is to be interpreted as an adverbial of purpose ('he laboured to be the first'/'he laboured in order to be the first'), rather than a direct object" (1969, 1336).

Even if such adverbial construals can be set aside, it is still not always easy to pin down a semantic difference between the *at* -*ing* and infinitive constructions for the class of verbs in question. To the extent that a difference can be proposed, the *at* -*ing* construction focuses on the ongoing activity of S_2 as activity. For instance, as far as 13a is concerned, the focus is on John being busy with, or engaged in, clearing a path through the thicket. For its part, the infinitive in 13b highlights John's intention and goal and the sense of his working toward his goal. (There may perhaps be a slight echo of the purpose adverbial even in the infinitival complement clause construction.) However, the difference between the two constructions should not be exaggerated, at least not in the case of 13a–b. In particular, there does not seem to be any appreciable difference between 13a and 13b regarding the progress of the activity expressed by S_2. For instance, a *but* clause denying that any progress was made seems about equally possible with either construction, as witness 14a and 14b:

(14) a. John worked at improving his serve, but did not get anywhere.
b. John worked to improve his serve, but did not get anywhere.

The semantic and distributional overlap of class 3 verbs of the *at* -*ing* pattern here is typically with the infinitival pattern selected by some verbs of the major class of 1.1.3 of Rudanko (1989, 23), comprising verbs that, in the characterization proposed there, typically express (a degree of) endeavor on the part of NP_1 for the realization of S_2. Although some verbs that carry a meaning of endeavor have here been found to occur in both the *at -ing* and the infinitival patterns, it should be added that many other verbs of the infinitival pattern do not allow the *at -ing* pattern, at least not in present-day English. *Endeavor*, considered above, is a case in point. Other such verbs include *manage, seek,* and *try,* which are of course perfect with the infinitive but are quite inconceivable with *at -ing:* **John managed/sought/tried at breaking the code.* Some distributional overlap, then, is observed here, but it seems to be limited to a subset of verbs of the infinitival pattern.

This comparative survey has explored potential areas of distributional or semantic overlap between the *at -ing* pattern and others that seem relevant. It has uncovered some overlap but on the whole suggests a reasonable degree of homogeneity. In cases of obvious semantic overlap, not much distributional overlap was uncovered, and where there is distributional overlap, more delicate semantic distinctions are often possible. The conclusion of homogeneity, it may be suggested, holds especially for class 1 of the present pattern, mainly because the meaning 'draw the line at' seems rather specific to this prepositional pattern. As for verbs of class 2, these often select other prepositional patterns, such as NP_1 $Verb_1$ *over* $Verb_1 ing$, that are not always easy to distinguish semantically from the *at -ing* pattern. Sometimes such constructions may come close to having adverbial force. The connection between the matrix verb and *at*, then, may perhaps be felt to be looser, at least at times, which may be not unconnected with the availability of a choice of prepositions. As far as class 3 is concerned, the 'perform the act of' class of verbs selecting *in -ing* and the infinitive construction should be mentioned, with the latter meriting more attention. The meaning 'field of activity" carried by *at* and the meaning component of 'endeavor' carried by a major class of verbs taking the infinitive are related, since making an effort typically presupposes a field of activity in which the effort can be made. Apart from semantic overlap, there is also considerable distributional overlap between the two patterns, affecting several common verbs of the *at -ing* pattern.

The *at -ing* pattern is not very large in terms of the sheer numbers of verbs belonging to it, at least not in comparison with some of the patterns of complementation in English investigated in Rudanko (1989). Within the overall number, classes 1 and 3 are fairly small, whereas 2, the "reactive" class, comprises a larger number of verbs. As far as meaning is concerned, it seems difficult to characterize all verbs selecting *at -ing* on the basis of any one single semantic property of any great specificity. However, probably most verbs selecting the pattern can nevertheless be grouped into one of three semantic classes, and from the point of view of the preposition *at,* the ranges of meaning of the three classes may all be considered extensions of a basic locative sense of the preposition. The three classes, it may be suggested, constitute the core classes of the *at -ing* pattern. Further, it seems that the characterizations of the core classes exhibit a relatively high degree of internal coherence. As far as their mutual relationships are concerned, classes 1 and 2 are closer to one another than either of these is to class 3. (One or two verbs may indeed be viewed as constituting an intermediate category between classes 1 and 2.) On the other hand, it is not easy to decide whether any one of the three core classes is more prototypical of the *at -ing* pattern than the other two.

This investigation also points to some cases of "competition" or "struggle" for semantic or distributional space between the *at -ing* pattern and some others, including the infinitive pattern and certain other prepositional patterns. It seems that classes 2 and 3 are more affected here, whereas verbs of class 1 have a character that is more uniquely specific to them. Of course, when considering "competition" for space, it is important to be sensitive to differences of meaning expressed by the various alternatives. There is clearly some semantic and distributional overlap between the *at -ing* pattern and some other constructions. However, we have seen that fairly often the constructions in question express different meanings or different nuances of meaning. Consequently, it is possible to conclude that, on the whole, the *at -ing* pattern has a fairly well defined function in the complementation system of present-day English.

6

Concentrating on Laying the Foundations: On Verbs Governing *on -ing*

I

Consider sentence 1, modeled on a sentence from the LOB corpus, and 1', which is a partially bracketed representation of its structure:

(1) The conference concentrated on laying the foundations for winning the next election.
(1') [[The conference]$_{NP1}$ [concentrated]$_{Verb1}$ [on]$_{Prep}$ [[PRO]$_{NP2}$ [[laying]$_{Verb2}$ the foundations for winning the next election]$_{VP}$]$_{S2}$]$_{S1}$

    The purpose of the present chapter is to examine the *on -ing* pattern. In it the matrix verb is subcategorized as selecting the preposition *on* and a following complement clause. The first leg of the investigation is the task of compiling a list of such verbs, and sources of data include the Brown and LOB corpora, grammars of English, especially Poutsma (1929), Bridgeman et al. (1965), and of course, intuitions of native speakers. A semantic characterization is then proposed of verbs on the list, with the object of isolating—to the extent that this is possible—semantic properties typical of verbs governing the *on -ing* pattern and of providing a framework for the further analysis of the pattern.

The complement sentence pattern of 1' seems relatively easy to separate from adverbial sentences, such as 2:

(2) John stumbled on reaching the top step.

In 2 the connection between the higher verb and the lower sentence is looser than in 1. Thus the preposing of S_2 is more readily possible in 2 than in 1: *On reaching the top step, John stumbled*, versus **On laying the foundations for winning the next election, the conference concentrated*. In this connection it is also worth pointing out that if a question is to elicit 1 as a response, it is appropriately of the form *What did the conference concentrate on?* rather than **When/how did the conference concentrate?* whereas 2 is an appropriate response to the latter type of question, *When/how did John stumble?* The suitability of *what* questions for 1 is also evidence for the nominal status of the lower clause in 1'. This is confirmed by other criteria. Thus it is possible to replace the lower clause in 1 with the pronoun *it* or the pronoun *that*, as in *The conference concentrated on laying the foundations for winning the next election, but the fringe meeting afterwards did not concentrate on it/that*. Such replacement is not possible in 2: **John stumbled on reaching the top step, but Sue did not stumble on it/that*. Further, in the case of 1, the lower clause may be moved by Right Dislocation, but in the case of 2 this is not possible: *The conference concentrated on it, laying the foundations for winning the next election* versus **John stumbled on it, reaching the top step*. The lower clause of 1 is also much better in the focus position of a pseudocleft sentence than the lower clause of 2 is in that position: *What the conference concentrated on was laying the foundations for winning the next election* versus **What John stumbled on was reaching the top step*. Considerations such as these support a syntactic distinction between 1 and 2: in the former the lower clause is a nominal complement clause, while in the latter the lower clause is an adverbial clause. The present chapter focuses on constructions where the lower clause is a complement clause, and adverbial clauses will be set aside.

Another construction that will be excluded is the one where *on* is not a preposition, but has adverbial force, as in *John went on explaining that*.... This type of construction is worth investigating but is very different from that of 1. For instance, the criteria considered in the previous paragraph show that in the *go on* construction, the *-ing* clause is not nominal. For instance, to consider the Right Dislocation criterion, observe the ill-formedness of **John went on it, explaining that*....

From another point of view, it is also worth noting that the verbs that select the *on -ing* pattern are not necessarily the same as those that subcategorize for the pattern *on* NP where the NP is nonsentential. Admittedly, it does seem that verbs that govern the pattern of *on -ing* also allow the sentence to be replaced with a nonsentential NP (see below). However, the converse generalization does not hold, for there are verbs that select *on* NP but do not allow the NP to be sentential, or allow a sentential NP only with strain. For instance, *fawn* occurs with *on* NP, as in *John fawned on his superiors,* but a sentential NP here is out of the question, as witness the impossibility of **John fawned on serving his superiors.* *Chance* is another case in point. It is fine with a nonsentential NP, as in *John chanced on a new discovery,* but seems inconceivable with a sentential NP, as witness **John chanced on coming upon a new discovery. Descend* is a further example. It selects *on,* as in *Hordes of fortune seekers descended on the city,* but seems difficult or impossible to combine with *on -ing,* as witness **Hordes of fortune seekers descended on making a fast buck in the city.* In conclusion, the class of verbs selecting *on* and a following nonsentential NP does not coincide with the class of verbs selecting *on -ing.* This nonconvergence is of independent interest, confirming analogous results in other chapters. It also serves to justify the focus of the present chapter.

II

The following matrix verbs governing the *on -ing* pattern may be culled from the Brown and LOB corpora:

Verbs	Illustrations and Comments
center	*Now all his desires centered on "rediscovering and singing of the prosaic and yet beautiful world of men and objects so long barred from me by a barbed wire fence"* [Brown G27, 1470-1490, from M. Josephson, "Jean Helion: The Return from Abstract Art" *(The Minnesota Review* 1: 3].
concentrate	*So the conference will concentrate on laying the foundations on which to win the next election* (LOB A03, 87-88, from *The Times* 1/10).
depend	*The continued operation of this program depends on having his service* (Brown A23, 0470-0470, from *The Oregonian* 8/26).

hinge	*The scheme therefore hinges on finding a property group to take over this aspect of the Grunwald "empire"* (LOB A25, 32-34, from *Sunday Telegraph* 4/2).
insist	*And yet she has insisted on keeping her promise to the ordinary people of Ghana* (LOB B13, 47-48, from *The Sunday Express* 11/12).
plan	*The wear and tear of life have taught me that very few friends of mutual friends long to see foreign strangers, but I planned on being the soul of tact, of giving them plenty of outs was there the tiniest implication that their cups were already running over without us* [Brown G51, 0280-0320, from I. Chase, *The Carthaginian Rose* (Doubleday and Company)].
thrive	*As we know, the Soviet peasant today still very largely thrives on being able to sell the produce grown on his private plot; and it is still very far from certain how valid the party's claim is that in "a growing number of kolkhozes" the peasants are finding it more profitable, to surrender their private plots to the kolkhoz and to let the latter be turned into something increasingly like a state farm* (Brown B25, 0330-0400, from *The Nation* 193: 16).

Further verbs may be gleaned from Poutsma (1929, 911), with illustrations from the same source.

calculate	*The Boers calculated on being able to hold Belmont for six months.* Times
venture	*Lucy was in high favour enough to venture on asking for a tune.* G. Eliot, *The Mill on the Floss,* 1, chap. 10, 81. Poutsma suggests that "the infinitive-construction is more common than the gerund-construction, from which it mostly differs in meaning in implying less risk." Poutsma's remark, particularly about the infinitive being more common, is to the point, and it is worth adding that there are speakers who are dubious about the acceptability of the *on -ing* construction with *venture* in present-day English. (Such doubts make it difficult to compare the two construals.) The verb can be included only with considerable hesitation.

Poutsma (1929, 912) has a separate group of verbs "denoting a deciding or resolving." It contains the following:

decide	*So soon as the rich decide on adopting these devices in the name of the public, they become law.* Green, *A Short History of the English People,* chap., 4, par. 4, 317.
determine	*The Snobkys suddenly determined on leaving town.* Thackeray, *The Book of Snobs,* chap. 4, 25.
resolve	*You resolved on quitting Netherfield.* Austen, *Pride and Prejudice,* chap. 10, 52.

Other verbs may be gleaned from pattern 31.6A of Bridgeman et al. (1965, 36 ff.), with illustrations freely invented, except where otherwise noted.

agree	*They agreed on selling their car.*
bank	*John banked on winning the last hand.*
bargain	*John cannot bargain on being selected for promotion.*
bet	*I would not bet on winning this race.*
border	*John's use of the term bordered on adopting other people's ideas without acknowledgment.*
brood	*He was brooding on being poor.* Here *about* is generally preferred, and *on* is at best a second choice.
capitalize	*We should capitalize on finishing the job on schedule.*
cash in	*We should cash in on finishing the job on schedule.*
collaborate	*The two firms collaborated on building the dam.*
comment	*He commented on being unable to fulfil the requirement.*
confer	*The cricket umpires conferred on adding an extra over because of the slow over rate.* A construction with a *wh* complement, as in *The cricket umpires conferred on whether to add an extra over because of the slow over rate,* or with an NP head, as in *The cricket umpires conferred on the matter/question of adding an extra over because of the slow over rate,* may seem preferable, but the *on -ing* construal is perhaps also possible.
count	*I am counting on winning the next round.*

deliberate	*John deliberated on introducing a few changes.*
discourse	*He discoursed on having too much work.* The verb is not very common, but may perhaps be retained.
dwell	*He dwelled on being ready to help.* The construction with a head NP would be more natural, as in *He dwelled on the ideal/possibility of being ready to help,* and the verb can be included only with some hesitation.
ease up	*You should ease up on living recklessly.*
elaborate	*He would not elaborate on offering help to the poor.* A construction with a head NP is again perhaps preferred, as in *He would not elaborate on the possibility of offering help to the poor,* and the verb is included with some hesitation.
embark	*The board embarked on dismantling old structures.*
enlarge	*He would not enlarge on offering help to the poor.* A head NP is again readily inserted, as in *He would not enlarge on the possibility of offering help to the poor.*
exist	?*He existed on blackmailing his clients.* This is an unlikely construction and would be replaced, for instance, by *He existed on the proceeds from blackmailing his clients.* Nor does the verb seem much better in a figurative use with *on -ing,* as in ?*He existed on being the center of attention.* On balance, it is perhaps best to drop the verb.
expand	*He expanded on being willing to help.* Again, a construction with an NP would be more natural, as in *He expanded on the possibility of being willing to help.*
expatiate	*He expatiated on feeling concerned for his friend.*
expostulate	*John expostulated on losing his turn.*
expound	*John expounded on being willing to help.*
fall back	*John fell back on eating Spam.*
figure	The verb, informal in style, may be used in the sense of 'rely on' and 'plan on' (or 'take into consideration') [see Random House (1981, s.v.)]. These may be illustrated with *John should not figure on getting a pay raise* and *You had better figure on running into heavy traffic leaving the city,* respectively. [The second example is from Random

House (1981, s.v.).] The two senses are different but at the same time not very far apart.

fix	*How did you fix on selling your house?*
focus	*We should focus on improving the economy.*
gamble	*John was gambling on winning the last hand.*
hold out	*John is holding out on releasing any new information.*
improve	*We can improve on feeding our students with handouts.* The sense of the verb is close to 'do better than', and the example may be paraphrased 'we can do better than feed our students with handouts'. (I am indebted to Ian Gurney for commenting on the verb.)
labor	*John labored on developing a new language program.*
lecture	*John lectured on irrigating deforested areas.* The verb may also take *about*, as in *John lectured about living during the Blitz*. Here *on -ing* carries a connotation of a more formal lecture. (On the two construals, see also section III.)
live	*?He lived on blackmailing his clients.* This is not a very likely construction (cf. the comment on *exist* above), and although *live on -ing* is perhaps slightly better than *exist on -ing* in a more figurative sense, as in *?He lived on being the center of attention*, it may be best, on balance, to drop the verb.
look back	*He looked back on living in Spain with fond memories.*
meditate	*He meditated on being poor.*
moralize	*John moralized on obeying orders to the letter.*
muse	*John mused on losing his chance of promotion.*
plan	*He planned on selling his house by autumn.*
preach	*He preached on obeying orders.*
presume	*John presumed on knowing her intimately.* This can be included only with considerable hesitation, so strong is the preference for a nonsentential NP, as in *John presumed on his familiarity with her*. The meaning of the verb here is along the lines of 'make (possibly unfair)

use of' (cf. the OED). The verb, of course, also combines with the infinitive, much more commonly than with *on -ing*, as in *John would not presume to speak for his wife*, but then it carries the sense of 'venture', 'take liberties' (ALD).

reckon	He reckoned on selling his house by autumn.
reflect	He reflected on losing his chance for promotion.
rely	John relied on winning the last hand.
remark	John remarked on feeling unwell.
renege	John reneged on paying his share.
rest	The scheme rests on having John's cooperation.
revolve	The scheme revolves on having John's cooperation.
settle	John settled on selling his house.
speak	John spoke on spending a fortune on slot machines.
speculate	John speculated on changing his name.
start	The board started on dismantling old structures. A nonsentential NP complement is no doubt much more common with *start on*, as in *The board started on the job/task of dismantling old structures*, but *start on -ing* seems likewise acceptable to many speakers, though there are those who hesitate about it. As far as sentential complementation is concerned, the verb of course very commonly occurs both with *-ing* forms and with infinitives. The meaning of *start on -ing* seems close to 'make a start on' (Ian Gurney, personal communication), and perhaps for this reason it is inconceivable in a sentence such as *It started raining/to rain/*on raining*.
take a chance	We should not take a chance on hiring a person like him.
talk	He talked on living in the Mediterranean.
theorize	He theorized on devising new guidelines. *About* is the first choice here, but *on* is just about possible.
touch	John's use of the term almost touches on adopting other people's ideas without acknowledgment.
turn	The scheme turns on obtaining John's cooperation.

verge	John's use of the term verged on adopting other people's ideas without acknowledgment.
vote	The board voted on admitting new members.
wager	I would not wager on winning this hand.
work	John worked on developing a new language program.
write	John wrote on devising a new computer program.

Even though the list in Bridgeman et al. (1965) provides a large number of verbs, there are still one or two others that have suggested themselves, or have been suggested, to me:

enter	The board entered on dismantling old structures. This verb is not very common in the pattern but may perhaps be included on the analogy of *embark* and *start*.
miss out	John missed out on being promoted to professor. (I am indebted to Ian Gurney for the verb and the example.)
toil	John toiled on developing a new language program.

III

The list of verbs given in section II, incomplete as it no doubt is, may be considered an approximation to the range of verbs that select the *on -ing* construction in present-day English and will in this section be used as the basis for the analysis of the pattern.

From a syntactic point of view, it is clear that all the verbs listed allow not only sentential *on -ing* constructions but also constructions in which *on* is followed by a nonsentential NP. For instance, *bank* and *reflect* do allow them, to take two examples at random, as in *John banked on my help* (see the ALD) and *John reflected on my misfortune*. Indeed, as was observed, in some cases a nonsentential NP is preferable to a sentential one. In this respect, the *on -ing* pattern is in line with findings relating to other patterns. The two-part generalization that emerges from a consideration of these other construals is also supported by the *on -ing* construction: if a verb governs any of these patterns, which are of the more abstract form Prep *-ing*, it invariably allows the *-ing* clause to be replaced by a nonsentential NP. On the other hand, as illustrated here and elsewhere, a verb that co-occurs with the preposition in question and a following nonsentential NP does not necessarily allow the NP to be sentential.

From a semantic point of view, the verbs governing *on -ing* may be grouped in the following way:

1. $Verb_1$ expresses verbal communication, NP_1 comments on $Verb_2 ing$: *comment, discourse, dwell, elaborate, enlarge, expand, expatiate, expostulate, expound, lecture, moralize, preach, remark, speak, talk, theorize, write.*
2. $Verb_1$ expresses cogitation, NP_1 thinks or reflects on $Verb_2 ing$: *brood, deliberate, look back, meditate, muse, reflect, speculate.*
3. $Verb_1$ expresses deciding or planning on $Verb_2 ing$ . . . , NP_1 decides or plans on $Verb_2$ing: *decide, determine, fix, resolve, settle, vote; figure, plan.*
4. $Verb_1$ expresses a degree of commitment to $Verb_2 ing$:
    a. NP_1 is unyielding in its commitment to $Verb_2 ing$ or to not $Verb_2 ing$: *insist; hold out.*
    b. $Verb_1$ expresses a mode of relinquishment, NP_1 is yielding on $Verb_2 ing$: *ease up, renege.*
5. $Verb_1$ expresses concentration, NP_1 concentrates on $Verb_2 ing$: *center, concentrate, focus.*
6. $Verb_1$ expresses engagement NP_1 works on $Verb_2 ing$: *collaborate, labor, toil, work.*
7. $Verb_1$ expresses dependence:
    a. NP_1 hinges on $Verb_2 ing$: *hinge, rest, revolve, turn.*
    b. NP_1 banks on $Verb_2 ing$: *bank, bargain, calculate, count, fall back, figure, reckon.*
    a./b. NP_1 depends on $Verb_2 ing$: *depend, rely.*
    c. NP_1 gambles on $Verb_2 ing$: *bet, gamble, take a chance, venture, wager.*
8. $Verb_1$ has the approximate meaning 'make use of', 'turn to profit', or 'fail to make use of': *capitalize, cash in, presume, thrive; miss out.*
9. $Verb_1$ expresses initiation, NP_1 embarks on $Verb_2 ing$: *embark, enter, start.*
10. $Verb_1$ expresses proximity, NP_1 verges on $Verb_2 ing$: *border, touch, verge.*
11. Others, *agree, confer, improve.*

It seems clear that not all verbs governing the *on -ing* pattern can be subsumed under any one semantic label, at least not if the label is to be of any specificity. In the present classification the number of classes runs to ten, an eleventh class being a mixed bag not susceptible to generalization. The idea underpinning the taxonomy is again that although the verbs of each class are not synonymous with each other, they have important senses that share an ingredient of meaning, and that the taxonomy provides a systematic account of such major or dominant senses of the verbs in question. The glosses are offered as approximations to expressing common ingredients of meaning. No doubt their form and content can be improved upon. Also, it may be possible to devise a more adequate grouping of different semantic classes, thereby perhaps reducing their number. However, even in this form the characterizations provided give some indication of the semantic range of verbs governing *on -ing*. They also provide a basis for comparing this pattern with some others that seem close semantically, for it turns out that the objects of comparison depend largely on the semantic class in question.

As far as sheer numbers are concerned, the largest class of the taxonomy is that of verbal communication. If the spoken versus written language dichotomy (and the verb *write*) is set aside, and the description is limited to spoken language, the verb *speak*, with its sense of relatively "pure" verbal communication, comes close to expressing the ingredient of meaning that is shared by members of the class. This may be substantiated by considering combinations of verbs of the class with explicit denials of speaking. Such combinations are fairly incoherent, as in *?John expatiated/expounded on being ready to help others, but did not speak on it*.

Verbs of verbal communication may be the largest class of the present taxonomy, but these verbs do not always sound very natural or very likely with *on -ing* clauses. As was observed in section II, some of these verbs definitely prefer a construal with *on* NP *of -ing*, along the lines of *John expatiated/expounded on the subject of being ready to help*. The NP in question is abstract, like *the subject, the topic, the theme, the idea*, etc. Even those verbs of the class that do not definitely prefer the *on* NP *of -ing* construction, like *comment*, very readily allow it, as in *John commented on the fact of being unable to fulfil his commitments*, alongside *John commented on being unable to fulfil his commitments*. It bears adding that many verbs of this class also select the preposition *about*. The *about* construal seems relevant to at least *expand, expatiate, expostulate, expound, lecture, moralize, preach, remark, speak, speculate, talk, theorize, write*. From a syntactic point of view, these two factors, the fairly common preference for the insertion of an abstract NP, and the similarly fairly common availability of, or sometimes even a preference for, the *about* construction, go some way toward explaining why not a single example of the *on -ing* construction was found with verbs of this class in the two corpora. Appearances may therefore be slightly deceptive: even though class 1 is large in terms of members, these verbs are not necessarily very common in the construction.

There is also a semantic consideration that often distinguishes the *on -ing* and *about -ing* patterns when both construals are available to a verb of class 1 and that further serves to explain why verbs of the class are not very common with *on -ing*. For instance, consider *speak*, as in 3a–b.

(3) a. John spoke on spending a fortune on slot machines.
 b. John spoke about spending a fortune on slot machines.

Example 3a may be paraphrased 'John gave a speech on spending a fortune on slot machines' or 'John spoke on the subject of spending a fortune on slot machines'. The reference of PRO here is not primarily that of NP_1. Instead, PRO is arbitrary or unspecified in reference. This kind of interpretation seems relevant to many, perhaps most, verbs of class 1, including *elaborate, expand, expatiate, expound, lecture, moralize, preach,* and some others and it gives such construals a fairly narrow range of meaning. By contrast, although 3b can have the reading 'spoke on the subject of', it can also have a reading where the reference of PRO is primarily that of NP_1. Example 3b, therefore, has a broader range of interpretation than 3a, which may also be a factor in explaining why the latter is not a very common construal with verbs of class 1. Despite this lack of frequency, however, verbs of class 1 clearly constitute a core class of the pattern.

Another core class is class 2, of verbs expressing reflecting. It is similar to class 1 in that verbs of the class allow the insertion of the same set of abstract NPs in front of the lower clause. Another similarity is that the preposition *about* is often possible with verbs of the class. Thus both *John brooded/reflected on the subject of being poor* and *John brooded/reflected about (the subject of) being poor* are possible. Further, as pointed out by Ian Gurney (personal communication), verbs of class 2 are typically capable of expressing communication in a suitable context, as for instance in *In his reply John brooded/reflected on being poor.*

Verbs of class 3, another core class, express deciding or planning. Alternative construals of verbs of this class are not with *about*, but with infinitives, though it should be pointed out that not all these verbs allow the infinitive with equal ease. In particular, *fix* and *settle*, of the subclass of verbs of deciding, do not sound very natural with it; compare *John fixed/settled on selling one of his houses* with *??John fixed/settled to sell one of his houses*. Nor is *figure*, of the subclass of verbs of planning, entirely comfortable with the infinitive; compare *John had not figured on paying double* with *?John had not figured to pay double*. On the other hand, several other verbs of class 3 do allow the infinitive. To start with *plan*, of the subclass of verbs of planning, *plan on -ing* is the preferred variant for many speakers, especially, it seems, in American English, but the infinitive is likewise good. Indeed, this note on usage regarding *plan* is found in Random House (1981, s.v.): "Many teachers object to the phrase PLAN ON plus a gerund, considering it poor style for PLAN TO followed by an infinitive: *I had planned to go to the movies tonight* (not *I had planned on going to the movies tonight*)." There is little doubt that *plan on -ing* and *plan to* + an infinitive are often close or even inseparable in meaning, but the former may sometimes carry a suggestion of 'rely on' (cf. *figure* below) or of a larger set of circumstances than what is expressed by Verb$_2$*ing*, whereas the latter lacks any suggestion of 'rely on' and seems restricted to more 'pure' intention and perhaps to a more narrow focus on the goal expressed by the lower clause. For instance, consider 4a–b:

(4) a. John is planning on being in hospital for a week.
 b. John had been planning to be in hospital for a week.

Of these 4b sounds less likely. It suggests in a rather narrow way that to be in hospital for a week was in itself John's goal, which is pragmatically unlikely. On the other hand, 4a suggests a broader set of circumstances, for instance, that being in hospital for a week was part of a larger plan or program.

As far as *vote* is concerned, there is a clear difference in meaning between *The committee voted on restricting the franchise* and *The committee voted to restrict the franchise*, with the matrix verb of the former having the approximate meaning 'took a vote on' and the latter that of 'decided'.

With *decide* the infinitive, of course, is very common. We might compare 5a–b:

(5) a. John decided on selling one of his houses.
 b. John decided to sell one of his houses.

Both 5a and 5b mean that John made a decision and that the decision was to sell his house, but there is still a difference between them. The infinitival construction here is fairly neutral, more or less limited to expressing deciding, but the *on -ing* construction implies that John had a number of alternatives and that he chose the one of selling his house [cf. also Wierzbicka (1988, 32)]. The *on -ing* construction may also suggest a dependency relation: if he sells his house, then something else will follow. Such extra ingredients of meaning are not necessarily carried by the infinitive construal. The idea of a choice among alternative courses of action is also carried by such other verbs of the *on -ing* pattern expressing deciding as *fix* and *settle,* in spite of the fact that, as observed above, these do not allow infinitival construals as readily as does *decide.*

Infinitival variants also seem possible with *determine* and *resolve,* as in *John determined on living abroad for a time/John determined to live abroad for a time,* and *John resolved on living abroad for a time/John resolved to live abroad for a time.* However, not all of these four variants are equally common, and there are even speakers who are dubious about the acceptability of one or more of them. (Adjectival construals such as *be determined on* Verb$_2$*ing/to* Verb$_2$ are, of course, more common but not the focus here.) The task of teasing out differences in meaning between the two constructions with the two verbs is complicated by such doubts regarding acceptability. To the extent that speakers accept the four versions, the infinitival variants tend to imply that whatever is expressed by the lower clause is a more immediate prospect than is the case with the *on -ing* construals. There may also be a touch, for some speakers, of the idea of a choice among alternative courses of action associated with the *on -ing* construction, especially perhaps in the case of *determine,* but not all speakers feel it, and even for those who do, it is more attenuated than in the case of *decide, fix,* and *settle.*

Overall, verbs of class 3 often have infinitival variants, and with one or two of them such constructions are very common. However, not all verbs of the class show distributional overlap, and where there is overlap, there is also often a more or less noticeable semantic difference between the two constructions, especially where acceptability judgements are secure.

Verbs of class 4 express a degree of commitment or a lack of it on the part of NP$_1$ to Verb$_2$*ing.* The verbs of 4a express commitment but are very different in that *insist on -ing* implies commitment to Verb$_2$*ing,* as in *The Cabinet insisted on recognizing the new regime,* whereas *hold out on -ing* implies commitment to not Verb$_2$*ing,* as in *The Cabinet held out on recognizing the new regime.* The two verbs are also similar in that both imply that the commitment has been under challenge. On the other hand, verbs of 4b imply lack of commitment or taking back a commitment. (*Ease up* expresses treading more lightly on a pattern of behavior rather than going back on any one decision.) The verbs of the class are few in number, but *insist* is very common with *on* -*ing*. The other verbs are less common, *ease up* probably being the most marginal, but they are also quite idiomatic with *on* -*ing*, and it is not easy to think of alternative construals for any verb of the class.

Verbs of class 5 are also few in number, at least in this survey, but the class is cohesive semantically, with a specific and well-defined meaning. Also, the verbs of the class seem quite common in the pattern. Two of them occurred in the corpora, and the third, *focus on*, is also quite idiomatic in the pattern. The class may then be considered another core class of verbs governing the pattern. The verbs of the class also display distributional homogeneity, for alternative construals, either with other prepositions or with the infinitive, do not readily come to mind.

On the other hand, verbs of class 6, expressing the idea that NP_1 works on $Verb_2 ing$, do in general allow alternative construals with both infinitives and *at* -*ing* constructions, as in 6a–c:

(6) a. John worked on developing a new language program.
    b. John worked to develop a new language program.
    c. John worked at developing a new language program.

The sentences of 6a–c are not equivalent, but the nuances of meaning that separate them are subtle and not easy to tease apart. As a first approximation, it may be suggested that 6b gives prominence to John working toward his intended goal (of developing a new language program), whereas 6c has more of a focus on the activity that is going on (cf. chapter 5). Sentence 6a has a focus on ongoing activity as well, and separating it from 6c is a delicate matter. Schibsbye (1970, 327) considers *work at* NP, as in *He is working at a new invention*, and *work on* NP, as in *He is working on a poem* (Schibsbye's examples, the NP being nonsentential), and suggests that the former "simply expresses the direction of the activity" and that the latter "includes duration." This may be part of the story even in sentential construals, but it is perhaps possible to add that 6a has a focus on engagement, whereas 6c highlights the idea of striving or attempting.

Verbs of class 7, another core class, express the idea of dependence. (Those of 7c express the rather specific idea of betting on Verb$_2$*ing*.) The division between 7a and 7b is based on the nature of NP$_1$. For verbs of 7a the subject is typically inanimate and +abstract, something like *scheme, plan, enterprise, business*, etc., as in *The scheme of unseating the chairman hinged/rested on attracting wider support*, whereas an animate NP is not possible, as witness **John hinged/turned on attracting wider support*. By contrast, verbs of 7b typically combine with animate NPs, as in *John banked/calculated on attracting wider support*, not with inanimate NPs, **The scheme banked/calculated on attracting wider support*. As far as verbs of 7b are concerned, there is an echo of the meaning of planning (cf. class 3). (It may be noted that *figure* has been placed in both class 3 and class 7b). This may explain the limitation to animate subjects. On the other hand, one or two verbs of class 7, *depend* and perhaps *rely*, in particular, are general enough in meaning to allow either inanimate or animate subjects, as in *The scheme/John depended/relied on attracting wider support*, which is recognized by their inclusion in a separate class 6a/b.

As far as alternative construals are concerned, obvious candidates do not suggest themselves for verbs of class 7. (Regarding *venture*, see the comments in section II.) In general the same seems true of verbs of classes 8–10. (Regarding *presume* and *start*, see again the comments in section II.) These are small in terms of numbers of verbs belonging to them, since they contain less than a handful of verbs each, but some of the verbs in question, such as *thrive*, of class 8, and perhaps *embark*, of class 9, seem common enough in the pattern. (It will be recalled that *thrive* was encountered in the corpora.)

A semantic relation, albeit of a fairly abstract sort, may perhaps be discerned combining classes 7 and 8. The relation has to do with the meaning of the preposition *on* when it governs a nonsentential noun phrase. An important semantic property of the preposition in this case typically relates to the notion of a bearing or supporting surface. As Lindkvist (1976, 147) puts it, *on* occurs "with complements denoting surfaces which are not primarily conceived of as coated or overlaid by the object correlated, but instead above all as functioning to bear the object correlated, which is thus thought of as somehow held up by the surface on which it rests." He goes on to compare *He has a towel over his arm* and *He has a towel on his arm*, and comments that "from a physical point of view, the arm supports the towel in its position in both cases; but the mind perceives the cases somewhat differently: 'the arm' is primarily thought of as covered over in the former case, as bearing the towel in the latter" [Lindkvist (1976, 147); in this connection, see also Herskovits (1986, 49, 140 ff.)]. The meaning of a bearing or a supporting surface seems related to the meaning of dependence carried by verbs of class 7. For instance, the sentence *The scheme depended/relied on attracting wider support* implies that the scheme rested on getting wider support. Bringing in class 8 here does entail a further degree of abstraction, but the idea that (the entity designated by) NP_1 derives support from what is expressed the lower clause seems to extend to verbs of this class, verbs implying that NP_1 derives profit from $Verb_2$.

There is another semantic property typically associated with the preposition *on* when it governs nonsentential noun phrases that can be brought to bear on the analysis of sentential complementation dependent on the same preposition. This is the idea of contiguity [cf. Lindkvist (1976, 147) and Herskovits (1986, 144)]: the objects designated by noun phrases linked by *on* should be contiguous. This property is relevant to the example just cited from Lindkvist (1976, 147) and may be further illustrated by the noun phrase *the lock on his forehead* [Herskovits (1986, 144)]. In the case of sentential complementation, contiguity must necessarily be conceived of in a more abstract sense, but it seems possible to gloss verbs of class 10 *(border, touch,* and *verge)* as expressing contiguity or approaching contiguity.

The verbs of class 10 are also noteworthy because they require inanimate subjects. Typically, their subjects are abstract nominalizations of the type produced above: *John's use of the term bordered/verged on adopting other people's ideas without acknowledgment.* Sentences of this type exhibit interesting control properties. Strictly speaking, PRO (the understood subject of the lower sentence between *on* and *adopting*) in this example is not interpreted as coreferential with NP_1, the subject of the higher sentence: John's use of the term does not adopt other people's ideas without acknowledgment. Rather, the sentence implies that John does so (or comes close to doing so). The NP *John* is the subject of the larger NP *John's use of the term,* and PRO is interpreted as coreferential with this subject, which is an instance of remote control. This intuition may be substantiated by choosing an example in which the lower sentence has a reflexive verb. Thus although *?John's story of what happened borders/verges on perjuring himself* may not be completely well formed (and is certainly very awkward when compared with *John's story of what happened borders/verges on perjury*), it is still comprehensible, whereas **John's story of what happened borders/verges on perjuring itself/oneself* is not. It may be added that with verbs of class 10, remote control of PRO is not necessarily restricted to emanating from the subject position of NP_1, as witness *The use that John made of this term bordered/verged on adopting other people's ideas without acknowledgment,* where *John* may again be interpreted as the controller of PRO.

It seems that verbs governing the *on -ing* pattern in present-day English cannot be fitted into very few semantic classes of any specificity. From this point of view, the verbs in question seem rather more heterogeneous than those governing either the *in -ing* pattern, as analyzed in chapter 2, or the *at -ing* pattern, as analyzed in chapter 5. At the same time, verbs of the class show rather less distributional overlap with other patterns than do the other two patterns cited. Indeed, apart from verbs of verbal communication (class 1), of thinking and reflecting (class 2), or deciding (class 3) and of working (class 6), such distributional overlap seems fairly minimal. Also, where there is distributional overlap, it is sometimes possible to discern more delicate semantic distinctions between the *on -ing* pattern and the alternative in question. Such further distinctions are especially discernible in the case of verbs of deciding (class 3) and of working (class 6), though with the latter the distinctions are perhaps more subtle. These considerations suggest that in spite of the seemingly rather sprawling and heterogeneous character of verbs governing *on -ing* in present-day English, the pattern is a robust one, with a well-defined semantic domain. Further, to some extent it seems possible to associate the domain in question with the sense of the preposition *on*.

7

Coping with Putting the Baby to Bed and *Charging Someone with Stealing Something:* On Verbs Governing *with -ing*

I

Consider sentences 1a–b and structures 1'a–b, their partially bracketed representations:

(1) a. John coped well with putting the baby to bed.
    b. They charged John with stealing a car.
(1') a. [[John]$_{NP1}$ [coped]$_{Verb1}$ well [with]$_{Prep}$ [[PRO]$_{NP2}$ [[putting]$_{Verb2}$ the baby to bed]$_{VP}$]$_{S2}$]$_{S1}$
     b. [[They]$_{NP1}$ [charged]$_{Verb1}$ [John]$_{NP0}$ [with]$_{Prep}$ [[PRO]$_{NP2}$ [[stealing]$_{Verb2}$ a car]$_{VP}$]$_{S2}$]$_{S1}$

In 1'a, S_2 is a complement sentence dependent on the preposition *with*, which in turn is governed by the verb *cope*. In 1'b, S_2 is again a complement sentence dependent on *with*, this time governed by the verb *charged*. The term "*with -ing* pattern" will be used of the two constructions here. As in other patterns in this book, the subject of the two complement sentences is PRO, and in the pattern of 1'a it is often

135

controlled by NP_1, the subject of the matrix clause, whereas in the pattern of 1'b it is generally controlled by NP_0, the direct object of the matrix clause. (As will be shown below, this statement is an oversimplification, but it serves to distinguish the two patterns.) In referring to these constructions, 1'a will be called the intransitive (and generally subject controlled) *with -ing* pattern and that of 1'b the transitive (and generally object controlled) *with -ing* pattern.

In this chapter we examine the two *with -ing* patterns. As always, it is first necessary to base the discussion on a solid foundation by compiling a reasonably extensive list of verbs that govern each pattern. A semantic characterization of such verbs is then carried out in each case, and the balance of the chapter is devoted to discussion of verbs in the taxonomies.

As far as the *with -ing* patterns are concerned, the status of S_2 as a complement sentence in both 1'a and 1'b is clear without further argument. The same holds for virtually all other verbs to be considered. (For an exception, see below.) Also, using diagnostics employed in earlier chapters, it is again easy to show that S_2 is a nominal clause in the pattern. For instance, replacement of the lower clause with *it* or *that* is possible, as in *John coped with putting the baby to bed but Sam did not cope with it/that* and in *They charged John with stealing a car but they did not charge Sam with it/that*. Similarly, Right Dislocation yields expected results, as in *John coped with it, putting the baby to bed* and in *They charged John with it, stealing a car*. A pseudocleft sentence yields further confirmation of NP status, as in *What John coped with was putting the baby to bed* and in *What they charged John with was stealing a car*.

Data in the present chapter are taken from the same sources as in previous chapters. For presentational convenience, the pattern of 1'a is considered first, in section II, and the pattern of 1'b is considered in section III.

II

Verbs and illustrations of usage in this section come first from the two corpora considered in this book. Data from Poutsma (1929, 930) come next, and these are followed by verbs from Bridgeman et al. (1965, 46 ff.). In the case of Bridgeman et al., example sentences have been freely invented. (Ian Gurney helped in devising example sentences.) Next, a number of verbs that were suggested by Ian Gurney or that suggested themselves to me are likewise illustrated.

Verbs	Illustrations and Comments
accord	*That such points make up a prime section of S is known (see 5.2.2 in [5]), and that there are 63 of them accords with putting* $\kappa = \lambda = 2$ *in 8.2.4 of [5]* [LOB J21 44-46, from W. Edge, "A Permutation Representation of the Group of the Bitangents" *(London Mathematical Society Journal* 36)].
get away	*She can't get away with saying things like that!* (LOB L22 168-169, from Anon., "Whispering Tongues Blamed Her" *(Secrets* 3/4, D. C. Thomson and Co.)].
have to do	*But I don't see what that has to do with calling me a spy* (LOB N07 126-127, from B. Cloos, *Drury* (Ward Lock, Curtis Brown)].
start off	*I feel that it will bring the advantages of bulk handling to many who have previously been deterred by the thought of having to spend £4,000, because one can literally start off with spending only about £118 for one of these bins ex works* (LOB E38 147-150, from *The Field* 9/28).
dispense	*I could dispense with toying with their brats, if it gives them any pain* [Poutsma (1929, 930), from Lamb, *Essays of Elia*, 25].
put up	*He was forced to put up with only having the probable credit of it* [Poutsma (1929, 930), from Jane Austen, *Pride and Prejudice*, chap. 52, 317].
alternate	*Torturing the prisoners alternates with keeping them in solitary confinement.*
begin	Reactions to sentences such as *He began with clearing the snow* are not always very uniform. There are speakers, especially perhaps of American English, who only accept the sentence with an interpretation suggesting a list of actions or activities, along the lines of *He began with clearing the snow (and then did something else)*. The preposition *by* is a possible substitute for *with* here, with

a meaning that seems fairly similar, and it is indeed often preferred by speakers. Both construals have a slightly adverbial flavor. On the other hand, there are speakers, especially perhaps of British English, who accept the sentence in the sense of 'he made a start on clearing the snow', where the *with -ing* construction is more clearly a complement clause construal. A clearly complement clause construal may be observed in sentences such as *The day began with clearing the snow* and *His day began with clearing the snow*. (These two sentences were pointed out to me by Jane Hill, personal communication.) Whether these two sentences might be derivationally related to something like $NP_{1+animate}$ *began his day with clearing the snow* is a question that invites further investigation.

bother — *He did not bother with writing to me. Bother* also takes the *to* infinitive construal, as in *He did not bother to write to me*. The two constructions are not entirely equivalent, for the *to* infinitive construal at least potentially sounds more like an accusation, whereas *bother with -ing* is more tongue-in-cheek, more tolerant of NP_1's behavior, perhaps also implying that what is expressed by S_2 is at least potentially viewed as something less serious or less important than is the case with the *to* infinitive construction (Ian Gurney, personal communication).

clash — *For him, working full-time clashed with attending to his family.*

coincide — *For him, finishing his first book coincided with realizing the futility of writing.*

come — *Such a view comes with misinterpreting the facts.*

come about — *Higher productivity came about with lowering wages.*

commence — In meaning the verb is reminiscent of *begin*, and somewhat similar comments seem appropriate. Illustrations might include *He commenced with clearing the snow*, which is not universally acceptable as a complement clause construal, and *The day/his day commenced with clearing the snow*. It should be added that the verb is much less common than *begin*, and favorable judgments seem less secure. Even so, the verb may perhaps still be admitted.

compare   *Flying as a passenger does not compare with flying as a pilot.*

compete   *Traveling by bus does not compete with traveling by plane.*

continue   *John continued with painting the wall despite all distractions.* [On this verb, see also Dixon (1991, 241 f.); the illustration is modeled on Dixon's illustration of *continue + -ing*.]

cope   *He coped well with putting the baby to bed.*

contrast   *Flying as a passenger contrasts with flying as a pilot.*

correlate   *Being happy does not always correlate with being rich.*

deal   *He was unable to deal with having to put the baby to bed.* The meaning of *deal* here is reminiscent of that of *cope*. The verb may perhaps also select *with -ing* with the approximate sense of 'discuss', as in *In his talk he dealt with generating well-formed sentences*. There are speakers who prefer to insert an NP here, along the lines of *In his talk he dealt with the subject/question of generating well-formed sentences*, but the verb may perhaps still be included even in this sense.

do away   *He did away with serving wine in wine glasses.*

experiment   *The company experimented with omitting all soliloquies.* As observed in chapters 2 and 5, *experiment* also allows *in -ing* and *at -ing*. Differences between these three construals should not be exaggerated, but it still seems possible to tease them apart, at least to some extent. *Experiment with -ing*, as in the example given, focuses on something done by way of an experiment as a means of getting a better effect. *Experiment in -ing*, as in *He experimented in merging poetry and visual art*, abridged from the sentence cited in chapter 2, suggests a field or line of activity, and *experiment at -ing*, as in *The doctor experimented at grafting animal bones in nonhuman subjects*, veers in emphasis toward the sense of 'make attempts at doing something' or 'have tries at doing

	something'. (I am indebted to Robert MacGilleon for helpful comments on *experiment*.)
find fault	*He found fault with doing it this way.*
fit in	*Starting a career does not easily fit in with bringing up children.*
flirt	*He flirted with buying a new car.* Flirt with NP is clearly the more likely combination, and the verb is retained with some hesitation.
fool	*He fooled with starting up in business.* Again, *fool with something* or, more likely still, *fool with somebody* are much more common, and the sentential construction can be included only with hesitation.
fool around	*He fooled around with starting up in business.* This is more readily possible than the previous entry.
go	*Such behavior goes with being a politician.*
go along	*He went along with paying his share.*
grapple	*He grappled with being left destitute.*
happen	Q. *How did you catch a cold?* A. *It happened with going out with next to nothing on.* Not all speakers are entirely happy with this construction, and it can be included only with some hesitation.
harmonize	*Bringing up children does not easily harmonize with making a career.*
help	*He helped with clearing the snow.* As compared with the *help* constructions discussed in chapters 2 and 5, the present construction is close to 'helped with (the task or job of) the clearing of the snow'.
hold	*I do not hold with making public exhibitions of oneself.* Not all speakers are entirely happy with this construction, and it can be included only with some hesitation.
hurry	*He hurried with finishing his lecture.* This usage is not entirely acceptable to all speakers. The construal sounds slightly better in a negative context, as in *We should not*

	hurry with answering him, and the verb may then be included. [On *hurry with*, see also Dixon (1991, 243).]
identify	He identified with being a teacher.
interfere	His professional duties interfered with attending to his family.
make out	How are you going to make out with being on your own?
manage	*He managed with putting the baby to bed.* The *to* infinitive construction is of course possible as well, and indeed more common, as in *He managed to put the baby to bed.* In both cases the baby no doubt gets put to bed, but the *to* infinitive focuses on the result, whereas *manage with -ing* draws attention to the process (in this case, that of putting the baby to bed), so that the two constructions are felt to be different. Where there is no process involved, the *with -ing* construction sounds odd or impossible; compare *He managed to hand in his essay in time* with ??*He managed with handing in his essay in time.*
mess	He messed with starting up in business.
mess around	He messed around with starting up in business.
mix	Getting ahead in business does not mix easily with being a family man.
occur	These things can occur with being too careful.
originate	His problems generally originated with feeling inferior to others.
pair	Bridgeman et al. (1965, 47) mark the verb with an asterisk, which suggests that the verb is more or less marginal in the pattern (cf. also Alexander and Kunz 1964, 10). The verb is indeed not common, but a sentence such as *Lying under oath does not easily pair with maintaining a facade of respectability* seems reasonably acceptable to many speakers and the verb may perhaps then be included.
persevere	*He persevered with coming to class.* As noted in earlier chapters, *persevere* also commonly takes *in -ing,* as in

John persevered in asking stupid questions, but the two constructions are not equivalent, for *persevere with -ing* may suggest continuing to do something in spite of difficulty to oneself, as in *In spite of having to arrange for a baby-sitter, he persevered with/?in coming to class*, whereas *persevere in -ing* may suggest that what NP₁ is continuing to do is causing difficulty or annoyance for someone else, as in *She persevered in/?with requiring an explanation* (modified from the example cited in chapter 2).

play	He played with starting up in business.
play around	He played around with starting up in business.
proceed	He proceeded with asking his question.
rank	His achievement ranks with climbing Mount Everest.
rate	His achievement rates with climbing Mount Everest.
reckon	He did not reckon with being left alone.
tie in	His attitude ties in with being an author.
toy	He toyed with starting up in business.
trifle	You trifle with courting her at your peril. (The example is due to Robert MacGilleon, personal communication.)
trouble	Why should he trouble with paying his bills?
wrestle	He wrestled with being left destitute.
arise	Such problems arise with misinterpreting the facts.
carry on	John carried on with writing the letter.
come up	Several problems came up with inventing examples.
go on	John went on with writing the letter.
toy around	John toyed around with setting up in business. (I am indebted to Ian Gurney for most of these last five verbs.)

Perhaps a general comment is in order, in view of the fact that a consideration of the two corpora and of Poutsma (1929) yielded relatively few verbs governing the subject-controlled *with -ing* pattern, whereas Bridgeman et al. (1965) come up with a number of verbs that at least in the context of some other chapters, including that of the *in -ing* pattern, seems disproportionate. A tribute is due to the comprehensiveness of Bridgeman et al. (1965), but at the same time appearances may be slightly deceptive, in that a number of the verbs in question seem marginal when combined with *with -ing*. This is a point to bear in mind when a taxonomy is attempted.

Providing a taxonomy of verbs selecting *with -ing* is not very easy, for the verbs listed and illustrated above appear to be a fairly disparate lot. To ground the present discussion of them on a reasonably solid foundation, it seems useful to consider the nature of NP_1 and to separate cases in which it is at least generally +animate from those where it is often −animate. Making use of this distinction, the following taxonomy suggests itself as a first approximation:

A. NP_1 is typically +animate.
   1. $Verb_1$ has the approximate meaning 'deal with something formidable', 'grapple with', NP_1 grapples with $Verb_2ing$: *grapple, wrestle*.
   2. $Verb_1$ has the approximate meaning 'play around with', NP_1 plays around with $Verb_2ing$: *flirt, fool, fool around, play, play around, toy, toy around, trifle*.
      'to do so unnecessarily or unsuccessfully': *mess, mess around*.
   3. $Verb_1$ has the approximate meaning 'abolish', 'to do away with', NP_1 does away with $Verb_2ing$: *do away, dispense*.
   4. $Verb_1$ has the approximate meaning 'cope': NP_1 copes with $Verb_2ing$: *cope, deal, manage, make out*.
   5. $Verb_1$ has the approximate meaning 'take trouble', 'bother', generally in negative or interrogative contexts: *bother, trouble*.
   6. $Verb_1$ expresses beginning or continuation: *begin, carry on, commence, continue, go on, proceed, start off*.
   7. Others: *deal* ('discuss'), *experiment, find fault, get away, go along, help, hold, hurry, identify, persevere, put up, reckon*.
B. NP_1 is typically −animate.
   8. $Verb_1$ has the approximate meaning of 'go (or not go) together with', NP_1 goes/does not go together with $Verb_2ing$: *go, pair, tie in*.

NP$_1$ harmonizes/does not harmonize with Verb$_2$*ing*: *accord, fit in, harmonize, mix; clash, interfere.*

NP$_1$ originates with Verb$_2$*ing*: *arise, come, come about, come up, happen, occur, originate.*

NP$_1$ coincides or alternates with Verb$_2$*ing*: *coincide, alternate.*

NP$_1$ correlates or has to do with Verb$_2$*ing*: *correlate, have to do.*

9. Verb$_1$ has the approximate meaning 'compare' or 'compete', NP$_1$ compares/competes with Verb$_2$*ing*: *compare, contrast, rank, rate; compete.*

The taxonomy of verbs governing the subject controlled *with -ing* pattern is not the tidiest in this book. One reflection of this is the large number of verbs listed under "Others" in class 7. The +/−animate dichotomy serves to bring some order into the taxonomy, for verbs of classes 1 through 7 tend to take +animate subjects, whereas in the case of classes 8 and 9, subjects tend to be −animate. On the +animate side, the number of classes for which glosses have been provided is as high as six or seven. Some of these are small, but they have fairly distinctive meanings, and it seems difficult to combine them in order to reduce the number. Classes 2 and 6 have a larger number of verbs in them, and one or two comments might be made about them. Verbs of class 2 are under the heading of 'play around with'. Some of them, such as *flirt* and *toy*, express something in the mind, as in *John flirted/toyed with setting up in business*, which might be glossed as 'flirted/toyed with (the idea of) setting up in business', whereas others, including *fool around* and the "mess" verbs, entail that NP$_1$ undertakes some physical action. Verbs of class 6, expressing beginning or continuation, offer a more complex picture, and the present discussion, being limited in scope, cannot do full justice to their description. Verbs such as *begin*, in particular, are subject to differing judgments (cf. the discussion of the verb above), and the variation makes their classification difficult, for they straddle the animate/inanimate divide. Placing them in class 6 on the animate side here has only provisional status, pending further work on these verbs. By contrast, some other verbs of class 6, such as *proceed*, are more satisfactorily accommodated in class 6; inanimate NP$_1$s seem out of the question for them, as witness the inadmissibility of **The/his day proceeded with clearing the snow*, as opposed to *He proceeded with clearing the snow*. From another point of view, verbs of the class might also be further divided on the basis of a difference regarding the way in which the lower clause is viewed. Verbs such as *proceed* imply active control by NP_1 over the content of S_2, whereas a verb such as *start off* does not necessarily imply it. For instance, *John proceeded with clearing the snow*, which implies that clearing the snow was what John chose to do at his unprompted discretion, might be compared with *??John proceeded with having to pay 100 percent interest*, which is doubtful because the *have to* construction, implying imposition on—or lack of choice for—NP_1, is in conflict with the *proceed with -ing* construal. On the other hand, *John started off with having to pay 100 percent interest* sounds more readily possible. (I am indebted to Ian Gurney for commenting on the notion of control here.)

As far as remaining verbs selecting +animate subjects are concerned, their number is fairly high. They are accommodated in class 7. Some of the verbs listed there undoubtedly bear semantic relations to one another or to verbs of one of the classes 1 to 6. For instance, *go along* and *put up* are related in meaning, and *experiment* feels close to at least some of the verbs of class 2. However, there is a point of diminishing returns both with setting up additional very small subclasses and with stretching or diluting the boundaries and content of existing ones. Consequently, in the present taxonomy, the verbs in question have been left in a class of "Others."

On the –animate side, only two classes have been set up. Of these, class 9 is straightforward, its verbs expressing comparison. Class 8 has more verbs and is semantically more heterogeneous. Its verbs express a link or connection between NP_1 and the lower clause, such as one of harmony (or conflict), temporal sequence, or simultaneity or correlation. The verbs of the first list of verbs under 8 may express the general idea of a link between NP_1 and S_2, but this often blends with the idea of a harmonious link, so that the boundary between the first two lists of verbs is a fluid one. From a syntactic point of view, there are some verbs in class 8 with which the *with -ing* construal is fairly adverbial in flavor. This holds of most verbs of the "originate" subclass, for a sentence such as *These things occur with being too careful*, is close in meaning to 'these things occur as a result of (somebody) being too careful'. On the other hand, as far as verbs of the other subclasses are concerned, these take complement sentences with little or no adverbial flavor. This holds especially of verbs of the large 'harmonize' subclass.

No doubt with more ingenuity a neater taxonomy could be devised. Also, there may be verbs governing *with -ing* that were overlooked and that should be added. However, the present classification may serve as a first approximation of the kinds of verbs that govern subject controlled *with -ing,* and the rest of this section will be devoted to one or two additional questions that it helps to bring into focus.

First, the lists of verbs demonstrate that all verbs governing *with -ing* allow the subordinate clause to be replaced by an NP. For instance, consider *dispense* and *interfere*, to take two verbs at random. Both allow not only sentential complements—these were illustrated above—but also NP complements, as in *He dispensed with formalities* and *His hobbies interfered with his job*. At the same time, there are verbs selecting the preposition *with* with an NP complement that sound strained or impossible with the sentential *with -ing* pattern. For instance, consider *fight*. It is fine with an NP complement, as in *He fought with his enemy,* but sounds very unlikely with *with -ing,* as in ??*He fought with feeling low*. Similarly, *echo* and *resound* are idiomatic with NP construals, as in *The air echoed/resounded with gunfire,* but seem impossible with sentential complements, as in **The air echoed/resounded with sounding gunfire*. This finding is in line with conclusions reached in other chapters: verbs taking a preposition and an *-ing* clause always have the privilege of taking NP complements as well, but verbs taking a preposition and an NP do not necessarily take sentential complements (given that the preposition remains the same).

As far as the present taxonomy is concerned, it should further be added that some of the verbs listed in it are more comfortable, or likely, with NP complements than with sentential complements. Some verbs of class 2, such as *flirt, fool,* and *mess,* might be cited here, as might some verbs of classes 7 and 8, such as *coincide*. It is perhaps symptomatic that few of the verbs of these classes, and none of the verbs cited, were found illustrated either in the two corpora considered or in Poutsma's collections of recorded usage.

Second, the taxonomy is helpful from the point of view of considering the interpretation of PRO. In a sentence such as 1a, considered at the beginning of the chapter, PRO is coreferential with NP_1. In other words, PRO is controlled by the subject of the matrix sentence, and the control relation is thus local. Such an interpretation of straightforward subject control is not relevant to all verbs of the pattern. For instance, consider 2.

(2) Bringing up children does not easily harmonize with making a career.

In 2, NP_1 is the sentential subject *bringing up children,* but this complex NP does not control the reference of the PRO that is the understood subject of *making a career*. Rather, the understood subject of *making a career* is an arbitrary NP, where "arbitrary," as in earlier chapters, means 'people in general' or 'a certain subset of people in general relevant in the world of the discourse in question'. More interestingly, the complex subject of S_1 in 2, *bringing up children*, has a PRO subject as well, and the interpretation of this PRO is primarily along the same lines $NP_{arbitrary}$, where "arbitrary" again means 'people in general' or 'a certain subset of people in general', and the point is that it is the same set or subset of people that the other PRO, the subject of *making a career*, is interpreted as referring to. In other words, it is possible to propose 2' as a partially bracketed representation of 2, with coindexation indicating coreference:

(2') $[[[PRO_i]_{NP}$ bringing up children$]_{NP1}$ does not easily [harmonize]$_{Verb1}$ with $[[PRO_i]_{NP2}$ [making]$_{Verb2}$ a career$]_{S2}]_{S1}$

The kind of coreference between the arbitrary PROs in 2 might be termed "PRO-to-PRO coreference." PROs participating in PRO-to-PRO coreference may also be controlled. This situation may arise on account of a phrase such as *as for* NP, *as far* NP *is concerned,* or *in* NP*'s case,* as in *As for John, bringing up children does not easily harmonize with making a career, As far as John is concerned, bringing up children does not easily harmonize with making a career,* and *In John's case, bringing up children does not easily harmonize with making a career.* In the first two of these sentences, the two PROs are primarily coreferential with the NP in the initial phrase, and in the third sentence they seem exclusively so. The constructions *as for* NP, *as far as* NP *is concerned,* and *in* NP*'s case* might be seen as specifying what the sentence is about, with the NP identifying a "topic" for the sentence and the PROs then being coreferential with the topic. The kind of control that emanates from the topic of the sentence is not local, since the controller is neither the subject nor the object of the matrix verb. It seems to be a variety of remote control.[1]

In 2' NP_1 is sentential, but NP_1 may of course also be a nonsentential NP. (When it is, it seems generally to be +abstract.) For instance, consider 3:

(3) John's professional duties did not easily harmonize with bringing up children.

In 3 there is only one PRO, and it has coreference with the possessive NP in the determiner position of NP_1, at least primarily. The kind of control involved in this case is again remote. PRO may also be remotely controlled from a topic position. Thus in *As for John, professional duties did not easily harmonize with bringing up children* and *As far as John is concerned, professional duties did not easily harmonize with bringing up children*, PRO is again primarily controlled by the NP identifying the topic of the sentence, and in *In John's case, professional duties did not easily harmonize with bringing up children*, this seems the only interpretation. A remote controller for PRO may also be retrieved from outside the sentence. Thus in the second sentence of the sequence *Let me tell you about John's professional duties. They did not easily harmonize with bringing up children*, the controller of PRO is recovered from the first sentence.

This discussion suggests that verbs governing the intransitive *with -ing* pattern generally exhibit one of two control patterns: either PRO is locally controlled by the subject of the matrix verb or else PRO is arbitrary or remotely controlled. When the taxonomy is considered, a further and more specific generalization suggests itself: verbs of classes 1 through 7—those typically occurring with +animate NP_1s—tend to involve subject control; but verbs of classes 8 and 9—those typically occurring with −animate NP_1s—tend to involve arbitrary PROs or PROs that are remotely controlled. No doubt there are complexities to the analysis of control with verbs of the present pattern that are glossed over by this generalization. For instance, *hold*, accommodated in class 7, is something of an exception. It takes a +animate subject and may perhaps for some speakers be subject to local control, with the PRO of the complement controlled by the matrix subject in a regular fashion, as in *John does not hold with making a public exhibition of himself;* but it seems more readily to permit PRO to be arbitrary, as in *John does not hold with making a public exhibition of oneself.* [*Deal*, with the approximate sense of 'discuss' (class 7), may also involve an arbitrary PRO, as in *In his talk he dealt with generating well-formed sentences;* but the construction is less than perfect for some speakers. Cf. the discussion above.] On the other hand, the generalization seems to be supported by verbs such as *begin*, which, as observed, to some extent straddle the animate/inanimate divide: a sentence such as *He began with clearing the snow*—to the extent that it can be allowed here—exhibits subject control. By contrast, all of *John's day began with clearing the snow, As for John, the day began with clearing the snow, As far as John is concerned, the day began with clearing the snow,* and *In John's case, the day began with clearing the snow* exhibit remote control. So does the second sentence of the sequence *John had a difficult day. It began with clearing the snow.* Overall, the fairly systematic difference in control properties between classes A and B gives further substance to the basic distinction underlying the present taxonomy.

Third, the taxonomy also provides a basis for considering alternation between the *with -ing* pattern and other patterns. Such alternation seems surprisingly restricted. As far as the two verbs of class 1 are concerned, alternative construals do not come readily to mind. On the other hand, several verbs of class 2 allow alternative construals with *at -ing*. The most common of these with the *at -ing* construal is no doubt *play*, as in *The children were playing at keeping shop* (from the ALD); but the meaning of the verb here may be glossed as 'pretend, for fun, to be sth or do sth' (ALD), whereas the meaning of the verb with *with -ing*, as in *He is playing with setting up in business*, is something like 'consider lightly' (again see the ALD, which provides the example *He is playing with the idea of emigrating to Canada* of *with* + NP, where the sense of the verb seems close to what it is in the sentential pattern). Some other verbs of this class, such as *mess around, fool around*, and *play around*, likewise allow *at -ing*, as in *John messed/fooled/played around at setting up in business*, and such *at -ing* construals do not differ that much from *with -ing* construals, as in *John messed/fooled/played around with setting up in business*. These *at -ing* construals hark back to the class of verbs in chapter 5 expressing "intention, engagement, or effort, real or pretended, on the part of NP_1 with respect to the realization of S_2," and they may carry a trace of the sense of 'to have a try at doing something'. That is, there is a feeling of a goal, though NP_1 goes about achieving it in an unskillful or unsuccessful way. On the other hand, in the corresponding *with -ing* construals there is perhaps less sense of an activity directed at a goal. As for verbs of class 3, alternative construals do not easily come to mind. The same holds of verbs of class 4. *Manage* is an exception, but, as observed above, there is again a difference in meaning between the *with -ing* construal and the alternative infinitival construction. The infinitive construction is also quite idiomatic with *bother* and *trouble* of class 5, as witness 5a–b:

(4) a. John did not bother with returning my phone call.
    b. John did not trouble with returning my phone call.
(5) a. John did not bother to return my phone call.
    b. John did not trouble to return my phone call.

Again, the point should be made that the two constructions are not equivalent: 5a–b need not be accusations, but they could be, more readily than 4a–b.

Several verbs of class 6 are of course very common with *to* infinitives or with *-ing* forms, or indeed with both. *Begin* is probably the most prominent verb of the class, and even though the other verbs of the class do not necessarily select the same construals as this verb, the discussion here will in the main have to be restricted to it, with a focus on points that have a direct bearing on *begin with -ing*. *Begin* certainly allows both *He began to clear the snow* and *He began clearing the snow*, and sentences of both of these types are no doubt more common than *with -ing* construals governed by *begin*. Comparing these construals, it may be observed that in those dialects that allow *He began with clearing the snow* with the approximate meaning 'he made a start on clearing the snow', the *begin with -ing* construal differs from its *to* infinitival and *-ing* clause variants syntactically in that the former does not permit subject-to-subject raising (NP movement in later work), which the latter two do. Thus there is a clear difference between 6a, on the one hand, and 6b–c, on the other:

(6) a. * It began with raining hard./*There began with arriving visitors at the gate.
      b. It began to rain hard./There began to arrive visitors at the gate.
      c. It began raining hard./There began arriving visitors at the gate.

In this respect, the *begin with -ing* construction is closer to the *begin by -ing* construal, as in *John began by clearing the snow*, for sentences such as **It began by raining hard* and **There began by arriving visitors at the door* are also ill formed. The *begin with -ing* and *begin by -ing* construals are therefore both control constructions. (Looking beyond *begin*, it might be added at this point that not all verbs in class 6 that take *to* infinitival or *-ing* clause construals allow subject-to-subject raising. *Proceed* is a case in point, for it allows *to* infinitives, as in *He proceeded to clear the snow*, alongside of *He proceeded with clearing the snow*, but does not allow subject-to-subject raising, as witness the ill-formedness of **It proceeded to rain hard*. On *proceed* from another angle, see also Granath (1994, 218).)

Second, attention must be drawn here to a property of the *begin with -ing* construction that distinguishes it from both *to* infinitival and *-ing* clause construals, on the one hand, and from *begin by -ing* construals, on the other. This is the relevance of remote control assignment to the *begin with -ing* construal with an inanimate NP_1. For instance, we might compare the well-formed sentences *His day began with clearing the snow* and *In John's case, the day began with clearing the snow* and the well-formed sequence *He had a difficult day. It began with clearing the snow* (with *it* standing in for *a difficult day*) with the sentences and sequences in 7a–c. (In 7a–c *it* should again be interpreted as standing in for *a difficult day*.)

(7) a. *His day began to clear the snow./*In John's case, the day began to clear the snow./He had a difficult day. *It began to clear the snow.
   b. *His day began clearing the snow./*In John's case, the day began clearing the snow./He had a difficult day. *It began clearing the snow.
   c. ??His day began by clearing the snow./??In John's case, the day began by clearing the snow./He had a difficult day. ??It began by clearing the snow.

The sentences and sequences of sentences of 7a–b are all quite inconceivable. The sentences and the sequence of sentences in 7c are perhaps slightly less inconceivable but still not idiomatic. In this way, the availability of remote control for *begin with -ing* sets it apart from the other three construals selected by *begin*.

As far as verbs of class 7 "Others" are concerned, most of them seem limited to *with -ing*. Exceptions include *experiment, help, hesitate*, and *persevere*. These were discussed and illustrated above, with comments on the range of uses that are specific to their respective *with -ing* construals.

As far as verbs of classes 8 and 9, with generally –animate subjects, are concerned, alternative patterns do not readily come to mind. For instance, *interfere*, from class 8, and *rank*, from class 9, do not generally allow either the *to* infinitive or the *to -ing* construction, to consider two candidates for alternation that might come to mind. For instance, consider *For him, getting ahead in business did not interfere with bringing up a family/*For him, getting ahead in business did not interfere to bring/bringing up a family* and *His achievement ranks with climbing Mount Everest/*His achievement ranks to climb/climbing Mount Everest*. (*Interfere* may also be construed with *in -ing*, but then it typically selects a +animate NP$_1$; see chap. 2.) *Compare* is more permissive with the *to -ing* construction here, for although the *to* infinitive is impossible, as witness **His achievement compares to climb Mount Everest, His achievement compares to climbing Mount Everest* sounds possible to many speakers, alongside of *His achievement compares with climbing Mount Everest*.

This survey of alternation, then, shows that it is severely restricted. There is some limited distributional alternation, but broader and more systematic generalizations about it are difficult to formulate, for what alternation there is tends to be confined to individual verbs. At the same time, where alternation is found, the *with -ing* constructions are generally semantically distinct from the alternative or the alternatives available. The overall scarcity of distributional alternation and the semantic distinctiveness of the *with -ing* construal suggest that virtually all of the several classes of the taxonomy are core classes of the *with -ing* pattern. This means that *with -ing* has several characteristic semantic functions in present-day English, and that in spite of the relatively large number of such functions, it is scarcely under "threat" from other prepositional patterns in most of its functions.

III

Turning now to a consideration of the pattern of 1b', verbs will be listed again from the two corpora and from Poutsma (1929, 930), with illustrations mainly from the same sources. There will also be verbs from Bridgeman et al. (1965, 49 f.), illustrated with examples freely invented, as well as one additional verb that has suggested itself to me.

Verbs	Illustrations and Comments
associate	*Hay fever and other allergies may also be associated with lying in bed, due either to feathers in the pillow or mattress or (less commonly recognized as the cause) an accumulation of woolly dust under the bed* [LOB F06 57-60, from M. Eden and R. Carrington, *The Philosophy of the Bed* (Hutchinson)]. A second sentence, modeled on the authentic one, may help to confirm the inclusion of the verb: *The doctor associated hay fever with lying in bed.*
charge	*They were also jointly charged with stealing a car belonging to Herbert Arthur Peel at Bristol between January 1 and January 2* (LOB A11 73-74, from *The Times* 2/22). To judge by the evidence of the two corpora considered, this is the most common verb by far in either of the *with -ing* patterns. The sense of the verb in question is approximately that of 'accuse formally' (cf. Collins-Cobuild, s.v.). However, the verb is also capable of selecting *with -ing* in a different sense, approximately

'give (somebody) the task of', as in *The king charged his ambassador with delivering his message*. This second usage is perhaps slightly archaic in flavor, and to judge by the evidence of the corpora it is much less common than the first sense. However, it is still current, and both senses of the verb should be taken into account.

confuse   *For although snorkel diving is not to be confused with using an aqualung it is a proper introduction to it and it is within everybody's means* (LOB C14 148-150, from *The Times Educational Supplement* 11/3).

credit   *Local authorities credited the men with saving the girl's life* (Brown A24 1500-1510, from *The Providence Journal* 11/29).

accredit *Mr. Bright himself was accredited with having said that his effort to arouse a reforming spirit was like flogging a dead horse* [Poutsma (1929, 930), from McCarthy, *A History of our Own Times*, 3, 208 (OED, 3)].

reproach *She could not reproach herself with having missed any chance* [Poutsma (1929, 889), from Mrs. Ward, *Sir George Tressady*, chap. 2, 13a; cf. also Poutsma, MS, s.v.]. The construction is not limited to the reflexive, as witness *John reproached Sam with having overlooked an error*.

taunt   *He was taunted with becoming the adviser of the Nationalists* [Poutsma (1929, 930), from *The Review of Reviews*, No. 193, 86b].

tax   *The American woman has often been taxed with being extravagant* [Poutsma (1929, 930), from *The Pall Mall Magazine*].

upbraid   *He upbraided him gently with choosing so rude an abode* [Poutsma (1929, 889), from Scott, *Waverley*, chap. 18, 65a].

acquaint *They acquainted him with using an aqualung.*

burden	*They burdened him with filling unnecessary forms.*
busy	*They busied him with filling unnecessary forms.*
challenge	*They challenged him with being an excollaborator.*
combine	*They combined snorkel diving with using an aqualung.*
compare	*He compared writing a thesis with climbing Mount Everest.*
contrast	*He contrasted flying a plane with steering a ship.*
face	*They faced him with having to pay up.* This is not a very common combination, but it sounds better in the passive, as in *He was faced with having to pay up.*
familiarize	*They familiarized him with filling forms.*
hurry	*They hurried him with finishing the novel.* This is not a very likely construction.
identify	*He identified snorkel diving with using an aqualung.*
intrust	*They intrusted him with counting the money.*
occupy	*They occupied him with filling forms.*
overwhelm	*We should not overwhelm students with writing essays.* This is not a very common combination.
pair	*You would not normally pair being a teenager with being cautious.*
plague	*He plagued informants with making acceptability judgments.*
reconcile	*Nothing will reconcile me with being unemployed.*
saddle	*They saddled him with filling unnecessary forms.*
threaten	*They threatened him with having to pay the bill.* Not all speakers are sure or convinced about the acceptability of *threaten* in this pattern, and the verb can at best be included with some hesitation. It might be added that a sentence such as *They threatened him with cutting off power supplies* is acceptable—and indeed more readily so than the previous sentence—but displays subject control, PRO being controlled by *They*. At the same time, the verb is rather peculiar in that many speakers do not like omitting the NP between it and *with*, not even on the subject control reading, as in ?*They threatened with*

cutting off power supplies, which is the reason why the verb was not included in section II. As for the alternation between subject and object control, the nature of the lower predicate seems to play a role, in that when the predicate expresses something under the control of PRO and, consequently, of NP_1, subject control prevails, as with the predicate *cutting of power supplies*. On the other hand, when the lower predicate expresses something outside of the control of PRO and of NP_1, object control prevails, as with the predicate *having to pay the bill*. In this latter case it is even more difficult to omit the NP between the verb and *with*, which is the direct object in this case, as in **They threatened with having to pay the bill*, which no doubt has to do with B's generalization (either form of it; cf. chap. 4).

tie in We should tie in the restructuring of the department with improving security.

link They linked the restructuring of the firm with increasing its productivity.

Providing a taxonomy of verbs governing NP_0 *with -ing* seems slightly easier than characterizing verbs governing *with -ing*. One way of going about it is again first to consider the notion of animacy. NP_1s in the present pattern are generally +animate, so that it seems difficult to ground a taxonomy in their properties. The nature of NP_0, the direct object, is of more interest, for some verbs typically select +animate NP_0s, whereas others take −animate ones. The following taxonomy suggests itself:

A. NP_0 is typically +animate:

1. $Verb_1$ has the approximate meaning 'burden' or 'charge', NP_1 burdens or charges NP_0 with $Verb_2ing$: *burden, charge, busy, face, hurry, intrust, occupy, overwhelm, plague, saddle.*

    NP_1 threatens NP_0 with $Verb_2ing$: *threaten.*

2. $Verb_1$ has approximate meaning 'acquaint' or 'reconcile', NP_1 acquaints or reconciles NP_0 with $Verb_2ing$: *acquaint, familiarize; reconcile.*

3. $Verb_1$ implies that NP_1 ascribes or imputes to NP_0 the action or property expressed by S_2:
   a. $Verb_1$ implies that NP_1 credits NP_0 with $Verb_2 ing$: *accredit, credit*.
   b. $Verb_1$ implies that NP_1 reproaches NP_0 with $Verb_2 ing$: *reproach, tax, upbraid*.
   c. $Verb_1$ implies that NP_1 accuses NP_0 of $Verb_2 ing$: *challenge, charge*.
   d. $Verb_1$ implies that NP_1 taunts NP_0 with $Verb_2 ing$: *taunt*.

B. NP_0 is typically –animate:
   4. $Verb_1$ implies that NP_1 associates or links NP_0 with $Verb_2 ing$: *associate, combine, link, pair, tie in*.

   'by way of comparison, contrast, or similarity': *compare, contrast, identify*.

   'do so erroneously': *confuse*.

This taxonomy suggests that fewer classes are sufficient for the transitive *with -ing* pattern than were needed for the subject controlled variety. (Also, fewer verbs seem to fall outside of the main classes of the taxonomy.) At the same time, the classes in question seem closer to each other semantically than in the previous pattern. When NP_0 is typically +animate, the taxonomy has three groups, which might be described as the 'burden with', the 'familiarize with', and the 'ascriptive' or 'imputative' classes. Of these, the first two are close to each other, and the second might be seen as a subclass of the first, in that if one acquaints someone with doing something, there is generally a suggestion that someone will—or should—at some point do it. In other words, classes 1 and 2 tend to share the property of referring to something that is to take place later than the point in time of $Verb_1$. Further, that something that is to take place later is typically an action that is under the conscious control of NP_0. Where this is not so, as for instance in *??They saddled/ acquainted John with being too old for the job,* the sentence is pragmatically strange. On the other hand, verbs of the 'ascriptive' class are different in that $Verb_2$ generally expresses something that has happened in the past or that is true at the point of time of $Verb_1$. For instance, one typically credits or charges someone with what the person has already done or is already doing, not with what the person may do in the future. As for the notion of controllability, it seems relevant to the 'accuse' subclass and perhaps to the 'reproach' subclass, but not to the 'taunt' and 'credit' subclasses, since one can taunt or credit someone not only with some action but also with some property. For instance, one can taunt someone with being too old for a job or credit someone with being intelligent enough for a job.

As far as verbs taking −animate NP_0s are concerned, their number is not very large. Nor do they seem very common with *with -ing*. On the other hand, the meaning of verbs such as *associate* and *link* is rather general, general enough to bear a relation to meanings of verbs of classes 1 to 3 of the top half of the taxonomy. One might propose that the glosses of classes 1 to 3 specify more precisely the kind of association or link that there is between NP_0 and what is expressed by the lower clause. This might lead one to propose setting up *associate* and *link* as core verbs whose meaning is relevant to the description of the meanings of virtually all verbs of the present pattern. Under this proposal paraphrases of meanings of verbs of classes 1 and 2 would be of the form 'associate NP_0 with doing $Verb_2ing$' and those of verbs of class 3 would be of the form 'associate NP_0 with having done $Verb_2ing$' (or 'with being what is expressed by $Verb_2ing$'). This seems quite feasible. On the other hand, the more specific glosses given in the taxonomy will still need to be given.

As far as sheer numbers of verbs are concerned, class 1 is the largest of the present taxonomy. However, some of the verbs cited, including *busy* and *hurry*, are not at all common in the pattern with *with -ing*—nor indeed with *with*—so that appearances are slightly deceptive. To judge by the evidence of the two corpora considered, *charge*, from class 3c, with the meaning 'accuse', is the most common verb by far in the pattern.

The taxonomy invites one or two further analytic observations. First, the generalization observed in other chapters and in section II of this chapter that an *-ing* clause following the preposition of the pattern in question can always be replaced by a nonsentential NP holds of the present transitive *with -ing* pattern as well. For instance, to take two verbs at random, consider *saddle* and *reproach*. Both allow not only sentential complements, as illustrated above, but also NP complements, as in *They saddled him with all the awkward jobs* and *They reproached him with insensitivity to the feelings of others*. On the other hand, analogously to what was shown in earlier chapters and in section II of this chapter to be the case with other patterns, there are verbs that select an NP object and the preposition *with* and yet do not allow the complement of the preposition to be sentential. The verb *provide* is a case in point here. It is fine in sentences such as *They provided John with additional information*. In contrast, a sentence with a sentential complement seems excluded, as witness *They provided John with receiving/knowing additional information*.

It should be added that, analogously to the intransitive *with -ing* pattern, some verbs illustrated above and included in the present taxonomy are more likely with nonsentential NP complements. In particular, some verbs of class 1 have this property. *Face* and *overwhelm* are cases in point, as in *They faced him with an ultimatum* and *They overwhelmed him with new work*. This has the effect of further reducing the predominance of verbs of this class when actual usage is considered.

Second, the present pattern being one of object control, it is worth examining it from the point of view of the two versions of B's generalization that were distinguished in chapter 4. As was the case with verbs of chapter 4, the great majority of verbs of the present pattern observe the strong form of the generalization in that they do not permit intransitive uses. For instance, *saddle* and *taunt* do not, as witness the impossibility of omitting the object in *They saddled John with filling unnecessary forms* (*They saddled with filling unnecessary forms*) and in *They taunted him with becoming an adviser of the Nationalists* (*They taunted with becoming an adviser of the Nationalists*). However, there are also some verbs that observe the weak form but not the strong form of the generalization. For instance, *compare* allows a sentence such as *Climbing this mountain does not compare with climbing Mount Everest*, as was noted in section II. A closer look at the taxonomy reveals a two-part clustering: first, verbs of classes 1 through 3 observe the strong form of the generalization almost without exception, *hurry* perhaps being more or less the only exception (see also the comment on *threaten* above); second, *compare* is not the only verb in class 4 that does not, requiring instead the weak form of the generalization. Indeed, for verbs of class 4 the weak form of the generalization is more the rule than the exception, for not only *compare* but also *combine, pair,* and *contrast* allow intransitive uses with *with -ing*, as in *Working in secondary school contrasts with working at a University*. (For further illustrations, see section II.) So does *identify*, with NP_1 control, as *He identified with being a teacher*. The clustering of verbs that do not observe the strong form of B's generalization in class 4 of the taxonomy and the virtual absence of such verbs from classes 1 through 3 underline the correlation of the present semantic taxonomy with syntactic properties of the verbs involved.

Third, as far as control properties of the transitive *with -ing* pattern are concerned, it seems that verbs of classes 1 to 3, whose direct objects are typically +animate, involve object control, which is local in character, in a fairly straightforward way. For instance, in *They saddled John with organizing the end-of-term party* and *They reproached John with being late*, PRO is controlled by NP_0. By contrast, verbs of class B, whose direct objects are typically inanimate, do not in general involve object control. Instead, PRO often seems to be arbitrary in reference, referring to 'people in general' or 'a certain subset of people in general relevant in the discourse in question'. This is illustrated in *The doctor associated hay fever with lying in bed*. NP_0 may also at times be sentential and have its own PRO. In this case the two PROs are often not controlled and they refer to the same 'general' set or the same subset of people, as in *They compared PRO_i climbing this mountain with PRO_i conquering Mount Everest*. It seems that remote controllers for PRO are less likely in this transitive *with -ing* pattern than in the intransitive pattern discussed in section II; for instance, *??As far as $John_i$ is concerned, they compared PRO_i climbing this mountain with PRO_i conquering Mount Everest* is hardly coherent. The phrase *in NP's case* perhaps gives a less incoherent result, as in *In $John's_i$ case, they compared PRO_i climbing this mountain with PRO_i conquering Mount Everest*. Setting aside the seemingly rather unlikely possibility of remote control, it should be pointed out that when the object of a verb of class 4 is +animate, which seems possible for *associate* and *link*, straightforward local object control again comes into consideration, as in *They associated John with taking bribes*. Overall, with regard to control, the link between the two divisions of the taxonomy and control properties of verbs in the two parts serves to provide the system of classification with some motivation, independent of the glosses of verb meanings.

Object control, then, is primarily relevant to verbs of classes 1 to 3. Considering these verbs from the broader perspective of the analysis of object control in English, it seems that verbs of classes 1 and 2 tend to be amenable to analysis on the basis of the notion of influencing. As was observed in chapter 4, this notion underlies the analysis of the *order/ permit* verb type: the referent of NP_0 is influenced by the referent of NP_1 to perform (or toward performing) the action expressed by the lower clause. However, this kind of analysis, making use of the notion of influencing, is altogether inappropriate to verbs of class 3. As far as they are concerned, the referent of NP_1 does not try to influence the referent of NP_0 toward some course of action; rather the referent of NP_1 makes a claim about the referent of NP_0, ascribing or imputing to the referent of NP_0 some action or property that is presented in a certain light, by way of a reproach, an accusation, etc. The "discovery" of verbs of class 3 here means that the analysis of object control verbs in English cannot be reduced to the type of *order/permit*, central as this type undoubtedly is. Rather, it must be enriched to allow for an ascriptive or imputative type as well.

Finally, regarding alternative construals available to verbs of the present pattern, with the meaning of the verb staying at least approximately the same, it seems that such alternation is very limited. In class 1 there are some verbs, including *burden* and *saddle*, for which the *with -ing* pattern is quite idiomatic, and others for which, as was suggested, the construal is perhaps slightly less idiomatic and certainly not very common, either because they do not often select a direct object followed by the preposition *with*, or if they do, they prefer a nonsentential complement after *with*. In neither case do alternative construals spring easily to mind. The same goes for verbs of the small class 2. As far as class 3 is concerned, *with -ing* seems the only option available to verbs of class 3a. On the other hand, *for -ing* is a fairly systematic alternative for verbs of class 3b, as in 8a–b:

(8) a. They reproached/upbraided John with being late.
    b. They reproached/upbraided John for being late.

The two construals are not entirely equivalent, though. The *with -ing* construals are less factive about the nature of S_2, more in the nature of claims about NP_0, whereas the *for -ing* construals imply more definitely, or take it for granted to a greater extent, that what S_2 expresses holds of NP_0. It should be added that with one or two other verbs that are somewhat similar semantically, *with -ing* construals seem less good, whereas *for -ing* construals are fine, as witness *They blamed John for/ ??with letting the cat out*.

As for remaining subclasses of class 3, they are small, but *with -ing* seems the only construction available to *charge* and *taunt*. On the other hand, whereas *charge* selects only *with -ing*, *accuse*, fairly close in meaning to *charge* of class 3c, takes *of -ing*, not *with -ing*:

(9) a. They charged John with/*of stealing a car.
    b. They accused John of/*with stealing a car.

As for verbs of class 4, most seem restricted to *with -ing*. Exceptions are *link* and *compare*, which allow *to -ing*, as in *They linked the restructuring of the firm to/with increasing its productivity* and *They compared climbing this mountain with/to conquering Mount Everest*. The alternatives are perhaps not entirely equivalent with either verb, though the differences are fairly subtle and seem to depend idiosyncratically on the matrix verb in question. As far as *link* is concerned, there is perhaps a difference regarding the connection of the things linked: in the case of *with -ing* they seem to exist more independently of each other, but in the case of *to -ing* there is more of a causal link between them. As far as *compare* is concerned, *to -ing* may be used to establish a likeness, as in this example (devised by Ian Gurney): *They compared reading the work of certain linguists to eating shredded wheat without milk and sugar*. But *with -ing* tends to be used for a point-by-point comparison if the things being compared are of the same category, whether or not they are similar or different in some way, as in *They compared climbing this mountain with conquering Mount Everest, saying that conditions were almost equally hazardous in both cases;* admittedly, even *to -ing* is generally likewise acceptable in the latter case.

Our discussion has thus uncovered some distributional overlap between the transitive *with -ing* pattern and other patterns, but on the whole such overlap is severely limited and, as in the case of the subject controlled *with -ing* pattern discussed in section II, broader generalizations about the alternation seem difficult to formulate, because variation tends to be confined to individual verbs. At the same time, where overlap does occur, it is often possible to make a semantic distinction between the *with -ing* pattern and its alternative. The scarcity of alternation and the distinctiveness of the pattern suggest that the present *with -ing* construal has a fairly well defined functional domain in the system of complementation of present-day English.

8

Dreaming of Changing the World and *Accusing Somebody of Stealing Something:* On Verbs Governing *of -ing*

I

Consider sentences 1a–b and structures 1'a–b, their partially bracketed syntactic representations:

(1) a. John dreamed of changing the world.
 b. John accused Sue of stealing a car.

(1') a. [[John]$_{NP1}$ [dreamed]$_{Verb1}$ [of]$_{Prep}$ [[PRO]$_{NP2}$ [[changing]$_{Verb2}$ the world]$_{VP}$]$_{S2}$]$_{S1}$
 b. [[John]$_{NP1}$ [accused]$_{Verb1}$ [Sue]$_{NP0}$ [of]$_{Prep}$ [[PRO]$_{NP2}$ [[stealing]$_{Verb2}$ a car]$_{VP}$]$_{S2}$]$_{S1}$

In 1'a, S$_2$ is a complement sentence dependent on the preposition *of*, which in turn is governed by the matrix verb *dreamed*. In 1'b, S$_2$ is again a complement sentence dependent on *of*, which in turn is governed by the matrix verb *accused*. The term "*of -ing* pattern" will be used of the two constructions here. As in other patterns treated in this book, the subject of the lower sentence is PRO. In the pattern of 1'a, PRO is

163

typically controlled by NP_1, the subject of the matrix clause, whereas in that of 1'b it is typically controlled by NP_0, the direct object of the matrix clause. To distinguish the two patterns, that of 1a might be called the intransitive or subject controlled *of -ing* pattern, whereas that of 1b is the transitive or object controlled *of -ing* pattern.

As far as the *of -ing* patterns are concerned, there seems little danger of confusing them with adverbial or other patterns. Also, it is worth noting that S_2 in the two patterns is a nominal clause, as is shown by the criteria used in earlier chapters. For instance, the following are good:

(2) a. John dreamed of changing the world, but Sue did not dream of it/that. John dreamed of it, changing the world. What John dreamed of was changing the world.
 b. John accused Sue of stealing a car, but he did not accuse Sam of it/that. John accused Sue of it, stealing a car. What John accused Sue of was stealing a car.

The pattern of 1a will be considered in section II, and that of 1b in section III.

II

Verbs and illustrations of usage in this section are first taken from the two corpora considered in this book. These examples are followed by data from Poutsma (1929, 906), and then verbs from Bridgeman et al. (1965, 34). In the case of Bridgeman et al., example sentences have been freely invented.

Verbs	Illustrations and Comments
beware	*We must beware, however, of supposing that there must be any close analogy between the units of quite different sciences* [LOB F01 109-111, from P. Meredith, *Learning, Remembering and Knowing* (English Universities Press, Hodder and Stoughton)].
boast	*Grocery stores sell dozens of foods that boast of having almost no food value at all* (Brown C17 0300-0310, from *Time* magazine 1/13). The sentence cited is well formed, but a second example, freely invented, may be added to

illustrate the verb in the pattern: *John boasted of doing it all alone.*

come — No good can come of contemplating the sad, inevitable fact that once youth has passed "a worse and worse time still succeeds the former" [Brown G70 0330-0350, from J. Krutch, "If You Don't Mind My Saying So" (*The American Scholar* 31:1)].

complain — Better than almost any other, this example of the science fiction of pure idea acts as a test case, in that those learned in the medium will at once salute its ingenuity and elegance, while those whose study is but little will complain of not being illuminated, of being offered an unworthy escape from the universe of man and fact, of being presented with a pseudo-question instead of a question [LOB G36 181-187, K. Amis, *New Maps of Hell: A Survey of Science Fiction* (Victor Gollancz, A. D. Peters and Co.)].

consist — (His "holiday," incidentally, has consisted of working on his farm with a vigour which would dismay most other men on the shady side of 50) (LOB A40 34-36, *Evening Argus*, 6/2).

despair — He should not despair of keeping a large part of his copper revenue (LOB B02 152-153, from *The Guardian* 9/15).

dream — No auto maker would dream of putting the head on the engine before he fitted the pistons in the block [Brown E35 0250-0260, from Anon., "The Industrial Revolution in Housing" (*House and Home* 20:4)].

speak — We cannot now speak of maximizing the value of the objective function, since this function is now known only in a probabilistic sense [Brown J79 1460-1470, from R. Aris, *The Optimal Design of Chemical Reactors* (Academic Press)].

talk — M. Tshombe has once or twice been brought to see the discrepancy, and has even talked of sharing his revenues (LOB B02 125-127, from *The Guardian* 9/15).

tell — In an anonymous interview with a French newspaper the financier told of spending several months with her (Brown F09 0730-0740, from *Confidential* 9:1).

think	He declared the government is thinking of asking for foreign troops if the situation worsens (Brown A21 1470-1480, from *The Detroit News* 4/19). To judge by the evidence of the two corpora, this is the most common verb selecting the pattern.
admit	*These views admit of being argued to their consequences* [Poutsma (1929, 906), from Huxley, *Darwiniana*, chap. 1, 10].
repent	*You will never repent of being patient and sober* [Poutsma (1929, 906)]. Poutsma also has one or two examples of *repent* followed by *for -ing*, and most speakers appear to find either construction acceptable, though sometimes with some hesitation, as witness also *John repented of/for denigrating his opponent*. There may be a subtle difference between the two construals, with the *of -ing* variant emphasizing a sense of more inward contrition.
approve	*John approved of giving Sue her share.*
brag	*He bragged of finishing first.*
conceive	*I cannot conceive of admitting John to the club.*
die	*He died of eating mushrooms.*
disapprove	*John disapproved of reneging on promises.*
get out	*He got out of teaching beginning syntax.* Here it may be felt that the choice of *of -ing* is linked to the particle, *out of* being an independent grammatical unit.
hear	*Yesterday John heard of being selected for promotion.*
learn	*Yesterday John learned of being selected for promotion.*
perish	*He perished of eating mushrooms.*
smack	*What John said smacks of demanding something for nothing.*
tire	*John tired of being alone.*

On the analogy of *get out, back out, chicken out,* and *wriggle out* may also be included, as in *John backed/chickened/wriggled out of teaching beginning syntax* (Ian Gurney, personal communication). As in the case of *get out*, the choice of *of -ing* may be linked to the particle.

On the basis of the survey above, it is safe to say that verbs selecting *of -ing* typically select +animate subjects. The following semantic taxonomy suggests itself:

A. NP_1 is +animate.

   1. $Verb_1$ expresses communication.
      a. NP_1 speaks of $Verb_2 ing$: *speak, talk, tell.*
      b. $Verb_1$ expresses reception of communication: *hear, learn.*
      c. $Verb_1$ expresses boasting, NP_1 boasts of $Verb_2 ing$: *boast, brag.*
      d. Others: *complain.*
   2. $Verb_2$ expresses a mental activity or a mental state:
      a. $Verb_1$ expresses thinking or dreaming: *conceive, think; dream.*
      b. $Verb_1$ expresses approval or disapproval, NP_1 (dis)approves of $Verb_2 ing$: *approve, disapprove.*
      c. Others: *beware, despair, repent, tire.*
   3. $Verb_1$ expresses dying: *die, perish.*
   4. $Verb_1$ expresses backing out of (doing something): *back out, chicken out, get out, wriggle out.*

B. NP_1 is –animate: *come; consist; admit; smack.*

From a syntactic point of view, it is easy to see that all verbs governing the pattern allow the sentential complement to be replaced with a nonsentential NP. *Complain* and *tire* may serve as cases in point, as witness the well-formedness of *John complained of my behavior* and *John tired of the long walk.* As far as the question of whether all verbs taking *of* followed by a nonsentential NP also govern *of -ing* is concerned, the discussion of analogous constructions involving other prepositional patterns in earlier chapters leads us to expect that the answer will be no. Examples here seem slightly harder to come by than in corresponding constructions in earlier chapters, but *dispose* and, as Ian Gurney has pointed out, *taste* and *smell,* in contrast to *smack,* do appear to be cases in point. They take *of* with NP complements with ease, as in *John's resolute action disposed of the problem* and *The stuff tastes/smells of rubber*, but sentential complements seem out of the question for these verbs. The existence of such verbs provides further confirmation of the conclusions reached in earlier chapters regarding the set versus subset relation of NP and sentential complements dependent on the preposition of the pattern in question.

The taxonomy seems useful in providing a framework for discussing control properties of the intransitive *of*-*ing* construction. Here verbs with +animate subjects overwhelmingly display a pattern of straightforward subject control, which is local in character. For instance, in *He told of spending several months with her* (modified from the example cited above), PRO is controlled by NP_1. *Approve* and *disapprove*, of A2b, do often allow—or even prefer, it may be felt—a PRO that is arbitrary, as in *John does not approve of making a public exhibition of himself/oneself*, but verbs of this kind appear to be a minority in class A. Further, the fact that most verbs of the intransitive *of*-*ing* construal are in class A emphasizes the role of local subject control in the analysis of the pattern.

As far as verbs of class B are concerned, NP_1 is generally inanimate, and typically it does not control PRO. Instead, arbitrary PROs seem common with most of these verbs, as, for instance, in *No good can come of contemplating these sad facts*, modified from the authentic example produced above. However, it is not the case that verbs of class B do not ever permit PROs in their subordinate clauses to be controlled. Whereas NP_1 does not in general act as a controller, a more remote controller may be recovered from elsewhere in the sentence, or indeed from outside the sentence, in ways that seem analogous to some patterns of remote control assignment observed in earlier chapters, including chapter 7. For instance, in *John's holiday consisted of working on a farm*, modified from the authentic example produced above, the NP_1, *John's holiday*, of course does not control PRO, the subject of *working on a farm*. However, the possessive *John's* does control PRO. It is also possible to shift the controller to the topic of the sentence, in a manner reminiscent of some control patterns in chapter 7. Thus in *As for John, a holiday consisted of working on a farm, As far as John is concerned, a holiday consisted of working on a farm,* and *In John's case, a holiday consisted of working on a farm*, the controller may be retrieved from the initial constituent that announces the topic of the sentence. (The first two sentences also permit arbitrary PROs.) Further, a remote controller may be recovered from outside the sentence, as in the sequence *John took a holiday. It consisted of working on a farm.*

With one or two verbs of class B, NP₁ may also be sentential with its own PRO. In this case, the PRO within the sentential NP₁ is typically coreferential with the PRO in the *of -ing* complement, which seems to be another instance of the PRO-to-PRO coreference phenomenon observed in chapter 7. For instance, a sentence such as *Giving a speech there consisted of standing on a box and haranguing the crowd* may be partially analyzed as in *[[[PRO]ᵢ giving a speech there] consisted of [[PRO]ᵢ standing on a box] and [[PRO]ᵢ haranguing the crowd]]*. The PROs in the sentence are arbitrary, referring to 'people in general' or to 'a certain subset of people in general relevant in the discourse in question,' but they refer to the same set or subset of people. The interpretation of PRO may also be restricted to involving a specified subset of people, and even to involving a subset of one, by providing the sentence with a suitable controller for PRO in a topic phrase, as in *As for John, giving a speech there consisted of standing on a box and haranguing the crowd*, *As far as John is concerned, giving a speech there consisted of standing on a box and haranguing the crowd*, or in *In John's case, giving a speech there consisted of standing on a box and haranguing the crowd*. In the first two of these sentences, an arbitrary PRO is not excluded, but in all three it is possible to interpret *John* (or *John's*) as the controller of PRO. (The third sentence seems restricted to this latter interpretation.)

In the light of this discussion, it appears that verbs of class B with inanimate NP₁s often involve arbitrary or remotely controlled PROs. However, this is not a categorical rule. For instance, *admit*, as in *These views admit of being argued to their consequences*, which is the example cited above, follows the pattern of NP₁ control, with PRO locally controlled by the subject of the matrix clause *these views*. Categorical rules cannot therefore be given, but it remains true that matrix verbs taking +animate NP₁s (class A) tend to go together with control by the NP in question, but those selecting –animate NP₁s tend to involve remote control or, when this fails for lack of a suitable controller, to have an arbitrary PRO.

The taxonomy also provides a suitable basis for considering the possibility of alternative patterns. In the case of A1a, alternative patterns with *about* and *on* are often available. *Speak* may serve as a case in point. Consider 3a–c.

(3) a. John spoke of feeling unwell.
　　b. John spoke about feeling unwell.
　　c. John spoke on feeling unwell.

Regarding *speak of -ing*, it seems closer to *speak about -ing* than to *speak on -ing*—on the latter two, see chapter 7—but conveys the idea of a "pure" assertion about NP_1 more straightforwardly and more exclusively than does *speak about -ing*. For instance, in 3a it is clear that PRO is controlled by NP_1 and although this control relation is likewise possible in 3b, the latter also allows a more general (or arbitrary) interpretation of PRO. The difference in control may contribute to a feeling that the *of -ing* construal is the more specific of the two. It may also be felt that *speak of -ing*, as in 3a, is slightly formal in flavor. (At the same time, *speak about -ing* is not necessarily informal; an informal way of phrasing the sentence might be *John said something about feeling unwell*.) The sense of the verb in *speak of -ing* may also be slightly different from what it is in *speak about -ing*: often, as in 3a, the former may be glossed as 'mention', whereas the latter may often, as in 3b, be glossed as 'mention and discuss'.[1] (I am indebted to Ian Gurney for discussing the alternation between *speak of -ing* and *speak about -ing*.)

Alternation with *about -ing* is also commonly found with verbs of A1b. *Hear* might be considered here. *Hear of -ing* seems the only possibility in *I will not hear of taking advantage of his predicament*, where the verb is construed with *will* and *not* and has the sense 'refuse to listen to' (OED, s.v., 7b), but otherwise the meanings of the two prepositional construals are not always very easy to tease apart, and there seems to be overlap between them, as in *John heard of/about being selected for promotion too late*. [At the same time, Schibsbye's (1970, 307) suggestion that *"I've heard about it* = 'I have heard talk of it' " deserves to be mentioned.] As far as verbs of boasting (A1c) are concerned, *about -ing* is again often an alternative. However, *boast* may have an inanimate subject and carry or emphasize the meaning of 'have', as in the example cited above from the Brown Corpus (*foods that boast of having almost no food value at all*), and in this meaning *about -ing* is not a very likely alternative (*??foods that boast about having almost no food value at all*). With +animate NP_1s, *about -ing* is an alternative, but with a slightly different meaning, as witness 4a–b:

(4) a. John boasted/bragged of doing it all himself.
    b. John boasted/bragged about doing it all himself.

Both 4a and 4b express self-aggrandizement, but *boast of -ing* and *brag of -ing* in 4a tend to imply the meaning of 'assert', the boast being an assertion, and quite possibly a contested one. For their part, *boast about -ing* and *brag about -ing* in 4b may suggest an assertion, but they may also suggest that the content and the truth of S_2 is viewed as something not so much asserted as more generally recognized or accepted by the speaker and the hearer. The difference may be substantiated in at least two ways. First, if a *that* clause variant is constructed for 4a–b, as in *John boasted/bragged that he had done it all himself,* it is observed that it is closer in sense to 4a than to 4b. Further, if the content of the boast is presented as a fact in a sentence, there is a clear preference for the *about* construal, as in this example devised by Ian Gurney: *He is a rich man, but he does not boast about/??of being rich.*

A similar kind of difference may often be felt in the case of *complain* from A1d, as in *John complained of/about being passed over for promotion.* Intuitions here are sometimes hazier, but for at least some speakers, the meaning of *complain of -ing* veers toward 'claim that', while that of *complain about -ing* is often felt to be more factive and even paraphrasable as 'take exception to the fact that'. (These paraphrases are due to Robert Cooper.)

As far as verbs of class 2 are concerned, prepositional patterns other than *of -ing* do not easily come to mind for most of them, including *conceive, beware, despair and repent. Approve,* of A2b, allows a nonprepositional *-ing* pattern, but there is a fairly clear difference in meaning between the two construals. For instance, if we compare *The Cabinet approved of calling off the campaign against the opposition* and *The Cabinet approved calling off the campaign against the opposition,* the former may be paraphrased 'the Cabinet thought that it was a good idea to call off the campaign against the opposition' and the latter 'the Cabinet gave the go-ahead to calling off the campaign against the opposition'. On the other hand, for *think* and *dream,* construals with *about -ing* are very common, often with meanings resembling those of corresponding *of -ing* construals. Of the range of meanings available to *think of -ing,* that of 'come up with the idea of' seems specific to this construal, as in *How did you think of/??about solving the problem that way?* This usage aside, we might consider 5a–b:

(5) a. John thought of visiting Italy./John was thinking of visiting Italy.
    b. John thought about visiting Italy./John was thinking about visiting Italy.

It may be suggested that *think of -ing* in 5a may convey awareness of the option or course of action expressed by the lower clause, and that

5b may imply more prolonged or deliberate consideration of it. Some support for this kind of distinction may perhaps be garnered from a difference that arises if the insertion of manner adverbs such as *very carefully* is considered. This adverb is not very compatible with *of -ing*, although it is fine with *about -ing*: ??*John was thinking very carefully of visiting Italy* and *John was thinking very carefully about visiting Italy*. At the same time, the difference between the two patterns in sentences such as 5a–b may be fairly subtle and should not be exaggerated. [On comparing the *think of -ing* and *think to* infinitive construals, see Wierzbicka (1988, 30 f.).]

As for *dream*, it may have the sense of 'conceive', 'imagine', especially when combined with a negative (cf. OED, s.v., 5). In this sense of *dream*, *of -ing* is clearly more idiomatic than *about -ing*, as in *I would not dream of/??about suggesting anything like that to him*. However, when dream means 'have hopes of', it is often more difficult to separate the two patterns, as in *John dreamed about/of winning the pools*.

As for verbs of class 3, construals with *from -ing* are available, with meanings that seem similar to those of *of -ing*, as in *They died of/from eating mushrooms*. *Come*, from class B, allows *from -ing*, with a meaning similar to that of *of -ing*, as in *This comes of/from misinterpreting the facts*; but with the remaining verbs alternative construals do not come to mind as easily, it being taken for granted that meanings should remain at least approximately constant. (*Consist in -ing*, with a slightly different sense from *consist of ing*, was treated in chapter 2.)

Overall, this survey of distributional alternation suggests that quite a high percentage of verbs governing *of -ing* also select some other pattern of complementation. To a significant extent, alternation interacts with the taxonomy proposed in that the choice of an alternative construction varies depending not only on individual matrix verbs but on classes of verbs in the taxonomy. Overall, *about -ing* is the most common and the most systematically occurring alternative construal available, especially with verbs of A1a–c and with *think* and *dream* of class A2. In some cases semantic differences, of a more or less delicate nature, are discernible between *of -ing* and the alternative. This holds for alternation between *of -ing* and *about -ing* as far as verbs of class A1c are concerned, where *of -ing* construals tend to imply assertions and *about -ing* construals tend to present the content of S_2 as something given or accepted. Further, some uses and senses of other verbs governing both are restricted to *of -ing*. However, in other cases—especially with verbs expressing communication, or reception of communication—the two alternative constructions may sometimes be rather close semantically. From a historical perspective, it appears that *about* constructions (with *about* carrying the approximate sense 'concerning'), at least with NP complements, have been in general spreading over the last few centuries [see Brorström (1963, 11ff.)]. Today there are a number of verbs for which the *of -ing* pattern is the only construal possible, including *beware, despair, disapprove,* and *smack*. However, neither the overall number nor the proportion of such verbs that only govern *of -ing* is very large, and verbs of this type that do exist do not appear to be very common in the pattern. On the other hand, verbs such as *think* and *speak* that select both *of -ing* and *about -ing* occur much more frequently in these construals. Such ready availability of alternative construals with meanings that are sometimes not that much different and the relative dearth of frequently occurring verbs restricted to the intransitive *of -ing* pattern mean that the future of the intransitive *of -ing* pattern will bear watching, with respect to both the degree and the nature of semantic differentiation of the two patterns, and with respect to the overall status and stability of the intransitive *of -ing* pattern.

III

In this section verbs governing the transitive *of -ing* pattern will be presented and illustrated, first from the two corpora and then from Poutsma (1929, 906). Then I will present verbs from Bridgeman et al. (1965, 35), with freely invented illustrations.

Verbs	Illustrations and Comments
accuse	*Uncle Sam would then accuse them of creating a monopoly by "unfair competition"* [Brown A36 0580-0590, from W. Gomberg, "Unions and the Anti-Trust Laws" (*The Nation* 193: 16)]. To judge by the evidence of the two corpora, this is the most common verb selecting the pattern.
assure	*Since charges are relatively the same, reserving a car before you leave for Europe will assure you of having one on tap when you want it* [Brown E36 0440-0460, from E. Norling, "Renting a Car in Europe" (*Playbill* 5:11)]. The verb may also be acceptable, at least to some speakers, in a different pattern of control, as in *?John assured*

me of being ready to help, where PRO is controlled by NP₁. However, the usage seems so marginal that it will not be considered further here.

convict — Let us look at the heavy-electrical-goods industry in which General Electric, Westinghouse and a number of other manufacturers were recently convicted of engaging in a conspiracy to rig prices and allocate the market [Brown A36 0440-0460, from W. Gomberg, "Unions and the Anti-Trust Laws" (*The Nation* 193: 16)].

suspect — The questions women asked at baseball games were standard grist for amateur comedy, as were the doings of women automobile drivers; for every grown man (except a few who were always suspected of being shy on virility) knew at least the fundamentals of baseball, just as every male American in this era liked to imagine (or pretend) that he could fight with his fists [Brown F38 1640-1680, from R. Smith, *Baseball in America* (Holt, Rinehart and Winston)]. The evidence of the corpora suggests that this is the second-most-common verb selecting the pattern.

acquit — We cannot acquit him of having done what, if not in itself evil, was yet of evil example [Poutsma (1929, 906), from Macaulay, *Lord Clive*, 522a].

cure — If you can compass it, do cure the younger girls of running after the officers [Poutsma (1929, 906), from Jane Austen, *Pride and Prejudice*, chap. 10, 56].

absolve — John's statement absolved me of feeling guilty for the accident.

clear — The jury cleared the prisoner of conspiring to assassinate the president.

condemn — The jury condemned John of conspiring to pervert the cause of justice. Not all speakers are happy with this construction in present-day English, with the approximate meaning of 'pronounce guilty of a crime or a fault' (cf. the OED, s.v. 4, with illustrations of NP complements), where S_2 names the crime or fault in question. (*Condemn* may, of course, select infinitival or *to -ing* construals, in which case S_2 names something that NP_0 is to suffer or to undergo. For illustration and discussion of these construals and their meanings, see chap. 4.) At best, the verb can be included here only with considerable hesitation.

disabuse	*His words disabused me of feeling kindly toward him.*
exonerate	*John exonerated me of interfering in his affairs.*
free	*New information freed John of feeling guilty for the accident.*
insure	*Making a reservation will insure the traveler of having a car on tap on arrival.* The example is modeled on the authentic example of *assure* above. The verb is not very common in this pattern. This comment also appears to apply to the British English spelling variant *ensure*.
relieve	*What John said relieved me of feeling under any obligation toward him.*
remind	*Working in this department reminds me of being a recruit in the Army.*

It seems that a fairly small number of semantic classes is sufficient to characterize meanings of verbs governing the object controlled *of -ing* pattern. The following taxonomy suggests itself:

1. Verb$_1$ expresses freeing or clearing, NP$_1$ frees or clears NP$_0$ of Verb$_2$*ing*: *absolve, acquit, clear, disabuse, exonerate, free; cure, relieve.*
2. Verb$_1$ implies that NP$_1$ places the responsibility for what S_2 expresses on NP$_0$: *suspect; accuse; condemn, convict.*
3. Others: *assure, insure; remind.*

The small number of semantic classes that are required for the characterization of matrix verbs governing NP$_0$ *of* Verb$_2$*ing* in the taxonomy above is no doubt connected with the relatively small number of such verbs. Among the verbs listed, *accuse* and *suspect* are the most frequent by far, to judge by the evidence of the two corpora, with *acquit* and *convict* being the only other verbs that are found in the pattern with any frequency. Three of these belong to class 2, with *acquit* in class 1.

Both class 1 and class 2 are clearly core classes of the pattern. Indeed they are not unrelated. Rather in a sense they are antithetical. Verbs of class 2 mean basically that NP_1 lays something, a suspicion, an accusation—whatever is expressed by S_2—to the charge of NP_0: those of class 1, on the other hand, mean that NP_1 relieves NP_0 of something, again of a suspicion, an accusation—whatever is expressed by S_2. In either case S_2 expresses something that is compromising or in some sense disreputable or undesirable in the world of values of NP_0 and NP_1.

As far as semantic features of NP_0 are concerned, it seems that verbs in the present pattern typically select +animate direct objects. In the case of classes 1 and 2, this no doubt follows from the meanings identified as characteristic of them, but the finding also holds for the more disparate verbs of class 3.

Verbs of class 1, then, carry the meaning of absolving or freeing: NP_1 absolves or frees NP_0 of Verb$_2$*ing*, as in *absolve someone of feeling guilty, clear someone of conspiring to assassinate the president, cure someone of running after somebody* (see the illustrations above). In view of such a meaning, there is what may be called a presupposition to the effect that at one (earlier) point in time, NP_0 had the property, or was assumed to have the property, that is expressed by the lower clause. For instance, it would not make much sense to say *The experience cured them of running after the soldiers* if the speaker did not believe that they had done so at one time. [See here Ladusaw and Dowty's (1988, 66) comments on the semantics of *cure, deprive,* and other similar verbs.] (In the case of *clear*, it is more a question of NP_1 harboring a suspicion about what NP_0 had done.) In the case of verbs of class 2, it seems harder to speak of a presupposition (which would be reversed in this case). After all, one can accuse or suspect someone of doing something even if the person in question has already been accused or is already under suspicion. At the same time, there may still be a weaker Gricean implicature, of an earlier "innocent" state of NP_0, present in the case of verbs of class 2, to give point to an accusation or a suspicion.

The present pattern is similar to many of those illustrated above in that all verbs governing it allow the sentential complement to be replaced with a nonsentential NP, as witness the well-formedness of *They exonerated John of all responsibility for the debacle* and *They assured John of their continued support*. On the other hand, there are verbs allowing a pattern with *of* followed by a nonsentential complement that do not allow the complement to be sentential. *Rob* and *strip* are cases in point, as witness *The muggers robbed John of his watch/*The muggers robbed John of possessing a watch*, and *They stripped John of his shirt/*They stripped John of wearing his shirt*. In this pattern, then, analogously to many others in earlier chapters, it can be seen that the set of verbs governing NP_0 *of* *-ing* is a subset of those selecting NP_0 *of* $NP_{nonsentential}$.

A second syntactic generalization, more specific to the present transitive object control pattern, suggests itself in the light of the verbs brought together in the taxonomy. It concerns the syntactic status of NP_0 and the relation of the present object control pattern to the two versions of B's generalization, as introduced in chapter 4. It appears that NP_0 is typically obligatory and nonomissible with verbs of all classes and that these verbs do not have intransitive uses, at least not with *of -ing*. For instance, *accuse* and *remind*, chosen from different classes, are cases in point. Neither **Uncle Sam would then accuse of creating a monopoly*, from *Uncle Sam would then accuse them of creating a monopoly*, nor **Working in this department reminds of being a recruit in the Army*, from *Working in this department reminds me of being in the Army*, is possible. In other words, the present discussion suggests that verbs of this object control pattern observe the strong form of B's generalization. This conclusion is significant from a comparative perspective. As will be recalled, most verbs of the other two object control patterns treated in this book, those of NP_0 *to -ing* and NP_0 *with -ing*, also observed the strong version of B's generalization. Verbs of the present pattern are now seen to observe the strong form of the generalization even more overwhelmingly. From a broader perspective, this finding emphasizes the need to distinguish the two versions of the generalization, for they make possible a structured discussion of the data.

Control properties of the present transitive *of -ing* pattern seem relatively straightforward, for if the examples of usage above are considered, it seems that PRO is locally controlled by NP_0 in a very regular fashion. This is so, for instance, in *They accused John of stealing a car*. In view of control properties that came to light in the treatment of the transitive *with -ing* pattern in chapter 7 (for instance, recall *link* and *associate*), it is possible to surmise that the regularity with which verbs of the present pattern involve straightforward local object control is related to the typically obligatory presence of a +animate direct object with verbs of the pattern. One or two verbs of the pattern, including *remind*, select or may select sentential subjects with PROs of their own, as in *Working in this department reminds me of being a draftee in the Army,* but this does not affect object control. (The two PROs are both controlled by *me,* which means that they are also coreferential with each other.)

Regarding the position of the *of -ing* object control construction in the broader system of object control in English, it will be recalled that verbs selecting the NP_0 *to -ing* construal (chap. 4), such as *reduce,* are amenable to analysis on the basis of the notion of influencing (emanating from the referent of NP_1 to that of NP_0). In chapter 7 it was observed that the same notion is useful in the analysis of two subclasses of the NP_0 *with -ing* pattern, but that an additional object control type had to be admitted, viz., the ascriptive or imputative type. (The ascriptive type has to do with NP_1 making claims about the actions or properties of NP_0.) As far as verbs of the present NP_0 *of -ing* pattern are concerned, it seems that the notion of influencing as an analytic tool is of rather limited usefulness. The imputative type of object control is far more widely relevant, especially with regard to verbs of class 2, which includes such common verbs as *suspect* and *accuse.* Many verbs of class 1 may be analyzed in basically similar terms, by way of reversal: now it is not a question of the referent of NP_1 ascribing some action or property to the referent of NP_0 but of exonerating or absolving the latter of such an imputation. Because of the notion of reversal relevant here, it seems that no new control type is needed. On the other hand, the present NP_0 *of -ing* control pattern confirms the status of the ascriptive or imputative type as a major type in the analysis of object control.

With regard to distributional alternation between the present pattern and others, there seems to be little of it. The *of -ing* pattern seems specific and even unique to most verbs of classes 1 and 2. It is especially noteworthy that with respect to sentential complementation, the four verbs that are by far the most frequent in the pattern, viz., *accuse, suspect, acquit,* and *convict,* all are uniquely restricted to the *of -ing* pattern. Virtually the only area of distributional overlap in regard to classes 1 and 2 concerns some verbs of class 1 that allow *from -ing,* as in *What the witness said freed John from feeling guilty.* Apart from this area, *condemn* allows *for -ing,* as in *They condemned John for stealing a car,* which is possible alongside of *They condemned John of stealing a car.* (It must be repeated that not all speakers accept the *of -ing* construal with *condemn* at all.) However, this has a different flavor, in that the *of -ing* construal, to the extent that the latter is possible at all, suggests that the condemnation came about as a result of a judicial proceeding, whereas the *for*

-ing construal, which is more generally acceptable, lacks that narrow implication. As for verbs of class 3, alternative construals do not immediately spring to mind. *Remind* is an exception, for it is not limited to *of -ing* but also takes *about -ing*. However, the meanings of the two construals are rather different. With *of -ing*, as in *Working in this department reminds me of being a recruit in the Army*, the verb may be glossed 'bring to mind because of a likeness' (Ian Gurney, personal communication), whereas with *about -ing*, as in *He reminded me about going to the meeting*, the verb has the approximate sense "point something out that the addressee ought to remember'.

Overall, the present discussion suggests that as far as distributional alternation is concerned, the transitive *of -ing* construal is more clearly delimited against alternative patterns than is the intransitive *of -ing* pattern. The number of verbs in the present transitive pattern is admittedly rather small. However, four of these verbs are quite common. These four are all restricted to *of -ing*. Further, the semantic range of meanings of verbs of the transitive *of -ing* pattern is relatively well defined. Indeed, the two core classes seem semantically related to each other. The four verbs are all members of one of these two core classes. These considerations suggest that the transitive *of -ing* pattern is a healthy one in present-day English, with a well-defined grammatical domain.

9

Concluding Observations

The preceding seven chapters provide a discussion of nine predicate complement constructions in present-day English. In each of them the type of complementation in question is identified on the basis of syntactic properties as explicitly as possible. This prepares the way for the task of collecting a reasonable sample of verbs that select the pattern. The discussions provided in individual chapters demonstrate that the task of data collection is by no means a trivial exercise. They also demonstrate that the Brown and LOB corpora are very valuable resources, especially in providing authentic data in a context that can easily be checked by the investigator. However, it was also seen repeatedly that even actually occurring corpus data cannot be accepted without reflection. A case in point occurred as early as in chapter 2, where it was shown how the verb *concentrate* is attested in one of the corpora as occurring with the *in -ing* pattern. In spite of this, speakers today in general do not find this construal acceptable and instead prefer the *on -ing* construction for *concentrate*. Conflicts of this type are infrequent, but they show the need for constant vigilance even with corpus data. When such conflicts do occur, intuitions of native speakers must be arbiters, provided that these are sufficiently definite and sufficiently widely held.

Data from the Brown and LOB corpora are valuable when used with care. However, it will also have become clear how desirable it is to have access to other sources of data—quite apart from native speaker intuitions, which ultimately play an overriding role. Even if additional and larger standard corpora had been available to me, it may be suspected that other sources of recorded usage would still have been welcome and necessary. As far as such other sources that were available are concerned, a tribute is due here to Poutsma (1905, 1929, MS). Of course, not even what he says can be accepted blindly, at least not from the point of view of present-day English. However, his collections of usage are a most valuable resource. Further, his observations on usage and alternations of usage are almost invariably to the point and a continuing source of inspiration for work on English grammar. Indeed from the vantage point of today, it almost strains credulity how he was often able to sum up a complex issue with a simple statement that expresses what is essential. Apart from Poutsma, Bridgeman et al. (1965) was also a most valuable resource. Verbs there are given in the form of lists, without any illustration, for the most part. This means that anyone using the lists will sometimes need imagination and ingenuity to think up examples. This task is generally the more difficult the more marginal a verb is in a given construction.

It would be presumptuous to claim that the sets of verbs that are considered here exhaust the resources of the English language as far as the nine patterns of complementation are concerned. No doubt other verbs can be found. At the same time, the reliance on the corpora and other sources of recorded usage in this book may insure that additional verbs are not likely to be very frequent in the patterns under review here.

The business of data collection, on a syntactic basis, is an essential task if the investigation of the nine patterns is to be placed on a solid foundation. However, data collection is only an initial step. In order to shed light on the patterns in question, it is essential systematically to characterize the matrix verbs collected. Here this is done on a semantic basis. The taxonomies are proposed to express generalizations about sense relations of matrix verbs, and it is often possible to substantiate them with the help of notions such as entailment. No doubt there are details of the taxonomies proposed here that can be improved upon in subsequent work, for instance, by capturing more sense relations of verbs and by making the groupings more tightly coherent. However, even in their present form, the taxonomies are significant because they offer characterizations of senses of matrix verbs in a systematic and structured way. One important aspect here is that they are designed to provide representations of the core classes of verbs that govern individual patterns of complementation. Such core classes may be taken to provide an answer to the question of what meaning or meanings are typically associated with matrix verbs in each pattern.

Concluding Observations

It is probably useful to summarize some of the findings of the individual chapters here, so as to flesh out the notion of core classes. In the case of the *in -ing* pattern, discussed in chapter 2, matrix verbs typically express such senses as 'be equated with', 'feel joy or pleasure in', 'perform the act of' (or 'carry out the activity of'), and 'agree in'. Verbs governing the subject controlled *to -ing* pattern, covered in chapter 3, have either + or –animate subjects. In the former case, they typically have meanings such as 'turn to', 'keep to', or they express communication with some rather special shade of additional meaning, such as admitting. Verbs governing the object controlled *to -ing* pattern, discussed in chapter 4, were found to be semantically rather homogeneous in that their range of meanings is restricted to senses such as 'act on' or 'move'—NP_1 moves NP_0 to realize/realizing S_2—'limit' or 'give over'. Verbs governing *at -ing*, treated in chapter 5, are more numerous, but they may still be accommodated in relatively few classes. They may carry meanings such as 'show unwillingness (to do something)', they may express emotions such as criticism, anger, disgust, pain, sorrow, etc., or they may express intention, engagement, or effort, real or pretended, on the part of NP_1 with regard to, or directed to, the realization of S_2. Verbs governing *on -ing*, discussed in chapter 6, are again plentiful in number, even though it should be added that not all of them are very common in the pattern. Their analysis, it is suggested, requires the setting up of some ten classes, with verbs expressing notions such as thinking, verbal communication, deciding or planning, concentration, engagement, dependence, making use of, initiation, and proximity. The class of verbs selecting the subject controlled *with -ing* pattern, treated in the first part of chapter 7, is similarly very large in terms of the number of verbs belonging to it, but some of the verbs in question are more common with nonsentential NPs following *with*. Matrix verbs of the pattern divide into groups depending on whether NP_1 is typically +animate or –animate. Most subclasses are on the +animate side, with meanings such as 'grapple with', 'play around with', 'to do away with', 'cope with', 'bother with', and 'begin with'. On the –animate side, verbs of the pattern express meanings such as 'compare with' or 'harmonize with'. Verbs selecting the transitive *with -ing* construal are far fewer in number, but not necessarily less common in terms of actual usage. On the +animate side here, core classes express meanings such as 'burden someone with', 'acquaint someone with', or 'ascribe to someone what is expressed by S_2'. On the –animate side, matrix verbs typically mean 'associate someone with doing something or being something'. Verbs governing *of -ing*, discussed in chapter 8, are much fewer in number, though some of them are quite common, even in the *of -ing* construal. Most verbs of the intransitive (subject controlled) *of -ing* pattern select +animate subjects and express communication, reception of communication, boasting, thinking, or dreaming. Verbs governing the transitive (object controlled) *of -ing* pattern also select +animate subjects, even more exclusively than verbs of the intransitive *of -ing* pattern, and they express two families of meanings that are almost diametrically opposed to each other: either 'free or clear someone of what is expressed by the lower clause' or 'lay to someone's charge what is expressed by the lower clause'. The overall number of verbs in either class is small, but there are some very common verbs that govern the pattern, and most of these have the second type of meaning.

The setting up of core classes on the basis of meaning is an important feature of the taxonomies. It is also observed repeatedly in the book how the taxonomies and the core classes provide a framework for analyzing additional properties, both syntactic and semantic, of the nine patterns. They are helpful in particular in structuring the discussion of distributional alternation permitted by the verbs in question, considered here in the individual chapters with a focus on cases where the meaning of the matrix verb remains at least approximately constant. In some of the patterns, there is little or relatively little distributional alternation, whereas in others there is more of it. Where alternation is found, it is perhaps inevitable that some of it should be random or idiosyncratic. However, it is seen in virtually every chapter that the availability of alternation and also the type of alternation available vary in significant ways depending on the semantic type of the verb in question as specified in the taxonomy and as reflected in the core classes. The consideration of alternation is also observed to shed light, from a comparative point of view, on the question of the characteristic meaning or meanings associated with the pattern in question. This is especially so when patterns of fairly widespread and systematic alternation are found. A case in point here is provided by the transitive *to -ing* construal, treated in chapter 4, in that it displays a noticeable degree of systematic variation with the corresponding *to* infinitive pattern, perhaps partly because of the obvious surface-level similarity of the two constructions, but no doubt also because of a striking semantic similarity of matrix verbs governing them. (It is observed in chap. 3 that matrix verbs governing the intransitive *to -ing* pattern display less semantic similarity with verbs governing the corresponding *to* infinitive pattern, and that even though there is some alternation between the two intransitive patterns, it is less widespread.) Suggestions are offered in chapter 4 on the typical meaning or meanings of the transitive *to -ing* pattern when found in alternation with the corresponding *to* infinitive construal.

Further, and again from a semantic point of view, the taxonomies are seen to shed light on control properties of the nine patterns. For the majority of verbs considered here, it is observed that PRO, the understood subject of a complement clause, is necessarily controlled and not arbitrary in reference. More specifically, it is in general the case that in subject control constructions, PRO is necessarily and exclusively controlled by the subject of the matrix clause, and in object control constructions it is necessarily and exclusively controlled by the object of the matrix clause. Control assignment of these types is local in nature. However, the investigation of the grammatical patterns also brings to light verbs that are associated with other types of control relations. Thus PRO may sometimes be arbitrary in reference, or it may be subject to control assignment by a more remote controller. It is argued that different types of control do not occur randomly but are linked to aspects of the semantic taxonomies presented, in that control properties of matrix verbs vary in systematic ways depending on the semantic type of the verb in question.

Three object control patterns are considered. Their investigation is seen to relate to Bach's generalization, which has so far been substantiated in the literature, at least for the most part, on the basis of infinitival patterns. To accommodate the range of data uncovered here, it is suggested that the generalization should be split up into a strong and a weak form. Both preserve the idea that the direct object is not omissible in an object control construction, but the strong form of the generalization, renamed B's generalization, in addition excludes intransitive subject control uses for verbs that trigger object control, whereas the weak form does not. It is suggested that the strong form of B's generalization holds for the overwhelming majority of matrix verbs in all three object control structures. At the same time, the investigation identifies a number of verbs for which the strong form of the generalization does not hold. The weak form of the generalization holds for these. Further, it is observed that the incidence of such verbs varies depending on the type of syntactic pattern in question. In particular, verbs of the transitive *of -ing* construal, it is suggested in chapter 8, observe the strong form of B's generalization in a most regular fashion. Further, as far as the other two object control patterns are concerned, it is observed that the alternation of the strong and the weak form of the generalization and the necessity of the latter are not random but rather at least to some extent related to the taxonomies in question.

Another broad syntactic result of the book is the finding that all matrix verbs in all of the patterns considered allow the lower sentence to be replaced with a nonsentential NP. That is, to use a term from traditional grammar, the lower clause is invariably a nominal clause. Of equal or even greater significance is the concomitant finding that the converse generalization does not hold. There are verbs selecting a preposition found in a sentential pattern considered here that do not allow a following nonsentential NP to be replaced with a sentential complement. This finding was substantiated in the individual chapters of the book, and it was seen to hold for virtually all of the nine patterns. The regularity with which this conclusion holds suggests a generalization to the effect that classes of verbs selecting sentential complementation patterns introduced by prepositions are a subset of classes of verbs selecting the prepositions in question. This conclusion also provides justification for the focus of the book on sentential constructions.

It should be recognized that the full grammar of prepositional complementation in present-day English remains a major research task for the future. However, it may be hoped that the discussions and conclusions of this investigation will remain intact even when this undertaking is complete, and indeed that they may represent a contribution to such a comprehensive grammar.

Notes

Notes to Chapter 1

1. Poutsma (MS) should be added to these works by Poutsma, but regrettably, it still remains unpublished. I am indebted to Frits Stuurman, of the University of Utrecht, for drawing my attention to it in the first place and for making the unpublished manuscript available to me, with the kind permission of Oxford University Press. Thanks to this, it is possible to supplement data from Poutsma's published grammars with data from Poutsma (MS) where this seems appropriate, as will be indicated in the individual chapters.

2. The attention I devote to the investigation of alternation and of the typical semantic function or functions of each type of complementation considered may perhaps be viewed in relation to, and against the background of, such earlier work on complementation in English as Bolinger (1968), Dixon (1984), Wierzbicka (1988, 24 ff.) and Langacker (1991, 438 ff.). Work in this tradition has emphasized the semantic distinctiveness of different types of constructions in the field of English complementation and the desirability of identifying the semantic distinctions involved in as systematic a way as possible. Bolinger's (1968, 127) dictum that "a difference in syntactic form always spells a difference in meaning" may be extreme and is no doubt hard to verify completely, but it expresses a heuristic strategy, or a default assumption, that seems fruitful in guiding the investigation of alternation, as is seen repeatedly in the individual chapters of this book when the patterns considered here are

compared with other construals selected by the same matrix verbs. This perhaps only stands to reason, for as Bolinger (1968, 127) goes on to say, "a language that permitted syntactic divergences to be *systematically* redundant would represent a strange kind of economy" (emphasis in the original).

Notes to Chapter 2

1. For X bar theory in general, see Chomsky (1970), Jackendoff (1977), Stuurman (1985), Chomsky (1986a), and Pollock (1989). The problem in the present context is that a rule such as NP → S, which would express the nominal character of gerund clauses in a simple and economical way, runs afoul of the X bar convention, to the effect that "for any major category X, an XP is always headed by an X" (Baker 1985, 2). The problem has been addressed, of course. Thus Chomsky (1981, 49), when referring to "gerunds or clauses (if these are NPs)," speaks of "NPs that have no lexical N as head." This renders such NPs exceptions to the X bar convention. Also, Baker (1985, 2ff.) proposes ingeniously that gerunds are sentences in deep structure but are turned into NPs in surface structure, on account of *-ing*. Such proposals serve to underline the continuing importance of the concept of a nominal clause, but their details cannot be pursued here. In any case, X bar theory itself is still in the process of being refined, as is clear from Kornai and Pullum (1990).

2. Information on sources of corpus texts is from Francis and Kučera (1979, 33 ff.), for texts of the Brown corpus, and from Johansson et al. (1978, 42 ff.), for texts of the LOB corpus. All the Brown and LOB corpus texts relevant here are from the year 1961, and the date of publication is therefore not repeated in references to individual texts from the two corpora.

3. For discussion of control and of approaches, partly conflicting with each other, to its analysis, see Manzini (1983), Mohanan (1983, 1985), Lebeaux (1984), Comrie (1984, 1985), Huang (1984, 1989), Culicover and Wilkins (1986), Chomsky (1986b, 124 ff.) and Sag and Pollard (1991). The discussion of control here is indebted to Chomsky (1986b, 124 ff.), especially with regard to the notion of local control.

4. Thompson (1973) proposes interesting generalizations for predicting which matrix verbs and predicates selecting *-ing* complements require a control interpretation and which allow a noncontrol interpre-

tation. Her main generalizations are that predicates that allow a noncontrol interpretation are "public," describing an activity "which is generally shared" (Thompson 1973, 381). Thus "verbs of communication... are 'public' verbs almost by definition; so are causative verbs..., which involve objectively perceivable results" (Thompson 1973, 381). As for control interpretations: "The semantic property shared by the predicates in..., which require a controlled interpretation, is what we might call 'privateness'. These verbs involve an individual and his private thoughts, feelings, and personal welfare; no one but the individual himself need know that the proposition expressed by one of these verbs is true." (Thompson 1973, 381). In the first group, public verbs, she lists verbs such as *advocate, denounce, criticize, propose, object to, (dis)approve of, bring up,* and others. The second group, private verbs, includes *contemplate, like, dread, endure, prefer, remember, risk, conceive of, enjoy, relish, imagine, forget, feel like,* and others.

Thompson's project of interrelating control properties of matrix verbs with their semantic properties is to be commended. At the same time, her conclusions need careful attention. Her lists of verbs include one or two that select prepositional constructions, but her focus is undoubtedly on matrix verbs selecting nonprepositional *-ing* clauses. Conclusions based on nonprepositional *-ing* clauses cannot automatically be extended to the analysis of prepositional *-ing* clauses. One example of this is provided by Comrie (1985, 65), who considers the *from -ing* construal selected by *dissuade* and observes that object control is found in *He dissuaded us from going.* (It seems hard not to regard *dissuade* as a verb of communication and therefore as a public verb; yet it requires control.) With regard to the verbs of the *in -ing* pattern, verbs of class 2 are private, in Thompson's terms, and her generalization therefore accounts for control found with them. However, *believe* is likewise private, and the possibility of an arbitrary interpretation is therefore not predicted. Further, it seems hard to regard class 3 verbs such as *engage* as private. Control found with them therefore indicates the need for a more nuanced treatment of matrix verbs governing prepositions and *-ing* clauses.

    5. The term "remote control" is often used to characterize control in sentences such as *John thinks it is illegal [PRO to feed himself]* [Chomsky (1986b, 125, 144ii)] and *John thinks that PRO to behave himself is important for Mary* [from Huang (1989, 210, iii in n. 13)]. As Huang (1989, 210, n. 13), who uses the term "long-distance control,"

observes, notions such as c-command and command may play a role in the determination of the controller in such sentences [see also Chomsky (1986b, 125 f.)]. In the case of the kind of remote control observed with verbs of class 1, c-command and command seem less relevant to the determination of the controller, as witness the sentences considered in the text. Rather, it seems that control patterns with verbs of class 1 are similar in a significant respect to those with the verb *be* in sentences such as *All he wanted was to be able to wash himself in the morning* and *He had just one wish. It was to be able to wash himself in the morning.* [Cf., in this connection, also the interpretation of PRO in this sentence from Lebeaux (1984, 272, n. 1): *PRO to see Mary is a thing that I think John enjoys.*] Admittedly, the two patterns are not entirely identical. Thus when NP_1 expresses communication, a sentence with *be to* tends to express a paraphrase of what was communicated, as in *His advice to me was PRO to read his own book,* where PRO is controlled by *me* (the NP expressing the addressee), whereas verbs of class 1 mean that the content of NP_1 is equated, or nearly equated, with the content of S_2, as in *His advice to me consisted in PRO reading his new book,* where PRO is controlled by *his,* the subject of NP_1, analogously to 17a–b. This difference aside, control patterns across verbs of class 1 and across *be* seem similar with regard to the possibility of recovering a remote antecedent for PRO, in the absence of c-command or command. The similarity regarding control seems to be underpinned by semantic proximity. The meaning of *be* in the relevant examples is specificational [cf. Higgins (1973a, chap. 4); cf. also Lebeaux (1984, 272, n. 1)]. For instance, the sentence *All he wanted was to be able to wash himself* might be paraphrased 'all he wanted was this: to be able to wash himself'. As Higgins (1973a, 163) observes with reference to the verbs *lie* and *consist* (in patterns that are relevant to the present discussion), these verbs "can be construed as having a meaning close to that of specification." The equative gloss given to verbs of class 1, it may be suggested, expresses the specificational flavor of sentences with these verbs.

Notes to Chapter 3

1. A further criterion of NP status, proposed by Emonds (1976, 132ff.) but not adopted in this book, concerns the focus position of a cleft sentence, as in *It was borrowing money that John resorted to.* Since this sentence is good, the complement clause of the present pattern

passes this test as well. However, care should be exercised here, for Emonds's cleft sentence test does not necessarily define the same class of sentences as the four tests cited in the text. For instance, consider the *that* clause in *Bill regretted that Sue had cashed the check* [modeled on one of Emonds's (1976, 133) examples]. This passes the four tests: Q. *What did Bill regret?* A. *That Sue had cashed the check; Bill regretted that Sue had cashed the check, but others did not regret it/that; Bill regretted it, that Sue had cased the check; What Bill regretted was that Sue had cashed the check.* The *that* clause would no doubt be a nominal clause in the description of, for instance, Quirk et al. (1985, 1047 ff.). However, it does not pass the cleft sentence test, because *It was that Sue had cashed the check that Bill regretted* is bad [cf. Emonds (1976, 133)]. In view of such differences, the cleft sentence test is not cited in the text.

Notes to Chapter 7

1. The kind of coreference observed between the PROs in sentence 2 seems similar to the interpretation of arbitrary PROs in a number of sentences discussed by Lebeaux (1984, 260 ff.). He does not focus on *with -ing* construals, but his observations on sentences such as those reproduced as i and ii are of interest here.

i. PRO making a large profit (as a landlord) requires PRO exploiting tenants.
ii. PRO becoming a movie star entails/involves PRO being recognized by everyone.

As Lebeaux (1984, 260) observes with regard sentences such as i–ii, "while the reference of each PRO ranges over some universal set of entities (the domain restricted by context), the element picked out by the two PRO_{arb}s must be identical." To account for this kind of coreference, Lebeaux (1984, 260 ff.) proposes the rather radical step that arbitrary PROs are in fact bound, by nonovert operators that stand in certain structural configurations to PROs. One consequence of the proposal is to raise the question of the assignment of antecedents to such nonovert operators [cf. Lebeaux (1984, 265)]. Restricting the present treatment to overt controllers, it may be noted that if a topic phrase is added to Lebeaux's sentences, control can emanate from the overt NP in the phrase, as in *As for John, PRO making a large profit (as a landlord)* requires PRO exploiting tenants, *As far as John is concerned, PRO making a large profit (as a landlord) requires PRO exploiting tenants,* and in *In John's case, PRO making a large profit (as a landlord) requires PRO exploiting tenants.* (In the third of these, such control seems the only interpretation.)

Notes to Chapter 8

1. For an extended treatment focused on the alternation between *of* and *about* with special reference to *say, tell, talk, speak,* see Brorström (1963, especially chap. 2), who points to the significance that rhythmical and stylistic factors may have for the choice between the prepositions. His treatment is not focused on sentential complements; for instance, as far as Brorström's pattern of *speak* lacking a prepositional personal object (as in *John did not want to speak of/about it*) is concerned, he has sixteen examples of *speak about* and sixty-seven examples of *speak of,* and in not one of the approximately one hundred sentences is the complement of the preposition sentential (1963, 93ff.). Conclusions based on constructions with nonsentential complements cannot automatically be generalized to constructions with sentential complements; for instance, recalling the distinction made with regard to control between *of -ing* and *about -ing* construals, it may be pointed out that although the question of control is always and necessarily present in construals with sentential complements, it does not necessarily arise in sentences with nonsentential complements in the same way. (For instance, consider the *it* sentence just cited.) At the same time, although Brorström's treatment cannot be reviewed here at length, it is clear that his observations are also often significant for sentential complements. With regard to *speak,* he shows, for instance, that in his data *speak of* may sometimes carry the sense of 'discuss', but that the usage is "chiefly by writers who affect a literary or somewhat old-fashioned style" (1963, 93), whereas in negative sentences, *speak* in the construction *speak of it* "easily takes on the sense 'mention' " (1963, 98). Another factor that may play a role is the presence of a manner adverbial: "a large number of quotations show that *speak* is rarely construed with *about* in sentences expressing the idea 'speak of sy. or sg. in a certain way' " (1963, 98; emphasis in the original). With regard to sentential complements, the last point may be illustrated with a sentence such as *John spoke calmly of/about committing perjury,* where the presence of the manner adverbial may indeed render the *of -ing* construal more likely in present-day English.

Bibliography

Abney, Steven. 1987. "The English Noun Phrase in Its Sentential Aspect." MIT Doctoral Dissertation.

ALD = *Oxford Advanced Learner's Dictionary of Current English*, ed. by A. S. Hornby, with the assistance of A. P. Cowie and J. W. Lewis. 1979. 3rd ed. Oxford: Oxford University Press.

Alexander, D., and W. J. Kunz. 1964. *Some Classes of Verbs in English*. Linguistics Research Project, Indiana University. Bloomington, Ind.: Indiana University Linguistics Club.

Austin, J. L. [1962] 1975. *How to Do Things with Words*. 2nd ed. Edited by J. O. Urmson and Marina Sbisà. Cambridge, Mass.: Harvard University Press.

Bach, Emmon. 1980. "In Defense of Passive." *Linguistics and Philosophy* 3: 297–341.

Baker, Mark. 1985. "Syntactic Affixation and English Gerunds." In J. Goldberg et al., eds., 1985, 1–11.

Bennett, David C. 1975. *Spatial and Temporal Uses of English Prepositions*. London: Longman.

Bolinger, Dwight. 1968. "Entailment and the Meaning of Structures." *Glossa* 2(2): 119–127.

Bresnan, Joan. 1970. "On Complementizers: Toward a Syntactic Theory of Complement Types." *Foundations of Language* 6: 297–321.

———. 1972. "Theory of Complementation in English Syntax." Cambridge, Mass.: MIT Doctoral Dissertation.

Bridgeman, Loraine I., Dale Dillinger, Constance Higgins, P. David Seaman, and Floyd A. Shank. 1965. *More Classes of Verbs in English*. Linguistics Research Project, Indiana University. Bloomington, Ind.: Indiana University Linguistics Club.

Brorström, Sverker. 1963. *The Increasing Frequency of the Preposition* About *during the Modern English Period*. Stockholm Studies in English 9. Stockholm: Almqvist and Wiksell.

Brown Corpus = *The Standard Corpus of Present-Day Edited American English*. 1964. Assembled under the direction of W. N. Francis at Brown University. (Abbreviated as Brown.)

Brugman, Claudia. 1988. *The Story of* Over: *Polysemy, Semantics, and the Structure of the Lexicon*. New York: Garland.

Brugman, Claudia, M. Macaulay, A. Dahlstrom, M. Emanatian, B. Moonwomon, and C. O'Connor, eds. 1984. *Proceedings of the Tenth Annual Meeting of the Berkeley Linguistics Society*. University of California, Berkeley: Berkeley Linguistics Society.

Budde, E. H. 1956. "Infinitiv oder Gerundium nach 'to'?" *Praxis des neusprachlichen Unterrichts* 3: 106–109.

Cattell, Ray. 1976. "Constraints on Movement Rules." *Language* 52: 18–50.

Chomsky, Noam. 1970. "Remarks on Nominalization." In R. A. Jacobs and P. S. Rosenbaum, eds., 1970, 184–221.

———. 1981. *Lectures on Government and Binding*. Dordrecht: Foris.

———. 1986a. *Barriers*. Cambridge, Mass.: MIT Press.

———. 1986b. *Knowledge of Language: Its Nature, Origin, and Use*. New York: Praeger.

Chomsky, Noam, and Howard Lasnik. 1993. "The Theory of Principles and Parameters." In J. Jacobs, A. Stechow, W. Sternefeld, and T. Vennemann, eds., 1993, 506–569.

Collins-Cobuild = *Collins Cobuild English Language Dictionary*. 1987. Reprint, 1993. Editor in chief John Sinclair. London: HarperCollins.

Comrie, Bernard. 1984. "Subject and Object Control: Syntax, Semantics, Pragmatics." In Claudia Brugman et al., 1984, eds., 450–464.

———. 1985. "Reflections on Subject and Object Control." *Journal of Semantics* 4: 47–65.

Culicover, Peter, and Wendy Wilkins. 1986. "Control, PRO, and the Projection Principle." *Language* 62: 120–153.

Curme, George O. 1931. *Syntax*. Boston: D. C. Heath.

Dixon, R. M. W. 1984. "The Semantic Basis of Syntactic Properties." In Claudia Brugman et al., eds., 1984, 583–595.

———. 1991. *A New Approach to English Grammar, on Semantic Principles*. Oxford: Clarendon Press.

Ellinger, Joh. 1910. "Gerundium, Infinitiv und *That*-Satz als adverbiale oder adnominale Ergänzung." *Anglia* 33: 480–522.

Emonds, Joseph. 1976. *A Transformational Approach to English Syntax*. New York: Academic Press.

Fellbaum, Christiane, and George Miller. 1990. "Folk Psychology or Semantic Entailment? A Reply to Rips and Conrad (1989)." *Psychological Review* 97: 565–570.

Francis, W. N., and H. Kučera. 1979. *Manual of Information to Accompany a Standard Corpus of Present-Day Edited American English, for Use with Digital Computers*. Providence, R.I.: Brown University, Department of Linguistics. First published 1964, revised 1971, revised and amplified 1979.

Goldberg, Jeffrey, Susannah MacKaye, and Michael Wescoat, eds. 1985. *Proceedings of the West Coast Conference on Formal Linguistics*, vol. 4. Stanford University: Stanford Linguistics Association.

Granath, Solveig. 1994. "Verb Complementation in English: Variation between Clauses and Prepositional Phrases." Doctoral Dissertation. University of Göteborg: Department of English.

Herskovits, Annette. 1986. *Language and Spatial Cognition: An Interdisciplinary Study of the Prepositions in English*. Cambridge: Cambridge University Press.

Higgins, F. R. 1973a. "The Pseudo-Cleft Construction in English." MIT Doctoral Dissertation.

———. 1973b. "On J. Emonds's Analysis of Extraposition." In John P. Kimball, ed., 1973, 149–196.

Huang, Cheng-Teh James. 1982. "Lexical Relations in Chinese and the Theory of Grammar." MIT Doctoral Dissertation.

———. 1984. "On the Distribution and Reference of Empty Pronouns." *Linguistic Inquiry* 15: 531–574.

———. 1989. "Pro-Drop in Chinese: A Generalized Control Theory." In O. Jaeggli and K. Safir, eds., 1989, 185–214.

Jackendoff, Ray. 1977. *$\bar{X}$ Syntax: A Study of Phrase Structure*. Cambridge, Mass.: MIT Press.

Jacobs, Roderick A., and Peter S. Rosenbaum, eds. 1970. *Readings in Transformational Grammar*. Waltham, Mass.: Ginn.

Jacobs, Joachim, Arnim von Stechow, Wolfgang Sternefeld, and Theo Vennemann, eds. 1993. *Syntax: An International Handbook of Contemporary Research*. Berlin: Walter de Gruyter.

Jaeggli, Osvaldo, and Kenneth Safir, eds. 1989. *The Null Subject Parameter*. Dordrecht: Kluwer.

Jespersen, Otto. [1940] 1965. *A Modern English Grammar on Historical Principles*. Part 5: *Syntax*. London: Allen and Unwin.

Johansson, Stig, in collaboration with Geoffrey Leech and Helen Goodluck. 1978. *Manual of Information to Accompany the Lancaster-Oslo/Bergen Corpus of British English, for Use with Digital Computers*. Oslo: University of Oslo, Department of English.

Jones, Charles, and Peter Sells, eds. 1984. *Proceedings of NELS 14*. Amherst, Mass.: GLSA, University of Massachusetts/Amherst.

Kajita, M. 1967. *A Generative-Transformational Study of Semi-Auxiliaries in Present-Day American English*. Tokyo.

Karttunen, Lauri, 1971. "Implicative Verbs." *Language* 47: 340–358.

Kimball, John P., ed. 1973. *Syntax and Semantics*, vol. 2. New York: Seminar Press.

Kornai, András, and Geoffrey Pullum. 1990. "The X-Bar Theory of Phrase Structure." *Language* 66: 24–50.
Ladusaw, William, and David Dowty. 1988. "Toward a Nongrammatical Account of Thematic Roles." In Wendy Wilkins, ed., 1988, 61–74.
Langacker, Ronald. 1991. *Foundations of Cognitive Grammar.* Vol. 2, *Descriptive Application.* Stanford, Calif.: Stanford University Press.
Lebeaux, David. 1984. "Anaphoric Binding and the Definition of PRO." In C. Jones and P. Sells, eds., 1984, 253–274.
Lehrer, Adrienne. 1970. "Verbs and Deletable Objects." *Lingua* 25: 227–253.
Lindkvist, Karl-Gunnar. 1976. *A Comprehensive Study of Conceptions of Locality in Which English Prepositions Occur.* Stockholm Studies in English 35. Stockholm: Almqvist and Wiksell.
LOB Corpus = *The Lancester-Oslo/Bergen Corpus of British English, for Use with Digital Computers.* 1978. By S. Johansson in collaboration with G. Leech and H. Goodluck. Department of English, University of Oslo. Abbreviated as LOB.
Manzini, M. Rita. 1983. "On Control and Control Theory." *Linguistic Inquiry* 14: 421–446.
McCloskey, James. 1988. "Syntactic Theory." In F. Newmeyer, ed. 1988, 18–59.
———. 1993. "Constraints on Syntactic Processes." In J. Jacobs, A. Stechow, W. Sternefeld and T. Vennemann, eds., 1993, 496–506.
Miller, George, and Christiane Fellbaum. 1991. "Semantic Networks of English." *Cognition* 41: 197–229.
Mohanan, K. P. 1983. "Functional and Anaphoric Control." *Linguistic Inquiry* 14: 641–674.
———. 1985. "Remarks on Control and Control Theory." *Linguistic Inquiry* 16: 637–648.
Mustanoja, Tauno F. 1960. *A Middle English Syntax.* Part 1. Helsinki: Société Néophilologique.
Newmeyer, Frederick J. 1988. *Linguistics: The Cambridge Survey.* Vol. 1, *Linguistic Theory: Foundations.* Cambridge: Cambridge University Press.
OED = *The Compact Edition of the Oxford English Dictionary.* 1971. Reprint, 1980. Oxford: Oxford University Press.
Pollock, Jean-Yves. 1989. "Verb Movement, Universal Grammar, and the Structure of IP." *Linguistic Inquiry* 20: 365–424.
Poutsma, H. 1905. *A Grammar of Late Modern English.* Part 1, The Sentence. 2nd ed., 1929. Groningen: P. Noordhoff.
———. 1926. *A Grammar of Late Modern English.* Part 2, *The Parts of Speech.* Section 2, *The Verb and the Particles.* Groningen: P. Noordhoff.
———. MS. *Dictionary of Constructions of Verbs, Adjectives, and Nouns.* Unpublished. Copyright Oxford University Press.
Quirk, Randolph, Sidney Greenbaum, Geoffrey Leech, and Jan Svartvik. 1985. *A Comprehensive Grammar of the English Language.* London: Longman.

Random House Dictionary of the English Language. Unabridged edition. [1966] 1981. New York: Random House.

Rizzi, Luigi. 1986. "Null Objects in Italian and the Theory of *pro.*" *Linguistic Inquiry* 17: 501–558.

Rosenbaum, Peter S. 1967. *The Grammar of English Predicate Complement Constructions.* Cambridge, Mass.: MIT Press.

Rudanko, Juhani. 1976. *On Raising and Underlying VSO Order in English.* Tampere, Finland: Department of English and German, University of Tampere.

———. 1984. "On Some Contrasts between Infinitival and *That* Complement Clauses in English." *English Studies* 65: 141–161.

———. 1985. "Classes of Verbs Governing Subject-Controlled Forward Equi in Present-Day English." *English Studies* 66: 48–73.

———. 1989. *Complementation and Case Grammar: A Syntactic and Semantic Study of Selected Patterns of Complementation in Present-Day English.* Albany, N.Y.: State University of New York Press.

———. 1991. "On Verbs Governing *in -ing* in Present-Day English." *English Studies* 72: 55–72.

Sag, Ivan, and Carl Pollard. 1991. "An Integrated Theory of Complement Control." *Language* 67: 63–113.

Sager, Naomi. 1981. *Natural Language Information Processing: A Computer Grammar of English and Its Applications.* Reading, Mass.: Addison-Wesley.

Schibsbye, Knud. [1965] 1970. *A Modern English Grammar with an Appendix on Semantically Related Prepositions.* 2nd ed. London: Oxford University Press.

Seppänen, Aimo. 1986. "The Syntax of *seem* and *appear* Revisited." *Studia Linguistica* 40: 22–39.

Shumaker, Nancy W. 1977. "A Conceptual Analysis of Spatial Location as Indicated by Certain English Prepositions." Doctoral Dissertation, University of Georgia.

Söderlind, Johannes. 1958. *Verb Syntax in John Dryden's Prose.* Part 2. Uppsala: A.-B. Lundequistska Bokhandeln.

Somers, Harold L. 1984. "On the Validity of the Complement-Adjunct Distinction in Valency Grammar." *Linguistics* 22: 507–530.

———. 1987. *Valency and Case in Computational Linguistics.* Edinburgh: Edinburgh University Press.

Stuurman, Frits. 1985. *Phrase Structure Theory in Generative Grammar.* Dordrecht: Foris.

Sweet, H. 1903. *English Grammar Logical and Historical.* Part 2, *Syntax.* Oxford: Clarendon Press.

Thompson, Sandra A. 1973. "On Subjectless Gerunds in English." *Foundations of Language* 9: 374–383.

Visser, F. Th. 1969. *An Historical Syntax of the English Language.* Part 3, first half, *Syntactical Units with Two Verbs.* Leiden: E. J. Brill.

Wesche, Birgit. 1986/1987. "At Ease with 'At'." *Journal of Semantics* 5: 385–399.
Wierzbicka, Anna. 1988. *The Semantics of Grammar.* Amsterdam: John Benjamins.
Wilkins, Wendy, ed. 1988. *Thematic Relations. Syntax and Semantics,* vol. 21. New York: Academic Press.
Wood, Frederick T. 1956. "Gerund versus Infinitive." *English Language Teaching* 11: 11–15.

Index

Abney, Steven, 2
about -ing. See *at -ing*, *in -ing*, *of -ing*, *on -ing*
Adverbial clauses, 3, 4, 11–13, 15–18, 22, 34–35, 44, 61, 63, 96–97, 99, 164; introduced by *at*, 95; introduced by *by*, 10, 14, 34; introduced by *in*, 10, 34; introduced by *when*, 10; of attendant circumstances, 11, 14; of cause, 112; of instrumentality, 10, 14, 16; of manner, 11, 14, 16, 192n.1; of means, 16; of purpose, 114; of reason, 112; of time, 10–11, 16, 44, 112; with infinitive, 44; with *wh* constituent, 13
against -ing. See *at -ing*
ALD, 20, 49, 64, 102, 110, 113, 124, 125, 149
Alexander, D. and W. J. Kunz, 141
American English, 129, 137
at, 108–109; and cause, 95, 109; and location, 109, 116; and source, 109; and time, 95. See also *on*
at -ing, 109; versus *about -ing*, 101, 110–112; versus *against -ing*, 100, 111; versus *from -ing*, 109–110; versus *in -ing*, 99–102, 111-113, 115; versus infinitive, 99–101, 111, 113–115; versus nonsentential complement, 94, 102–103, 131; versus *over -ing*, 101, 110–112, 115; versus *to -ing*, 113; versus *upon -ing*, 111; versus *with -ing*, 110, 111; with adverbial force, 96–99, 102, 115. See also *in -ing*, *on -ing*, *with -ing*
Austin, J. L., 40

B's generalization, 83–85, 155, 158, 177, 185–186. See also Bach's generalization
Bach, Emmon, 80
Bach's generalization, 80–84, 185
Baker, Mark, 188n.1
Bennett, David C., 109
Bolinger, Dwight, 187n.2
Bresnan, Joan, 2, 67

Bridgeman, Loraine I. et al., 5, 18, 27, 44, 50, 51, 75, 93, 95, 101, 109, 110, 117, 121, 125, 136, 141, 143, 152, 164, 173, 182
British English, 74, 138, 175
Brorström, Sverker, 173, 192n.1
Brown Corpus, 4, 5, 7, 9, 18, 19, 20, 23, 24, 28, 29, 43, 44, 45, 46, 47, 48, 61, 67, 70, 71, 72, 73, 74, 87, 93, 117, 119, 120, 128, 132, 136, 142, 146, 152, 153, 157, 164, 165, 166, 170, 173, 174, 176, 181, 182, 188n.2
Brugman, Claudia, 112
Budde, E. H., 58, 62, 76
by -*ing*: with adverbial force, 138. See also *in* -*ing*, *with* -*ing*

Cattell, Ray, 13
Chomsky, Noam, 188n.1, 188n.3, 189n.5; and IP and CP projections, 2; and PRO, 33; and projection principle, 2; and theta criterion, 2
Chomsky, Noam and Howard Lasnik, 13
Collins-Cobuild, 49, 51, 152
Complement clauses, 3, 5, 6, 10–18, 22, 34–35, 43, 44, 63, 69, 94, 96–97, 106, 107, 112, 117, 118, 135, 136, 138, 146, 157, 163, 181; and nonsentential complement, 83, 84, 102; with *wh* constituent, 13
Comrie, Bernard, 188n.3, 189n.4
Control: arbitrary control, 33–34, 36–37, 56–58, 128, 147–148, 159, 168–170, 185, 191n.1; object control, 3, 33, 37, 57, 69, 70, 72, 77, 79–83, 84, 85, 90, 136, 155, 158, 159, 160, 164, 177–178, 185, 188n.4; remote control, 37, 57–58, 133–134, 147–148, 150–151, 159 168–169, 185, 189n.5; subject control, 3, 4, 33–34, 36–37, 56–57, 62, 65, 72, 79–83, 84, 85, 90, 93, 106, 108, 135–136, 143–144, 146, 148, 154–155, 164, 168, 169–170, 174, 185, 189n.5. See also PRO
Cooper, Robert, 52, 171
Culicover, Peter and Wendy Wilkins, 188n.3
Curme, George O., 44, 58

Dixon, R. M. W., 66, 101, 110, 139, 141, 187n.2

Ellinger, Joh., 58
Emonds, Joseph, 190n.1
Entailment, 29, 30, 182
Extraction of *wh* constituent, 13, 15, 96

for -*ing*. See *of* -*ing*, *with* -*ing* (transitive)
Francis, W. N. and H. Kučera, 188n.2
from -*ing*, 109, 189n.4. See also *at* -*ing*, *of* -*ing*

Granath, Solveig, 21, 23, 87, 150
Gurney, Ian, 16, 17, 23, 25, 27, 31, 40, 61, 66, 71, 73, 75, 76, 78, 79, 86, 88, 89, 94, 95, 102, 104, 112, 113, 123, 124, 125, 128, 136, 138, 142, 145, 161, 167, 170, 171, 179

Hall, Cristopher, 29
Herskovits, Annette, 133
Higgins, F. R., 12, 189n.5
Hill, Jane, 87, 138
Huang, Cheng-Teh James, 13, 188n.3, 189n.5

Implicative versus nonimplicative dichotomy, 39–41
in -*ing*, 3, 9, 10, 29, 30, 32, 37, 41, 42, 44, 56, 57, 66, 68, 96, 99, 183, 188n.4; omitting of, 14, 30–31; versus *about* -*ing*, 25; versus *at* -*ing*, 41, 42; versus *by* -*ing*, 15; versus infinitive, 21–23, 25, 38, 41; versus -*ing* form, 41; versus nonsentential complement, 24, 29, 32–33, 39; versus *of* -*ing*, 20–21, 41; versus *on* -*ing*, 5, 20, 25, 181; versus *over* -*ing*, 25; versus *when* -*ing*, 14, 15; with adverbial force, 11, 12, 13, 16, 17, 34. See also *at* -*ing*, *of* -*ing*, *to* -*ing*, *with* -*ing*
Infinitive, 7, 25, 55, 58, 61, 74. See also *at* -*ing*, *in* -*ing*, -*ing* form, *of* -*ing*, *on* -*ing*, Poutsma, *to* -*ing*, *with* -*ing*
-*ing* form, 7, 15, 16, 58, 61, 85–89, 94, 96, 118, 124, 125, 188n.4; and nongerundive participle clause, 18; replaceability of, 55; versus infinitive, 58–59; with nominal character, 55. See also *in* -*ing*, *of* -*ing*, *to* -*ing* (transitive), *with* -*ing*
into -*ing*. See *to* -*ing* (transitive)
it, replacement of complement clause with *it*, 11, 44, 69-70, 80, 94, 96, 118, 136, 164, 190n.1

Jackendoff, Ray, 188n.1
Jespersen, Otto, 10, 58
Johansson et al., 188n.2

Kajita, M., 11, 12
Karttunen, Lauri: and *but* sentences, 40; and implicative versus nonimplicative dichotomy, 39–40
Kornai, András and Geoffrey Pullum, 188n.1

Ladusaw, William and David Dowty, 175
Langacker, Ronald, 187n.2
Lebeaux, David, 188n.3, 189n.5
Lehrer, Adrienne: and object deletion, 81
Lindkvist, Karl-Gunnar, 132–133
LOB Corpus, 4, 5, 7, 9, 18, 19, 20, 21, 22, 24, 25, 28, 29, 44, 46, 47, 61, 67, 70, 71, 72, 73, 93, 95, 97, 117, 119, 120, 128, 132, 136, 137, 142, 146, 152, 153, 157, 164, 165, 166, 173, 174, 176, 181, 182, 188n.2

MacGilleon, Robert, 31, 63, 101, 112, 140, 142
make and *cause* construals, 105, 108
Manzini, M. Rita, 188n.3
McCloskey, James, 13
Miller, George and Christiane Fellbaum: troponymy relation, 30
Mohanan, K. P., 188n.3
Mustanoja, Tauno F., 10

OED, 49, 54, 62, 85, 86, 100, 111, 124, 170, 172, 175
of -*ing*, intransitive pattern: 20, 21, 163; versus *about* -*ing*, 169–173, 192n.1; versus *for* -*ing*, 166; versus *from* -*ing*, 172; versus *in* -*ing*, 172; versus infinitive, 172; versus -*ing* form, 171; versus nonsentential complement, 167, 168, 192n.1; versus *on* -*ing*, 169–170; versus *that* clause, 171. See also *in* -*ing*. transitive pattern: 164, 184, 185; versus *about* -*ing*, 179; versus *for* -*ing*, 178, 179; versus *from* -*ing*, 178; versus infinitive, 175; versus nonsentential complement, 176–177; versus *to* -*ing*, 175, 178. See also *with* -*ing* (transitive)

on, 117; and meaning, 132, 133, 134; and time, 95; with adverbial force, 118
on -ing, 5; versus *about -ing*, 121, 123, 124, 127-128; versus *at -ing*, 131; versus infinitive, 120, 124, 129–131; versus nonsentential complement, 119, 121–122, 123, 124, 125, 127, 128, 131; versus *wh* complement, 121. See also *in -ing, of -ing*
over -ing. See *at -ing, in -ing*

Passive, 71, 88, 89, 154
Pollock, Jean-Yves, 2, 188n.1
Poutsma, H., 5, 7, 9, 10, 18, 19, 25, 26, 33, 44, 48, 49, 50, 52, 57, 63, 64, 70–71, 89, 90, 91, 93, 95, 97–100, 104, 110, 111, 117, 120–121, 136, 137, 142, 146, 152, 153, 164, 166, 173, 174, 182, 187n.1; and gerund versus infinitive, 21–23, 25, 49, 58, 60–63, 85–88, 120
Preposing, 4, 12, 15, 95–96, 98, 118
Present-day English, 1, 4, 5, 7, 18, 21, 28, 39, 41, 42, 45, 48, 60, 62, 63, 64, 65, 67, 68, 85, 86, 87, 93, 104, 108, 115, 116, 120, 125, 134, 152, 161, 174, 179, 181, 182, 186, 192n.1
PRO, 2, 9, 10, 18, 33, 38, 41, 43, 55, 56, 59, 62-63, 65, 70, 80, 93, 95, 106, 107, 108, 117, 135; and *as far as* NP, 147–148, 168–169, 191n.1; and *as for* NP, 147–148, 168–169, 191n.1; and *in* NP*'s case*, 147–148, 150–151, 159, 168–169, 191n.1; and PRO-to-PRO coreference, 147, 169; as a subject, 33, 95, 106–108, 135; with possessives, 37, 56–57, 147; with reflexive pronoun, 35–37, 56–57, 133
Projection principle: definition of, 2
Pseudocleft sentences, 12, 14–18, 34, 44, 55, 70, 80, 94, 96, 118, 136, 164, 190n.1; specificational 12; with double *in in*, 17, 34; with *what...in*, 15; with *where...in*, 17, 32

Question-and-answer pairs, 14–16, 32, 34, 55, 69, 80, 94, 96
Questions: *how*, 11, 12, 15, 16, 17, 34, 96, 118; *what*, 14–15, 17, 44, 59, 64, 96, 99, 118, 190n.1; *when*, 11, 12, 96, 118; *where*, 15, 16, 17, 32; *who*, 14; *why*, 11, 96, 105
Quirk, Randolph et al., 11, 12, 43, 51, 59, 69, 70, 74, 85, 191n.1; and collective nouns, 37; and nonassertive contexts, 104

Raising, 150
Random House, 122–123, 129
Right Dislocation, 11, 44, 59, 70, 80, 94, 96, 118, 136, 164, 190n.1
Rizzi, Luigi, 80–81
Rosenbaum, Peter S., 12
Royle, Nicholas, 31
Rudanko, Juhani, 1, 4, 7, 12, 38, 39, 41, 53, 59, 67, 68, 90–91, 94, 108, 111, 114, 115; and verbs taking the infinitive, 64–65

Sag, Ivan and Carl Pollard, 78, 188n.3
Sager, Naomi, 76
Schibsbye, Knud, 131, 170
Seppänen, Aimo, 12
Shumaker, Nancy W., 109
Söderlind, Johannes, 10

Somers, Harold L.: and complement versus adjunct distinction, 14
Stuurman, Frits, 187n.1, 188n.1
Sweet, H., 58

that, replacement of complement clause with *that*, 11, 44, 69, 80, 94, 118, 136, 164, 190n.1
Theta criterion: definition of, 2
Thompson, Sandra, 188n.4
to -ing, intransitive pattern: 3, 50, 51, 52, 54, 55, 60, 67, 85, 91; versus *in -ing*, 66–68; versus infinitive, 43, 55, 58, 60–65, 67–68, 184–185; versus *that* clause, 53–54, 67. *See also at -ing, with -ing*
transitive pattern: 84, 177, 183; versus infinitive, 70–71, 74, 85–92, 184–185; versus *-ing* form, 74, 85, 90–92; versus *into -ing*, 74; versus nonsentential complement, 75, 80, 82-84. *See also of -ing* (transitive), *with -ing* (transitive)
Troponymy relation, 30

Visser, F. Th., 114

Wesche, Birgit, 109
when -ing. *See in -ing*
Wierzbicka, Anna, 130, 172, 187n.
with -ing, intransitive pattern: 110, 135, 136, 152, 158, 159, 161, 191n.1; versus *at -ing*, 139, 149; versus *by -ing*, 137–138, 150–151; versus *in -ing*, 139, 141–142, 143, 151; versus infinitive, 138, 141, 149–151; versus *-ing* form, 150; versus nonsentential complement, 140, 146, 160, 183; versus *to -ing*, 151; with adverbial force, 138, 145. *See also at -ing*
transitive pattern: 136, 155–156, 177, 183; versus *for -ing*, 160; versus nonsentential complement, 157–158; versus *of -ing*, 160; versus *to -ing*, 160–161
Wood, Frederick T., 58

X bar syntax, 12, 188n.1

Index of Verbs

abandon, 75, 77, 89
abound, 32, 33
absolve, 174, 175, 176
abstain, 109, 110
accord, 137, 144
accredit, 153, 156
accrue, 55, 56
accuse, 1, 3, 160, 163, 164, 173, 175, 176, 177, 178
accustom, 75, 77, 79, 85
ache, 99, 103
acquaint, 153, 155, 156
acquiesce, 27, 28, 31, 32, 33, 40
acquit, 174, 175, 176, 178
adapt, 50, 54, 75, 77, 79
adhere, 50, 54, 66
adjust, 50, 54, 63
admit, 44, 54, 66, 166, 167, 169
advocate, 189
agree, 25, 28, 31, 32, 40, 50, 54, 55, 56, 62, 121, 126
aid, 19, 23, 28, 31, 32, 35, 37, 38
aim, 97, 99, 104, 108, 113
allocate, 76, 77, 79
allude, 48, 53, 54, 60
alternate, 137, 144

amount, 44, 53, 54, 55, 56, 57, 60, 66
approach, 48
approve, 166, 167, 168, 171, 189
arise, 142, 144
arrive, 99, 104
ascend, 52
aspire, 99
assent, 50, 54, 62
assert, 7
assign, 76, 77, 79, 89, 90
assist, 19, 23, 28, 31, 32, 34, 35, 37, 38
associate, 152, 156, 157, 159, 177
assure, 173, 175, 176
attend, 48, 54
attract, 76, 77
avoid, 7, 38, 39, 65

back out, 167
balk, 1, 3, 93, 94, 95, 96, 101, 103, 104, 105, 106, 107, 109
bank, 121, 125, 126, 132
bargain, 121, 126
be, 26, 27, 31, 49, 190
begin, 137, 138, 139, 143, 144, 148, 150, 151

205

believe, 19, 28, 31, 32, 35, 36, 38, 189
bet, 121, 126
beware, 164, 167, 171, 173
bind, 75, 77, 88
blame, 160
blush, 97, 99, 103
boast, 164, 165, 167, 170, 171
boggle, 101, 103, 107
border, 121, 126, 133, 134
bother, 138, 143, 149
brag, 166, 167, 170, 171
bridle, 102, 103, 107
bring up, 189
bristle, 101, 103, 105, 106, 107
brood, 121, 126, 128
burden, 154, 155, 160
busy, 154, 155, 157

calculate, 120, 126, 132
capitalize, 121, 126
carry on, 142, 143
cash in, 121, 126
cause, 105, 108
center, 119, 126
chafe, 101, 103, 105, 106, 107
challenge, 154, 156
chance, 119
change over, 52, 53, 54, 76, 77, 84
charge, 1, 3, 135, 136, 152, 153, 155, 156, 157, 160
chicken out, 167
clash, 138, 144
clear, 174, 175, 176
cling, 50, 54, 61, 66
coerce, 91
coincide, 138, 144, 146
collaborate, 27, 28, 31, 35, 38, 121, 126
combine, 154, 156, 158
come, 45, 138, 144, 165, 167, 168, 172
come about, 138, 144
come around, 45, 53, 54

come down, 45, 53, 54, 66
come up, 142, 144
commence, 138, 143
comment, 121, 126, 127
commit, 71, 77, 79
compare, 139, 144, 151, 154, 156, 158, 159, 160, 161
compete, 27, 28, 31, 139, 144
complain, 165, 167, 171
conceive, 166, 167, 171, 189
concentrate, 1, 3, 5, 19, 20, 117, 118, 119, 126, 181
concur, 26, 28, 30, 31, 32, 38, 40
condemn, 75, 77, 79, 89, 91, 174, 175, 178
condition, 75, 77, 79, 80, 88
confer, 121, 126
confess, 48, 54, 56, 57, 61, 66
confide, 33
confine, 71, 75, 77, 79, 80, 84, 85, 91
confuse, 153, 156
connive, 102, 104, 108
consent, 51, 54, 62, 63
consist, 20, 27, 31, 33, 36, 37, 41, 42, 56, 66, 165, 167, 168, 169, 172, 190
contemplate, 189
continue, 139, 143
contrast, 139, 144, 154, 156, 158
contribute, 45, 53, 54, 55, 59, 60
contrive, 65
convert, 51, 52, 53, 54, 75, 76, 77, 79, 82, 83, 84
convict, 174, 175, 176, 178
cooperate, 20, 28, 31, 32, 34, 35, 38
cope, 1, 3, 135, 136, 139, 143
correlate, 139, 144
count, 121, 126
credit, 153, 156
criticize, 189
cry, 98, 99
culminate, 27, 28, 31, 32
cure, 174, 175, 176

Index of Verbs

dabble, 27, 28, 30, 31, 39, 100, 104, 112
deal, 139, 143, 148
decide, 121, 126, 129, 130
dedicate, 72, 76, 77, 79
delegate, 76, 77, 84, 89, 90, 92
deliberate, 122, 126
delight, 1, 2, 4, 9, 10, 11, 12, 13, 14, 15, 17, 20, 27, 30, 31, 32, 33, 37, 40, 98, 103, 111
demote, 76, 77, 79, 89, 90
demur, 102, 103, 107
denigrate, 40
denounce, 189
depend, 119, 126, 132, 133
depose, 49, 54
deprive, 176
descend, 51, 53, 54, 61, 119
desist, 39, 110
despair, 165, 167, 171, 173
determine, 121, 126, 130
devote, 72, 76, 77, 78, 79, 85, 86, 90
die, 166, 167, 172
die away, 95
direct, 90
disabuse, 175
disapprove, 166, 167, 168, 173, 189
discourse, 122, 126
dispense, 137, 143, 146
dispose, 167, 168
dissuade, 189
do away, 139, 143
dread, 189
dream, 1, 3, 163, 164, 165, 167, 171, 172
drive, 72, 77, 80, 86, 88, 90, 92
dwell, 122, 126

ease up, 122, 126, 131
echo, 146
elaborate, 122, 126, 128
embark, 122, 125, 126, 132
end, 33
endeavor, 99, 115

endure, 189
engage, 27, 28, 29, 30, 31, 39, 40, 42, 66, 113, 189
enjoy, 189
enlarge, 122, 126
ensure, 175
entail, 191
enter, 125, 126
eschew, 41
excel, 20, 28, 31, 32, 40, 99, 100, 104, 112
exist, 122, 123
exonerate, 175, 176
expand, 122, 126, 127, 128
expatiate, 122, 126, 127, 128
experiment, 20, 28, 31, 102, 104, 112, 139, 140, 143, 145, 151
expostulate, 122, 126, 127
expound, 122, 126, 127, 128
extend, 46, 53, 54, 56, 57
exult, 98, 103, 111

face, 154, 155, 158
fail, 21, 22, 39, 101, 104, 113
fall, 44, 46, 53, 54, 56, 60
fall back, 122, 126
familiarize, 154, 155
fawn, 119
feel like, 189
feel up, 49
fight, 146
figure, 122, 126, 129, 132
find, 87
find fault, 140, 143
fit in, 140, 144
fix, 123, 126, 129, 130
flinch, 110
flirt, 140, 143, 144, 146
focus, 123, 126, 131
fool, 140, 143, 146
fool around, 140, 143, 144, 149
force, 70
forget, 189
free, 175, 178

gamble, 123, 126
gear, 72, 77, 79
get, 46, 54, 61, 85
get around, 46, 54
get away, 137, 143
get down, 46, 54
get out, 166, 167
give over, 73, 76, 77, 78, 79
glory, 26, 27, 31
go, 49, 118, 140, 143
go along, 140, 143, 145
go back, 46, 54
go on, 142, 143
go over, 52, 54, 61
grab, 94
grapple, 140, 143
grieve, 98, 103
groan, 98, 103, 112
grudge, 38, 39
grumble, 98, 103, 106, 107, 111, 112

happen, 140, 144
harmonize, 140, 144, 146, 147, 148
have to do, 137, 144
hear, 46, 166, 167, 170
help, 23, 28, 29, 31, 32, 34, 35, 36, 37, 38, 40, 41, 42, 100, 104, 112, 113, 140, 143, 151
hesitate, 97, 99, 103, 104, 106, 107, 109, 110, 111, 151
hinge, 120, 126, 132
hold, 76, 77, 140, 143, 148
hold out, 123, 126, 130
hurry, 140, 141, 143, 154, 155, 157, 158

identify, 141, 143, 154, 156, 158
imagine, 189
improve, 123, 126
indulge, 27, 28, 31, 42, 66, 113
insist, 120, 126, 130, 131
insure, 175
intend, 38, 41, 65

interfere, 27, 28, 31, 40, 141, 144, 146, 151
interrupt, 40
introduce, 75, 77
intrust, 154, 155
inure, 73, 77, 79
invest, 33
involve, 191

jib, 102, 103, 107
join, 23, 28, 31
jump, 94

keep, 52, 54, 102, 104, 113

labor, 102, 104, 108, 113, 114, 123, 126
laugh, 98, 99
lead, 46, 53, 54, 60, 80, 81, 82, 83
learn, 166, 167
leave, 95, 96
lecture, 123, 126, 127, 128
lie, 23, 27, 31, 190
like, 189
limit, 73, 77, 79, 82, 83
link, 155, 156, 157, 159, 160, 161, 177
live, 123
look, 49, 54, 63, 64, 102, 104
look back, 123, 126
look forward, 47, 54, 63
luxuriate, 27, 31

major, 33
make, 105, 108
make out, 141, 143
manage, 41, 65, 115, 141, 143, 149
marvel, 101, 103, 107
meditate, 123, 126
mention, 53
mess, 141, 143, 146
mess around, 141, 143, 149
miss out, 125, 126
mix, 141, 144

moralize, 123, 126, 127, 128
move, 73, 77, 78, 88, 89
move over, 52, 53, 54, 76, 77, 84
muse, 123, 126

neglect, 65
nibble, 94
note, 53

object, 47, 54, 56, 57, 62, 64, 189
observe, 53
occupy, 154, 155
occur, 141, 144, 145
order, 78, 159, 160
originate, 141, 144
overwhelm, 154, 155, 158
own, 50, 54, 61, 62
own up, 51, 54

pair, 141, 143, 154, 156, 158
participate, 24, 28, 29, 31, 34, 35, 38, 42
perish, 166, 167
permit, 78, 159, 160
persevere, 26, 28, 29, 31, 40, 66, 102, 104, 112, 113, 141, 142, 143, 151
persist, 14, 15, 17, 24, 28, 29, 30, 31, 32, 39, 40, 42, 66, 113
persuade, 91
pin down, 76, 77, 89, 90
plague, 154, 155
plan, 120, 123, 126, 129
play, 101, 104, 142, 143, 149
play around, 142, 143, 149
preach, 123, 126, 127, 128
prefer, 189
presume, 123, 124, 126, 132
proceed, 142, 143, 144, 145, 150
promise, 95
propose, 189
provide, 157
put, 90
put back, 73, 77, 90

put off, 38, 39
put up, 76, 77, 87, 90, 137, 143, 145

rail, 101, 103, 106, 111
rank, 142, 144, 151
rate, 142, 144
react, 47, 54
rebel, 100, 103
rebuff, 1
reckon, 124, 126, 142, 143
recoil, 110
reconcile, 76, 77, 79, 88, 154, 155
reduce, 2, 69, 70, 73, 77, 78, 79, 86, 91, 178
refer, 51, 53, 54, 55, 60, 75, 80
reflect, 124, 125, 126, 128
refrain, 109, 110
regiment, 74
regret, 191
rejoice, 24, 27, 31, 32, 99, 103, 111
relate, 50, 53, 54, 55
relegate, 76, 77
relieve, 175
relish, 189
rely, 124, 126, 132, 133
remark, 124, 126, 127
remember, 189
remind, 175, 177, 178, 179
renege, 124, 126
repent, 166, 167, 171
reproach, 153, 156, 157, 159, 160
require, 191, 192
resign, 76, 77, 79
resolve, 121, 126, 130
resort, 1, 2, 43, 47, 54, 55, 60, 66, 67, 190
resound, 146
rest, 124, 126, 132
result, 24, 28, 31, 32, 38
return, 47, 54
revel, 24, 27, 31
revert, 52, 54
revolt, 98, 103

revolve, 124, 126
rib, 177
risk, 189
rouse, 76, 77, 88
run, 47, 53, 54

saddle, 154, 155, 156, 157, 158, 159, 160
say, 53, 192
scheme, 102, 104
scoff, 103
scruple, 102, 103, 109, 111
seek, 115
sentence, 75, 77, 79, 89, 91
set, 74, 77, 79, 87, 88
settle, 124, 126, 129, 130
settle down, 47, 54
share, 24, 28, 31, 35
shift, 47, 54
shrink, 110
shy away, 110
sicken, 99, 103
slip, 95
smack, 166, 167, 173
smell, 167, 168
sneer, 101, 103
speak, 55, 124, 126, 127, 128, 165, 167, 169, 170, 173, 192
specialize, 24, 28, 29, 31, 32, 37, 42, 113
speculate, 124, 126, 127
stammer, 4, 10, 11, 12, 13, 14, 17
stare, 99
start, 74, 77, 79, 88, 124, 125, 126, 132
start off, 137, 143, 145
stick, 47, 54, 100, 103, 104, 105
stickle, 100, 103, 109, 111
stoop, 52, 53, 54, 61
stop, 97, 103, 104, 105
strain, 101, 104
strip, 177
stumble, 10, 11, 12, 13, 14, 17, 118

subject, 75, 77
submit, 50, 54, 63
succeed, 15, 16, 17, 25, 28, 29, 31, 32, 33, 35, 36, 37, 38, 39, 42, 101, 104, 112, 113
suffer, 98, 103
suspect, 174, 175, 176, 178
swear, 50, 54
switch, 52, 54, 74, 77, 79, 84
switch over, 52, 54, 76, 77, 79, 84

take, 48, 54, 55, 60
take a chance, 124, 126
talk, 124, 126, 127, 165, 167, 192
taste, 167, 168
taunt, 153, 156, 158, 160
tax, 153, 156
tell, 165, 167, 168, 192
testify, 51, 54, 61, 67
theorize, 124, 126, 127
think, 166, 167, 171, 172, 173
threaten, 154, 155, 158
thrive, 120, 126, 132
tie in, 142, 143, 155, 156
tire, 166, 167
toil, 101, 104, 108, 113, 114, 125, 126
touch, 124, 126, 133
toy, 142, 143, 144
toy around, 142, 143
treat, 75
trifle, 142, 143
triumph, 98, 103, 111
trouble, 142, 143, 149
trust, 33, 50, 54, 63, 64
try, 115
turn, 48, 54, 60, 61, 67, 124, 126, 132

unite, 26, 28, 30, 31
upbraid, 153, 156, 160

venture, 120, 126, 132
verge, 125, 126, 133, 134

vie, 26, 27, 28, 30
vote, 125, 126, 129
vouch, 50, 54

wager, 125, 126
walk, 18
wallow, 27, 31
want, 7, 43, 65
warn, 75

wince, 103
wink, 102, 104, 108
work, 100, 104, 108, 113, 114, 125, 126, 131
wrestle, 142, 143
wriggle out, 167
write, 125, 126, 127
writhe, 103